Teach Yourself VISUALLY™

Photoshop® Elements 12

Mike Wooldridge
Brianna Stuart

Visual

A Wiley Brand

About the Authors

Mike Wooldridge is a writer and software developer based in the San Francisco Bay area. He has authored more than 30 books for the Visual series. For more information about him and his books, visit www.wooldridge.net.

Brianna Stuart is a writer, editor, and busy mom based in the Seattle area. She is also the author of *Creating Web Pages Simplified*, 2nd Edition and *Teach Yourself VISUALLY Photoshop CC*.

Authors' Acknowledgments

Mike and Brianna thank Sarah Hellert, Scott Tullis, Dennis Cohen, Carol Kessel, and everyone else at Wiley for their help with this book. Mike dedicates this book to his photographer wife Linda, who provided most of the photos in the examples, and his son, who loves posting photos to Instagram. Brianna dedicates this book to her husband and three-year-old twins, and her amazing extended family.

How to Use This Book

Who This Book Is For

This book is for the reader who has never used this particular technology or software application. It is also for readers who want to expand their knowledge.

The Conventions in This Book

① Steps

This book uses a step-by-step format to guide you easily through each task. **Numbered steps** are actions you must do; **bulleted steps** clarify a point, step, or optional feature; and **indented steps** give you the result.

② Notes

Notes give additional information — special conditions that may occur during an operation, a situation that you want to avoid, or a cross-reference to a related area of the book.

③ Icons and Buttons

Icons and buttons show you exactly what you need to click to perform a step.

④ Tips

Tips offer additional information, including warnings and shortcuts.

⑤ Bold

Bold type shows command names or options that you must click or text or numbers you must type.

⑥ Italics

Italic type introduces and defines a new term.

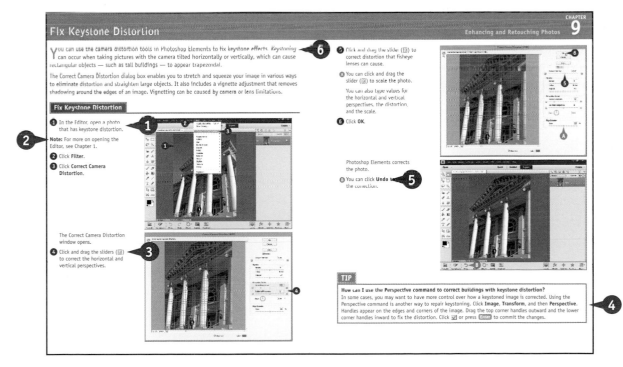

Table of Contents

Chapter 1   Getting Started

Introducing Photoshop Elements 12 4

Understanding Digital Images............................... 6

Start Photoshop Elements 8

Explore the Editor Workspace.................................. 9

Tour the Organizer Workspace 10

Switch between the Organizer and the Editor 11

Introducing the Photoshop Elements Tools 12

Switch Editor Modes.. 14

Work with Tools.. 16

Work with Panels 18

Set Program Preferences 20

View Rulers and Guides.. 22

Chapter 2   Importing and Opening Digital Images

Get Photos for Your Projects..................................... 26

Import Photos from a Digital Camera or Card Reader ... 28

Import Photos from a Scanner 30

Import or Search for Photos from a Folder 32

Open a Photo 34

Create a Blank Image 36

Save a Photo... 38

Duplicate a Photo 40

Close a Photo.. 41

Chapter 3   Organizing Your Photos

Introducing the Organizer 44

Open the Organizer 46

Create a Catalog 48

View Photos in the Media Browser 50

View Photos in Full Screen 52

Display a Slide Show in Full Screen 54

View Photo Information 56

Add a Caption 58

Work with Albums 60

Find Photos 62

Rate Photos 64

View Versions of a Photo.. 66

Remove a Photo from the Organizer 67

Chapter 4   Using Advanced Organizing Tools

Perform an Advanced Search.................................... 70

Work with Keyword Tags 72

Define People in Photos... 76

Define Places 78

View Places... 80

Define Events.. 82

Using Smart Events 84

Work with People, Place, and Event Tags 86

Apply an Instant Fix.. 88

Stack Photos 90

Find by Visual Similarity 92

Table of Contents

Chapter 5   Applying Basic Image Edits

Manage Open Images 96

Magnify with the Zoom Tool 100

Adjust the Image View 102

Change the On-Screen Image Size 104

Change the Image Print Size................................. 106

Change the Image Canvas Size.............................. 108

Work in Quick Mode... 110

Apply an Effect in Quick Mode 112

Add a Frame in Quick Mode 113

Crop an Image.. 114

Rotate an Image... 116

Undo Changes to an Image 118

Revert an Image... 119

Chapter 6   Making Selections

Select an Area with the Marquee 122

Select an Area with the Lasso 124

Select an Area with the Magic Wand 128

Select an Area with the Quick Selection Tool............. 130

Select an Area with the Selection Brush 132

Save and Load a Selection.................................... 134

Invert a Selection 136

Deselect a Selection 137

Chapter 7   Manipulating Selections

Add to or Subtract from a Selection 140

Move a Selection 142

Apply the Content-Aware Move Tool........................144

Duplicate a Selection..146

Delete a Selection..147

Rotate a Selection 148

Scale a Selection 149

Skew or Distort a Selection....................................150

Refine the Edge of a Selection 152

Feather the Border of a Selection 154

Chapter 8   Using Layers

Introducing Layers 158

Create and Add to a Layer 160

Hide a Layer...162

Move a Layer 163

Duplicate a Layer...164

Delete a Layer 165

Reorder Layers..166

Change the Opacity of a Layer 168

Link Layers 169

Merge Layers..170

Rename a Layer 171

Create a Fill Layer 172

Create an Adjustment Layer....................................174

Blend Layers 176

Add a Layer Mask...178

Edit a Layer Mask...180

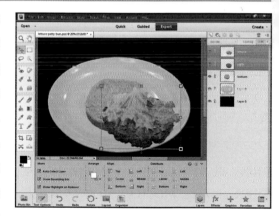

Table of Contents

| **Chapter 9** | Enhancing and Retouching Photos |

Quickly Fix a Photo 184

Remove Red Eye 186

Retouch with the Clone Stamp Tool 188

Remove a Spot 190

Sharpen an Image...................................192

Merge Group Shots.................................194

Recompose a Photo.................................196

Create a Photo Panorama 198

Fix Keystone Distortion............................200

| **Chapter 10** | Enhancing Lighting and Color |

Adjust Levels...204

Adjust Shadows and Highlights 206

Change Brightness and Contrast................208

Using the Dodge and Burn Tools 210

Fix Exposure...212

Using the Blur and Sharpen Tools..............214

Adjust Skin Color 216

Adjust Color with the Sponge Tool.............218

Replace a Color......................................220

Turn a Color Photo into Black and White 222

Add Color to a Black-and-White Photo 224

Adjust Colors by Using Color Curves 226

Apply the Auto Smart Tone Tool.................228

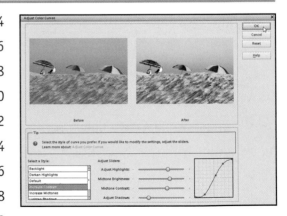

Chapter 11 — Apply Guided Edits

Restore an Old Photo.............................232

Improve a Portrait 234

Shift Colors......................................238

Apply a Lomo Camera Effect 240

Add Motion with Zoom Burst 242

Miniaturize Objects with Tilt Shift 244

Turn a Photo into a Puzzle 246

Apply a Reflection...............................248

Put an Object Out of Bounds 250

Apply a Low Key Effect 252

Chapter 12 — Painting and Drawing on Photos

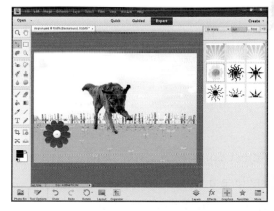

Set the Foreground and Background Colors 256

Add Color with the Brush Tool 258

Change Brush Styles.............................260

Using a Brush to Replace a Color................262

Adjust Colors with the Smart Brush.............264

Draw a Shape 268

Draw a Line.....................................270

Apply the Eraser 272

Apply a Gradient................................274

Add Content from the Graphics Panel.............276

Table of Contents

| Chapter 13 | Applying Filters |

Blur an Image 280
Distort an Image 282
Turn an Image into a Painting 284
Turn an Image into a Sketch...................286
Add Noise to an Image 288
Pixelate an Image...................................290
Emboss an Image....................................292
Apply Multiple Filters 294

| Chapter 14 | Adding Text Elements |

Add Text...298
Change the Formatting of Text................300
Change the Color of Text.........................302
Create Warped Text 304
Add an Effect to Text 306
Add Text along a Selection......................308
Add Text in a Shape 310

Chapter 15 Applying Styles and Effects

Add a Drop Shadow to a Layer 314

Add a Fancy Background 316

Add an Outer Glow to a Layer 318

Add a Fancy Covering to a Layer............................320

Add a Watermark 322

Apply a Photomerge Style 324

Apply an Effect with an Action 326

Add to Favorites 328

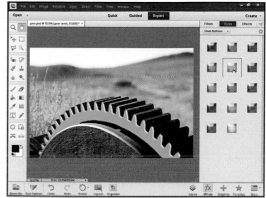

Chapter 16 Saving and Sharing Your Work

Save a Photo for the Web......................................332

Convert File Types...334

E-Mail Images with Photo Mail..............................336

Print Photos..340

Create a Slide Show...342

Create a Photo Book..346

Share Photos on Facebook.....................................350

Share a Photo on Twitter 354

Export Photos..356

Export Photos to Adobe Revel................................358

Back Up Photos 360

Index.. 362

CHAPTER 1

Getting Started

Are you interested in working with digital images on your computer? This chapter introduces you to Adobe Photoshop Elements 12, a popular software application for editing and creating digital images. Photoshop Elements also enables you to organize your collection of digital images so you can easily find what you are looking for.

Introducing Photoshop Elements 12. 4

Understanding Digital Images 6

Start Photoshop Elements 8

Explore the Editor Workspace. 9

Tour the Organizer Workspace 10

Switch between the Organizer and the Editor 11

Introducing the Photoshop Elements Tools 12

Switch Editor Modes 14

Work with Tools .16

Work with Panels 18

Set Program Preferences 20

View Rulers and Guides. 22

Introducing Photoshop Elements 12

Photoshop Elements is a popular photo-editing program you can use to modify, optimize, and organize digital images. You can use the program's Editor to make imperfect snapshots clearer and more colorful as well as retouch and restore older photos. With layers, you can isolate objects in your images and apply special effects just to those objects or combine multiple images into a collage. You can also use the program's Organizer to group your photos into albums, assign descriptive keyword tags, discover visually similar images, create slide shows, and more. When you are done with your images, you can use Photoshop Elements to save them for sharing on the web or print them out.

Manipulate Photos

As its name suggests, Photoshop Elements excels at enabling you to edit elements in your digital photographs. The program includes numerous image-

editing tools and commands you can apply to manipulate the look of your photos. Whether you import photos from a digital camera or a scanner, you can apply a wide variety of editing techniques to your images, from subtle adjustments in color to elaborate filters that make your snapshots look like paintings. See Chapter 7 for more on manipulating selected parts of your photos. See Chapter 12 for more on painting and drawing, and see Chapter 13 for more on using filters.

Retouch and Repair

You can use Photoshop Elements to edit new photos to make them look their best as well as retouch and repair older photos that suffer from aging problems. For example, you can restore a faded photo by using saturation controls to make it more vibrant, or you can use the Clone Stamp tool to repair a tear or stain. You can also use the program's exposure commands to fix lighting problems as well as edit out unwanted objects with the Healing Brush. See Chapter 9 for more on retouching your photos.

Add Decoration

The painting and drawing tools in Photoshop Elements make the program a formidable illustration tool as well as a photo editor. You can apply colors or patterns to your images with a variety of brush styles. See Chapter 12 to discover how to paint and draw on your photos. In addition, you can use the application's typographic tools to integrate stylized letters and words into your images. See Chapter 14 for more on adding text elements.

Create a Digital Collage

You can combine parts of different images in Photoshop Elements to create a collage. Your compositions can include photos, scanned art, text, and anything else you can save on your computer as a digital image. By placing elements on separate layers, you can move, transform, and customize them independently of one another. See Chapter 8 for more on layers. You can also merge several side-by-side scenes into a seamless panorama, which is covered in Chapter 9.

Organize and Catalog

As you bring photos into Photoshop Elements, the program keeps track of them in the Organizer. In the Organizer, you can place groups of photos into theme-specific albums, tag your photos with keywords, and search for specific photos based on a variety of criteria. You can also define the people who are in your photos, the places where photos were taken, and the events during which they were taken. See Chapters 3 and 4 for more on the Organizer.

Put Your Photos to Work

After you edit your photographs, you can use them in a variety of ways. Photoshop Elements enables you to print your images, save them for the web, or bring them together in a slide show. You can share your photos on Facebook or Twitter directly from the Organizer. You can also create photo books, calendars, and other projects. For more on creating and printing your photo projects, see Chapter 16.

Understanding Digital Images

To work with photos in Photoshop Elements, you must first have them in a digital format. When a computer saves a photographic file, it turns the image content into lots of tiny squares called *pixels*. Digital cameras capture their photos as files made up of pixels. Editing a digital image is mostly about recoloring and rearranging pixels, at least on a small scale. Using Photoshop Elements can be a little easier when you remember this. This section introduces you to some important basics about how computers store images in digital form.

Acquire Photos

You can acquire photographic images to use in Photoshop Elements from a number of sources. You can download photos to Photoshop Elements from a digital camera, memory card, or photo CD. You can scan photographs, slides, or artwork and then import the images directly into the program. You can also bring in photos that you have downloaded from the web or received via e-mail. For more on importing photos, see Chapter 2.

Understanding Pixels

Digital images that you download from a camera consist of pixels, each composed of a single color. Photoshop Elements works its magic by rearranging and recoloring these pixels. You can edit specific pixels or groups of pixels by selecting the area of the photo you want to edit. If you zoom in close, you can see the pixels that make up your image. Chapter 5 covers the Zoom tool.

Bitmap Images

Images composed of pixels are known as *bitmap images* or *raster images*. The pixels are arranged in a rectangular grid, and each pixel includes information about its color and position. Most of the time when you are working in Photoshop Elements, you are working with bitmap content.

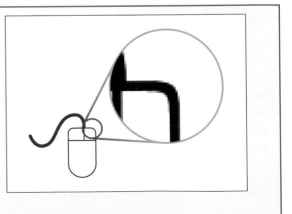

Vector Graphics

The other common way of displaying pictures on your computer is with vector graphics. Vector graphics encode image information by using mathematical equations instead of pixels. Unlike raster images, vector graphics can change size without a loss of quality. When you add shapes or text to your photos in Photoshop Elements, you are working with vector graphics.

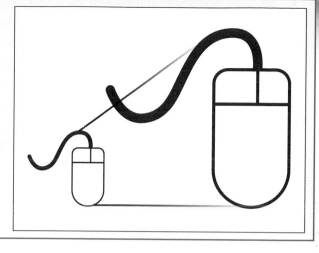

Supported File Formats

Photoshop Elements supports a variety of file types you can both import and export. Popular file formats include BMP, PICT, TIFF, EPS, JPEG, GIF, PDF, PNG, and PSD, which stands for Photoshop Document. Files that you save in the PSD, TIFF, and PDF formats can include layers and other information that cannot be saved with the other formats.

For images published on the Internet, JPEG, GIF, and PNG are the most common formats.

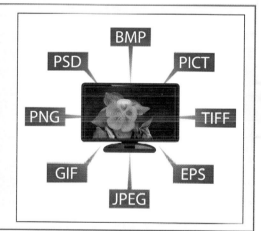

File Size

An important way file formats differ from one another is the amount of storage they take up on your computer. File formats such as PSD and TIFF tend to take up more space because they faithfully save all the information that your camera or other device originally captured. Those formats can also include multiple layers. JPEG, GIF, and PNG files, on the other hand, are built to be sent over the Internet and usually sacrifice some quality for the sake of compactness.

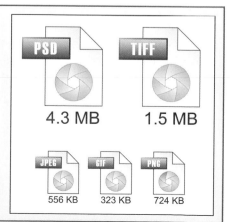

Start Photoshop Elements

After you install Photoshop Elements, you can start it to begin creating and editing digital images. Common ways of obtaining and installing the program include from a DVD or by downloading it from Adobe over the Internet. On a PC, you can access Photoshop Elements as you do other programs — through the Start screen. On a Mac, you can access it through the Finder in the Applications folder or through Launchpad.

Start Photoshop Elements

1 Open the Windows Start screen.

2 Click the **Adobe Photoshop Elements 12** button.

Note: Your location of the Photoshop Elements button may be different depending on how the Start screen is configured.

The Photoshop Elements welcome screen opens.

The welcome screen enables you to access the two different workspaces in Photoshop Elements.

3 Click **Photo Editor**.

The Photoshop Elements Editor opens.

A You can click **Organizer** to open the Organizer.

B You can click 🔧 to access the startup settings.

Explore the Editor Workspace

In the Photoshop Elements Editor, you can use a combination of tools, menu commands, and panel-based features to open and edit your digital photos. You can switch between editing modes to access different tool and panel arrangements. The main Editor pane displays the photos that you are currently modifying. To open the Editor, click **Photo Editor** on the welcome screen.

Ⓐ Image Window

Displays each photo you open in Photoshop Elements

Ⓑ Image Tabs

Clickable tabs for switching between open images in the Editor

Ⓒ Organizer Button

Clickable button for switching to the Organizer workspace, where you can catalog your photos

Ⓓ Mode Buttons

Clickable buttons for switching between Editor modes, each having a different arrangement of tools and panels (Expert mode is shown)

Ⓔ Panel Bin

A storage area for panels, which are the resizable windows that hold related commands, settings, and other information

Ⓕ Photo Bin

Enables you to open and work with multiple photos

Ⓖ Task Bar

Contains buttons for showing and hiding panels and executing common commands

Ⓗ Tools

Clickable icons that represent the editing tools in Photoshop Elements

Ⓘ Open Button

Clickable button for opening photos to start editing

Ⓙ Create Button

Clickable button for accessing a menu of photo-related projects

Tour the Organizer Workspace

In the Photoshop Elements Organizer, you can catalog, view, and sort your growing library of digital photos. The main Organizer pane, called the Media Browser, shows miniature versions of the photos in your catalog. To open the Organizer, click **Organizer** on the welcome screen.

A Media Browser

Displays miniature versions, or *thumbnails*, of the photos and other media in your catalog

B Photo Details

Shows ratings information and the categories associated with each photo

C Editor Button

Clickable button for switching to the Editor workspace, where you can edit your photos

D View Buttons

Clickable buttons for switching to different views in the Organizer

E Panel Bin

A storage area for panels, which are the resizable windows that hold related commands, settings, and other information

F Import Button

Clickable button for importing photos from a camera, folder, or other location to start organizing

G Task Bar

Contains buttons for showing and hiding panels, creating categories, and executing common commands

H Share Button

Clickable button for sharing via social networks, e-mail, and more

Switch between the Organizer and the Editor

Photoshop Elements has two main workspaces: the Organizer and the Editor. The Organizer lets you browse, sort, share, and categorize photos in your collection, and the Editor enables you to modify, combine, and optimize your photos. You can easily switch between the two environments.

You can use the Organizer to review your photos to find images for your projects. After you select your photos in the Organizer, you can open the Editor to adjust the colors, lighting, and other aspects of the photos, and then switch back to the Organizer to choose more photos to edit.

Switch between the Organizer and the Editor

1 Start Photoshop Elements in the Organizer view.

Note: See the section "Start Photoshop Elements" for more on starting the program.

You can browse and sort your photos in the Organizer.

Note: For more about adding photos to the Organizer, see Chapter 2.

2 Click a photo to select it.

3 Click **Editor**.

The photo opens in the Editor. If the Editor is not already running, it may take a few moments to launch.

A The Editor opens in whatever mode you last used.

B You can click **Organizer** to return to the Organizer.

Introducing the Photoshop Elements Tools

In the Editor, Photoshop Elements offers a variety of specialized tools that enable you to manipulate your image. You can select tools by clicking icons on the left side of the workspace or by typing a keyboard shortcut key. Keyboard shortcut keys are shown in parentheses. Each Editor mode features a different set of tools. Expert mode, which has the most tools available, is shown here.

A Zoom (Z)

Zooms your view of an image in or out

B Hand (H)

Moves the image to reveal off-screen portions of the image

C Move (V)

Moves selected areas of an image

D Marquee (M)

Defines an area of an image by drawing a box or ellipse around the area you want to edit

E Lasso (L)

Selects pixels by drawing a free-form shape around the area you want to edit

F Quick Selection (A)

Selects areas of an image based on color similarity and edges

G Red-Eye Removal (Y)

Corrects red-eye problems

H Spot-Healing Brush (J)

Repairs imperfections by copying nearby pixels

I Smart Brush (F)

Simultaneously selects and applies a wide variety of different effects

J Clone Stamp (S)

Paints pixels from one part of an image to another part

K Blur (R)

Blurs selected portions of your image

L Sponge (O)

Increases or decreases color saturation or intensity

Ⓐ Brush (B)

Paints strokes of color

Ⓑ Eraser (E)

Erases pixels by replacing them with background color or making them transparent on layers

Ⓒ Paint Bucket (K)

Fills a selected area with a single color

Ⓓ Gradient (G)

Fills areas with blended color effects

Ⓔ Eyedropper (I)

Samples color from an area of an image

Ⓕ Custom Shape (U)

Draws predefined shapes

Ⓖ Type (T)

Adds text to an image

Ⓗ Pencil (N)

Draws hard-edged lines of color

Ⓘ Crop (C)

Trims or expands an image to improve composition

Ⓙ Recompose (W)

Intelligently changes the size of a photo while keeping elements intact

Ⓚ Content-Aware Move Tool (Q)

Moves part of an image while replacing the original location with surrounding content

Ⓛ Straighten (P)

Straightens out a crooked image or changes the orientation of an image

Ⓜ Foreground and Background Color

Sets foreground and background colors to use with tools

Ⓝ Tool Options Panel

Displays settings to customize the selected tool

Switch Editor Modes

The Photoshop Elements Editor has three modes: Quick, Guided, and Expert. You can switch modes based on the tools you need and the workflow you are comfortable with.

Quick mode offers access to commonly used tools and optimization commands. It is perfect for the beginner or someone who wants to fix photos quickly. Guided mode features step-by-step instructions paired with tools for fixing photos and adding special effects. Expert mode gives you access to most of the program's tools and the more complex commands.

Switch Editor Modes

Note: This image and others from the book are available for download from www.wiley.com/go/tyvpse12. The images on the companion website are small, low-resolution images for you to practice the steps. You will get better results and learn more when you use your own photographs.

1 Open a photo in the Editor.

Note: See Chapter 2 for information about opening photos.

2 Click **Quick**.

Quick mode appears.

Ⓐ You can click here to select a tool.

Note: For more about tools, see the next section, "Work with Tools."

Ⓑ You can click here to access optimization settings.

3 Click a menu.

Photoshop Elements displays the menu commands.

Ⓒ Some commands are grayed out and disabled, depending on the mode.

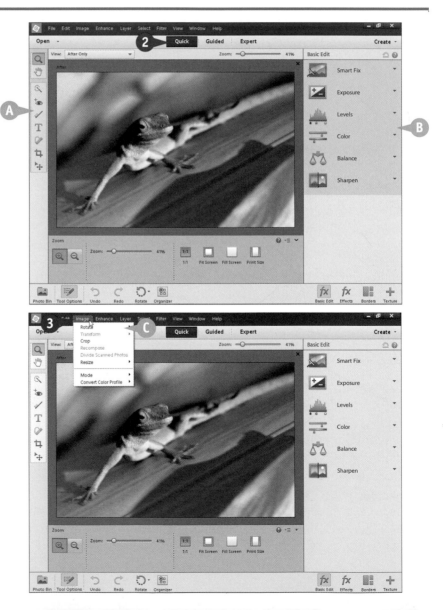

14

4 Click **Guided**.

Guided mode appears.

D You can click here to select a tool.

E You can click here to access step-by-step instructions for editing photos.

5 Click **Expert**.

Expert mode appears.

F You can click here to select a tool.

G You can click here to open and close panels.

Note: See the section "Work with Panels" for more information.

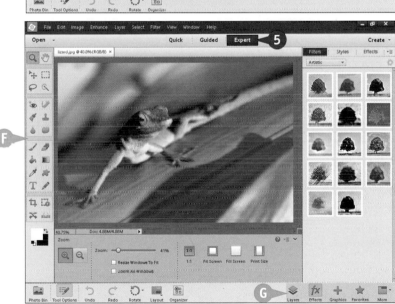

How do I view before and after versions of photos as I edit them?

In Quick mode and Guided mode, you can click the **View** menu in the upper left of the workspace. Select a Before & After view to display both versions of the current photo. You can choose horizontal and vertical versions, depending on the orientation of your photo.

How can I get extra help when learning about Photoshop Elements features?

Click the **Help** menu and then click a help-related command. The Key Concepts, Support, Video Tutorials, and Forum commands take you to the Adobe.com website. Accessing Adobe.com requires you to have an Internet connection.

15

Work with Tools

You can use the tools in Photoshop Elements to make changes to an image. After you click to select a tool, the Tool Options panel displays controls for customizing how the tool works. For example, after you select the Rectangular Marquee tool, you can adjust the Tool Options panel settings to determine the height and width of the tool.

Some tools display a tiny mark in the upper right corner when you position the cursor over them, indicating related tools you can select. For example, the Lasso tool includes two additional variations: Polygonal Lasso and Magnetic Lasso.

Work with Tools

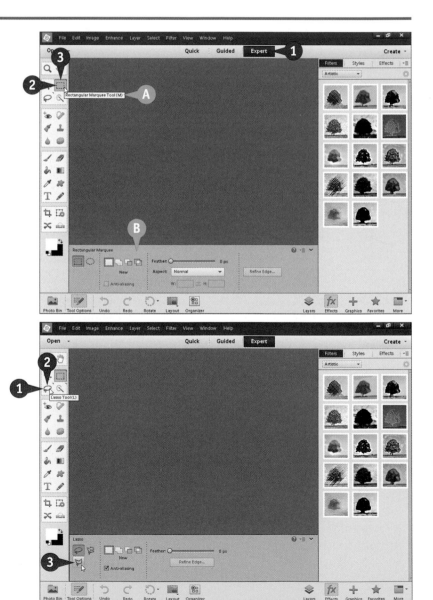

Select a Tool

1. Click an Editor mode.

2. Position the mouse pointer over a tool.

A. A screen tip displays the tool name and shortcut key. You can click the tool name to access help information about the tool.

3. Click a tool to select it.

B. The Tool Options panel shows settings for customizing the selected tool. Specify any options you want for the tool.

Select a Related Tool

1. Position your mouse pointer over a tool.

2. Click a tool that has a ⬛ in its corner.

   Photoshop Elements displays the clicked tool and one or more related tools in the Tool Options panel.

3. Click one of the related tools.

   You can also press a tool's shortcut key more than once to cycle through the related tools.

Close the Tool Options Panel

You can close the Tool Options panel to give you more space to view and edit your photos.

1 Click **Tool Options**.

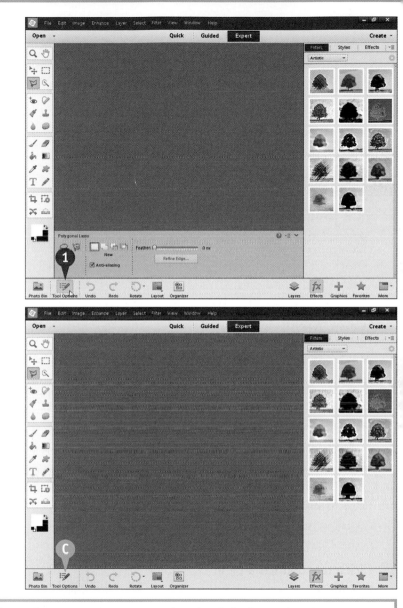

The Tool Options panel closes.

C You can click **Tool Options** again to reopen the Tool Options panel.

How can I keep the Tool Options panel hidden?

In the Tool Options panel, click the panel menu (⊡≡). By default, Auto Show Tool Options is selected and the panel is shown when a tool is clicked. Click **Auto Show Tool Options** to deselect the option and keep the panel hidden.

How can I reset a tool to its default settings?

With a tool selected, click the panel menu (⊡≡) in the Tool Options panel and then click **Reset Tool**. For painting tools, this resets the opacity to 100%, the blending mode to Normal, and other attributes to their startup values. For selection tools, the New Selection option is selected and any feathering is set to 0 px. You can click **Reset All Tools** to reset all the Photoshop Elements tools to their default settings.

Work with Panels

In the Photoshop Elements Editor, you can open resizable panes called *panels* to access different Photoshop Elements commands and features. In Expert mode, which is shown in this example, the more commonly used panels open in the Panel Bin located on the right side of the workspace. Other panels open in a tabbed, floating window.

The Layers panel gives you access to the one or more layers present in your image. Each layer can contain image content that can be moved and adjusted independent of the content in other layers. The Effects panel includes dozens of special effects that you can apply to your image.

Work with Panels

Using the Main Panels

1 Open the Photoshop Elements Editor.

Note: For more on opening the Editor, see the section "Start Photoshop Elements."

2 Click a button.

Ⓐ You can also access panels in the Window menu.

Ⓑ The clicked panel opens in the Panel Bin.

Ⓒ Buttons and menus enable you to filter available commands.

3 Click the panel button again.

The panel closes.

By closing panels, you can have more workspace for editing photos.

Open More Panels

1 Click **More**.

A window opens with tabbed panels.

2 Click a tab to access a panel.

D You can click ☒ to close the panel window.

E You can click and drag the panel header to move the window.

Resize Panels

1 To resize panels in the Panel Bin, position your cursor over the left edge of the bin and then click and drag.

2 To resize the panel window, click and drag the corner or edges. Not all panels in the panel window are resizable.

The panels resize.

TIPS

What are the panels in the modes other than Expert?
Quick mode has a single panel that contains optimization tools. Guided mode has a panel that lists step-by-step instructional tasks. You can hide the panel in Quick mode but not in Guided mode.

How do I reset my panels?
Click **Window** and then **Reset Panels**. This resets the size of the panels and, in Expert mode, sets the Panel Bin to the Layers panel.

Set Program Preferences

The Photoshop Elements Preferences dialog box enables you to change default settings and modify how the program looks. You can set preferences in both the Editor and Organizer workspaces to customize the program to match how you like to work.

When you make changes to the program in the preferences, the changes remain after you exit the program and then open it again. In the Organizer, you can restore all preferences to their original state by clicking **Restore Default Settings** in the General preferences.

Set Program Preferences

In the Editor

1 In the Editor, click **Edit**. (On a Mac, click **Adobe Photoshop Elements Editor**.)

Note: For more on opening the Editor, see the section "Explore the Editor Workspace."

2 Click **Preferences**.

3 Click **General**.

As an alternative, you can press **Ctrl**+**K** (**⌘**+**K** on a Mac).

The Preferences dialog box opens and displays General options.

4 Select any settings you want to change.

A For example, you can click the 🔽 to specify the shortcut keys for stepping backward and forward through your commands.

B You can click this option (☐ changes to ☑) to open images in floating windows instead of tabbed windows.

5 Click a different preference category.

C You can also click **Prev** and **Next** to move back and forth between categories.

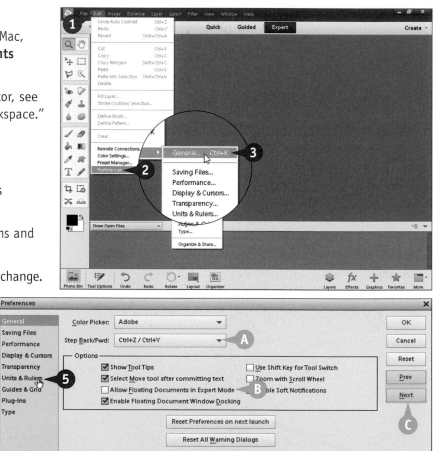

In this example, the Preferences dialog box displays Units & Rulers options.

6 Select any settings you want to change.

D For example, you can specify the default units for various aspects of the program.

7 Click **OK**.

Photoshop Elements sets the preferences.

In the Organizer

1 In the Organizer, repeat steps **1** to **3** in the subsection "In the Editor," or press **Ctrl**+**K** (**⌘**+**K** on a Mac).

Note: For more on opening the Organizer, see the section "Tour the Organizer Workspace."

The Preferences dialog box opens.

2 Select any settings you want to change.

E For example, you can specify date ordering and formatting preferences.

3 Click **OK**.

Photoshop Elements sets the preferences.

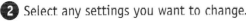

TIPS

What type of measurement units should I use in Photoshop Elements?
Typically, you should use the units most applicable to the type of output you intend to produce. Pixel units are useful for web imaging because monitor dimensions are measured in pixels. Inches, picas, centimeters, or millimeters are useful for print because those are standards for working on paper.

How do I allocate extra memory to Photoshop Elements for opening more image files?
The Performance preferences show how much memory, or *RAM*, you have available and how much of it Photoshop Elements is using. The Scratch Disks preferences enable you to allocate extra memory on your hard drive(s), called *scratch disk space*, to use if your computer runs out of RAM.

View Rulers and Guides

In Expert mode, you can turn on rulers and guides to help place objects accurately in your image. Rulers appear at the top and left sides of the image window and enable you to measure distances within your image. To change the units of measurement associated with the rulers, see the previous section, "Set Program Preferences."

Guides are the lines that help you position different elements in your image horizontally or vertically. These lines do not appear on your image when you save the image for the web or print it.

View Rulers and Guides

Show Rulers

1 Click **Expert**.

2 Click **View**.

3 Click **Rulers**.

You can also press Shift + Ctrl + R (Shift + ⌘ + R on a Mac).

A Photoshop Elements adds rulers to the top and left edges of the image window.

Create a Guide

1 Click one of the rulers and drag the cursor into the window (↖ changes to ↔).

Drag the top ruler down to create a horizontal guide.

Drag the left ruler to the right to create a vertical guide.

B A thin, colored line called a *guide* appears.

C You can also click **View** and then **New Guide** to add a guide.

You can use guides to align objects in the different layers of an image.

Note: See Chapter 8 for more about layers.

Move a Guide

1 Click the **Move** tool (⊞).

2 Position the mouse pointer over a guide (⬚ changes to ◄╫►) and then click and drag.

You can also press **Ctrl**+**'** (**⌘**+**'** on a Mac) to display a grid on your image. The lines of the grid can help you align objects in your image.

TIP

How do I make objects in my images "snap to" my guides when I move those objects?

The "snap to" feature is useful for aligning elements in a row or a column. Click **View**, **Snap To**, and then **Guides** (**A**). When you move an object near a guide, Photoshop Elements automatically aligns the object with the guide.

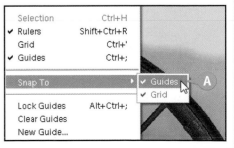

CHAPTER 2

Importing and Opening Digital Images

Before you can start working with photos, you must import them. This chapter shows you how to import photos into the Organizer and then open them in the Editor.

Get Photos for Your Projects 26

Import Photos from a Digital Camera or Card Reader 28

Import Photos from a Scanner 30

Import or Search for Photos from a Folder. 32

Open a Photo 34

Create a Blank Image. 36

Save a Photo. 38

Duplicate a Photo 40

Close a Photo 41

Get Photos for Your Projects

To work with images in Photoshop Elements, you must first acquire the images. You can get images and clip art to use in your creative projects from a variety of sources. Digital cameras have become ubiquitous, and you can get images using expensive digital SLRs, cheap point-and-shoot cameras, and camera phones. Scanned art is another option, as is content captured with a film-based camera. Finally, you can obtain photos that other people have posted to photo-sharing websites. Photoshop Elements makes it easy to bring in content from these different sources.

Digital Cameras

A digital camera is probably the most common way to take photographs and then import them into your computer. Most digital cameras save their images as JPEG or RAW files, both of which you can open and edit in Photoshop Elements. You can transfer images from most cameras by using a USB cable or a *card reader*, a device that reads a camera's memory card.

Scanned Photos and Art

A scanner gives you an inexpensive way to convert existing paper-based content into a digital form. You can scan photos and art into your computer, retouch and stylize them in Photoshop Elements, and then output them to a color printer. You can also use a slide attachment to digitize slides by using a scanner. For tips on cropping and rotating scanned photos, see Chapter 5.

Web Images

If you have photos or art stored on the web, you can easily save those image files to your computer and then open them in Photoshop Elements. In Internet Explorer on the PC, you can save a web image by right-clicking it and then choosing **Save picture as** (**Save Image As** in Firefox or in Safari on a Mac). Inexpensive stock photo websites, such as iStockphoto, offer professional-grade images for download. On photo-sharing sites such as Flickr, users often allow noncommercial use of their photos.

Start from Scratch

You can also create your Photoshop Elements image from scratch by opening a blank canvas in the image window. You can then apply colors and patterns with the painting tools in Photoshop Elements, or you can cut and paste parts of other images to create a composite. See the section "Create a Blank Image" for more on opening a blank canvas.

Film Photos

If you have a film camera, you can have your photos burned to a CD or DVD during film processing. Then, you can import the photos from the disc just as you would import photos from a folder on your computer. See the section "Import Photos from a Folder" for more. Hundreds or thousands of images can be saved on a single disc, depending on the type of disc and sizes of the images. Most photo-printing services can also burn photos from digital cameras to a disc for safekeeping.

Working with Imported Photos

Images imported into Photoshop Elements are stored in the program's Organizer workspace. There, you can browse miniature versions of your photos, called *thumbnails*, sort them, group them into albums, and assign keyword tags to them. You can edit your photos by opening them in the Photoshop Elements Editor. You can open them in the Editor from the Organizer or open them directly from folders on your computer. See Chapter 1 for more on the Editor and the Organizer workspaces.

Import Photos from a Digital Camera or Card Reader

You can import photos into Photoshop Elements from a digital camera or directly from the camera's memory card. After the import, the photos appear in the Organizer Media Browser. Most cameras and card readers manufactured today connect to a computer through a USB port. A typical PC or Mac comes with multiple USB ports. Make sure the device is properly connected before you begin. Also, most computers have special media slots that accept memory cards for transferring photos and other files. Every camera and card reader works differently. Consult the documentation that came with your device for more information.

Import Photos from a Digital Camera or Card Reader

1 In the Organizer, click **File**.

2 Click **Get Photos and Videos**.

3 Click **From Camera or Card Reader**.

The Photo Downloader dialog box opens.

Photo Downloader may automatically open when you connect your device to your computer, depending on the settings in Photoshop Elements.

4 Click the ▾ to choose your camera or memory card from the Get Photos From menu.

By default, Photoshop Elements downloads your photos into dated subfolders inside your Pictures folder. The dated subfolders are based on the time stamp associated with each photo.

Ⓐ You can click **Browse** to select a different download location.

Ⓑ You can click the ▾ to choose a different naming scheme for the subfolders.

5 Click the ▾ to choose a naming scheme for your files.

28

6 Click the ⬛ to choose whether to keep your photos on the device or delete them after downloading.

C You can click this option to enable Photoshop Elements to download your photos automatically using the current settings whenever a photo device is connected to your computer (☐ changes to ☑).

7 Click **Get Media**.

Photoshop Elements downloads the photos from the device.

D You can click **Stop** to abort the download.

After downloading the photos, Photoshop Elements adds them to the current Organizer catalog. There, you can add the photos to albums and perform other functions.

TIP

How do I use the Advanced dialog box in the Photo Downloader?
To open the dialog box, click **Advanced Dialog** in the bottom left corner of the Photo Downloader. All photos are selected and downloaded by default. You can click a check box to deselect a photo (☑ changes to ☐) (**A**). You can adjust other settings to turn on red-eye correction or apply copyright details to the imported photos. Click **Get Media** to import the photos.

Import Photos from a Scanner

You can import a photo into Photoshop Elements through a scanner attached to your computer in Windows. In Windows, the photo appears in the Organizer Media Browser after importing. On a Mac, you can use the Image Capture application to scan photos and send them to the Organizer. Some scanners include slide or film attachments that enable you to digitize slides or film.

Every scanner works differently. Consult the documentation that came with your scanner for more information. After scanning, you can rotate or crop the photo to fix any alignment issues. See Chapter 5 for details.

Import Photos from a Scanner

1 In the Organizer, click **File**.

Note: For more on using the Organizer, see Chapter 3.

2 Click **Get Photos and Videos**.

3 Click **From Scanner**.

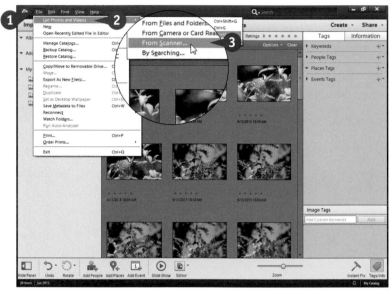

The Get Photos from Scanner dialog box opens.

4 Click the ▼ to choose your scanner.

By default, Photoshop Elements saves scanned photos in the Adobe folder inside your Pictures folder.

A You can click **Browse** to choose another location.

5 Click the ▼ to choose a file format.

B If you are importing as a JPEG, it is typically best to import at a high-quality setting.

6 Click **OK**.

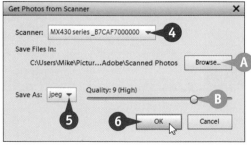

The software associated with your scanner opens. The window can look significantly different depending on the scanner make and model.

7 Change your scanning settings as needed. You may need to specify whether the photo is black and white or color. You may also get to preview the scan.

8 Click your scanner software's **Scan** button to scan your photo.

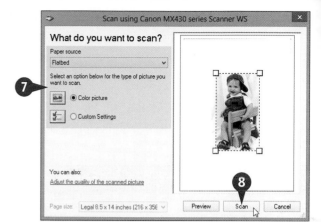

The image is scanned and added to the current catalog in the Organizer.

C Photoshop Elements displays the imported photo by itself.

9 Click **Back** to return to the previous Organizer view.

Note: To crop or rotate a scanned image, see Chapter 5.

Import or Search for Photos from a Folder

You can use the Organizer workspace in Photoshop Elements to import images from a folder on your computer or a disc. You may find this useful if you already have an archive of digital photos on your PC or on photo CDs. After the import, the images appear in the Organizer Media Browser.

You can also use the Organizer's search feature to discover folders on your computer that contain photos. Then you can choose the folders to import from. After importing, you can add photos to albums and also categorize them with keyword tags.

Import or Search for Photos from a Folder

Import Photos by Selecting a Folder

1 In the Organizer, click **File**.

Note: For more on using the Organizer, see Chapter 3.

2 Click **Get Photos and Videos**.

3 Click **From Files and Folders**.

The Get Photos and Videos from Files and Folders dialog box opens.

4 Click the ☑ to choose the folder containing your photos.

5 Ctrl+click (⌘+click on a Mac) to select the photos you want to import.

Ⓐ You can click this option to have Photoshop Elements automatically fix red eye (☐ changes to ☑).

Ⓑ You can import different types of files, such as PDF documents or Photoshop Elements projects, by clicking the ☑.

Note: For more on creating projects in Photoshop Elements, see Chapter 16.

6 Click **Get Media**.

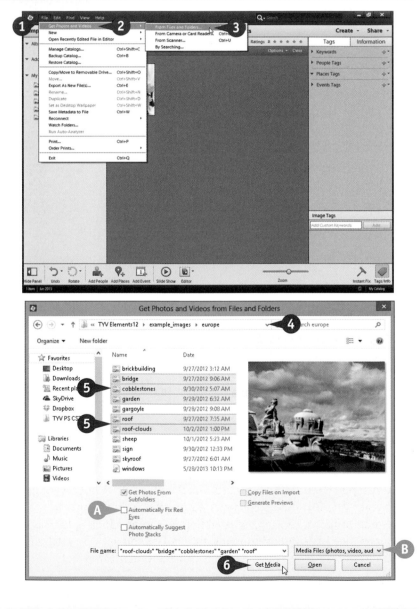

Photoshop Elements downloads the selected photos from the folder.

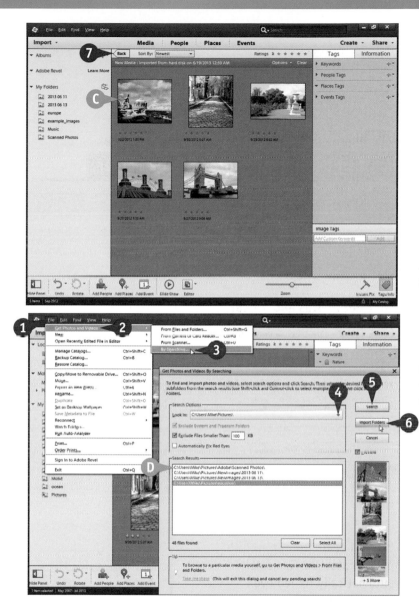

C Photoshop Elements displays the imported photos by themselves in the Organizer.

7 Click **Back** to return to the previous Organizer view.

Import Photos by Searching

1 Click **File**.

2 Click **Get Photos and Videos**.

3 Click **By Searching**.

The Get Photos and Videos By Searching dialog box opens.

4 In the Search Options section, click the ▼ to choose all hard drives, a single hard drive, or a folder.

5 Click **Search**.

D Your search results appear.

6 Select one or more folders and then click **Import Folders** to get the photos. Ctrl+click (⌘+click on a Mac) to select multiple folders.

How can I automatically add new images on my computer to the Organizer?

You can have Photoshop Elements watch certain folders on your computer. When new images are added to those folders, Photoshop Elements automatically adds them to the Organizer. Click **File** and then **Watch Folders**. A dialog box appears enabling you to add folders to watch and then add new images automatically. You can also have Photoshop Elements notify you with an alert window when new images are added. Then you can choose whether to add them to the Organizer or not.

Open a Photo

You can open a photo in the Editor to modify it or to use it in a project. After you open the photo, you can adjust its color and lighting, add special effects, and move objects in the photo to separate layers. You can also open photos from the Organizer for editing in the Editor.

You can open more than one photo at a time in the Editor. You can switch between photos using the window tabs. Open images also appear in the Photo Bin. For information about managing photos after you open them, see Chapter 5.

Open a Photo

Open a Photo from a Folder

1 In the Editor, click **Open**.

Note: For more on opening the Editor, see Chapter 1.

You can also press Ctrl+O (⌘+O on a Mac).

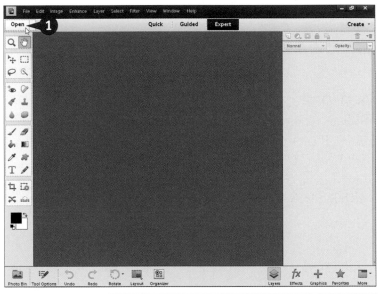

The Open dialog box appears.

2 Click the 🔽 to navigate to the folder containing the file you want to open.

3 Click the photo you want to open.

A A preview of the image appears.

4 Click **Open**.

Photoshop Elements opens the image.

Ⓑ The filename and zoom value appear in the tab for the image.

Note: The image may also open in a floating window depending on how your program preferences are set.

Ⓒ If the Photo Bin is open in the Editor, the image also appears in the Bin.

Ⓓ If you open multiple photos at one time, you can click **Window** to view a list of the open photos.

Open an Organizer Photo for Editing

① In the Organizer, right-click the photo you want to edit.

② In the menu that appears, click **Edit with Photoshop Elements Editor**.

Ⓔ You can also click **Editor**.

Photoshop Elements opens the photo in the Editor.

TIP

What types of files can Photoshop Elements open?
Photoshop Elements can open most of the image file formats in common use today. A partial list follows.

File Type	Description
BMP (Bitmap)	The standard Windows image format
TIFF (Tagged Image File Format)	A format for print
JPEG (Joint Photographic Experts Group)	A format for web images
PNG (Portable Network Graphics)	An alternative web format to GIF and JPEG
PSD (Photoshop Document)	Photoshop's native file format

Create a Blank Image

You can start a Photoshop Elements project by creating a blank image and then adding photographic, textual, and other content to the blank image. When you create a blank image, you specify the dimensions and the resolution. Photoshop Elements offers a number of useful preset sizes, including common paper sizes and web browser dimensions. For more about choosing a print size and resolution, see Chapter 5.

You can add content from other images to your blank image as separate layers. For more on layers, see Chapter 8. You can also use the Brush tool to add streaks of color. See Chapter 12 for information about using and customizing the Brush tool.

Create a Blank Image

1 In the Editor, click the next to **Open**.

Note: For more on opening the Editor, see Chapter 1.

2 Click **New Blank File**.

You can also press Ctrl+N (⌘+N on a Mac).

The New dialog box opens.

3 Type a name for the new image.

4 Type the desired dimensions and resolution, or choose a preset dimension and resolution from the pop-up menu.

If you have just previously performed a copy command in another image window or in another program, Photoshop Elements uses the dimensions of the copied content by default.

A You can click the 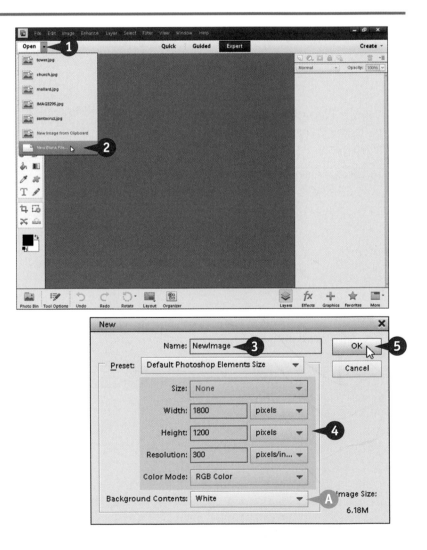 to change the background of the blank canvas.

5 Click **OK**.

Photoshop Elements creates a new image window at the specified dimensions.

6 Use the Photoshop Elements tools and commands to edit the new image.

B In this example, selections from other photos are cut and pasted onto the blank image.

Note: See Chapter 7 for more on how to duplicate a selection.

C The parts appear in different layers in the Layers panel.

Note: To save your image, see the next section, "Save a Photo."

TIPS

What should I choose as a resolution for a new image?

The appropriate resolution depends on how you will use the image. For web or multimedia images, select 72 pixels/inch, the standard resolution for on-screen images. To output images on a typical inkjet printer, use a resolution of 240 to 360 pixels/inch. A higher pixel/inch value is indistinguishable to the human eye.

How do I open a frame from a video clip?

Open a video frame in Photoshop Elements by clicking **File**, **Import**, and then **Frame from Video**. In the dialog box, you can browse for and open a video clip, scan through the clip, and import a frame into the Editor. Photoshop Elements supports importing from WMV, MPEG, and AVI files; Mac users can import MOV files.

Save a Photo

You can save a photo in Photoshop Elements to store any changes that you made to it. PSD is the default file format for Photoshop Elements. Photoshop Elements supports a variety of other image file formats, including the popular JPEG, GIF, and PNG formats commonly found on the web. If you have an image that includes multiple layers, you can save the image in the PSD, TIFF, or PDF format to preserve the layers.

You can have multiple versions of the same image saved as a *version set* in the Organizer. Version sets enable you to save copies of an image project at different stages or with different effects applied.

Save a Photo

Save a New Photo

1 In the Editor, click **File**.

Note: For more on opening the Editor, see Chapter 1.

2 Click **Save As**.

Note: For photos that you have previously saved, you can click **File** and then **Save**.

The Save As dialog box opens.

3 Type a name for the file.

 You can click the ⬇ to choose another folder or drive in which to store the file.

B You can click the ⬇ to choose another file format.

4 Click this option to include the saved file in the Organizer (☐ changes to ☑).

5 Click this option to save the edited file with other versions of the same file in the Organizer (☐ changes to ☑).

You can save a photo into a version set only when the photo already exists as a version in the Organizer.

6 Click **Save**.

Photoshop Elements saves the image file.

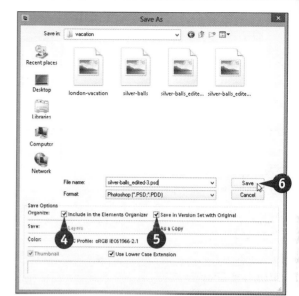

View a Version Set in the Organizer

1 In the Organizer, find a version set ().

ⓒ You can use the scroll bar to browse your photos.

2 Click ▶ to expand the version set so you can view all the photos in that set.

Photoshop Elements expands the version set.

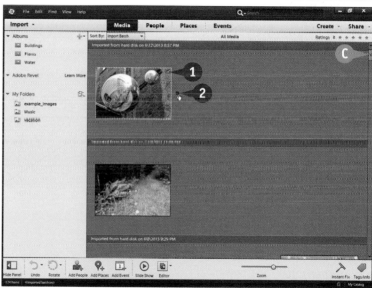

TIP

How can I save my open photos as an album in the Organizer?
In the Photo Bin, click the bin menu (▾≡). Click **Save Bin as an Album** (Ⓐ). In the Save Photo Bin dialog box, type a name for the album and click **OK**. The photos are saved as a new album in the Organizer.

Duplicate a Photo

In the Editor, you can duplicate a photo to keep an unchanged copy while you continue to work on the duplicate. Photoshop Elements puts the duplicate in its own window. You must save the copy to create a file for it on your computer. See the previous section, "Save a Photo," for more details.

If you perform changes to one of the images, you can compare the copies side by side by using a workspace layout that displays two image windows at one time. For more information about layouts and managing multiple open images, see Chapter 5.

Duplicate a Photo

1 In the Editor, click **File**.

Note: For more on opening the Editor, see Chapter 1.

2 Click **Duplicate**.

The Duplicate Image dialog box opens.

Ⓐ Photoshop Elements displays an editable name for the duplicate.

3 Click **OK**.

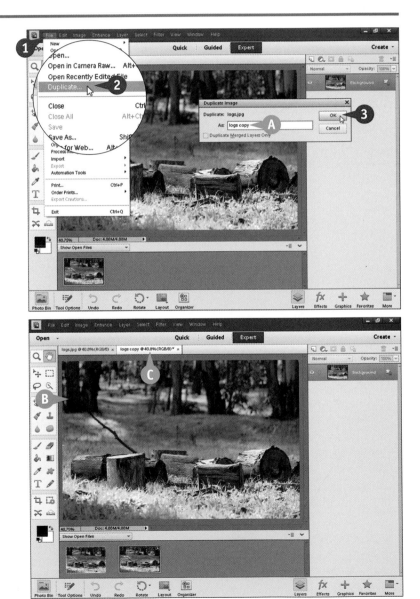

Ⓑ Photoshop Elements opens a duplicate of the photo as another tabbed window.

Note: For more on managing open images by using tabs, see Chapter 5.

Ⓒ The name and zoom value appear in the tab.

Note: See the previous section, "Save a Photo," for more on how to save the duplicate.

Close a Photo

Y ou can close a photo after you finish editing it. Although you can have more than one photo open at a time, closing photos you no longer need can free up system resources and speed up your computer's performance. Closing photos also reduces clutter in your workspace because every open item adds a tab along the top of the default workspace. If you try to close an image that has unsaved changes, Photoshop Elements warns you before closing the image. When you exit Photoshop Elements, it closes all open images and also warns you about unsaved changes.

Close a Photo

1 In the Editor, click **File**.

Note: For more on opening the Editor, see Chapter 1.

2 Click **Close**.

You can also press Ctrl+W (⌘+W on a Mac).

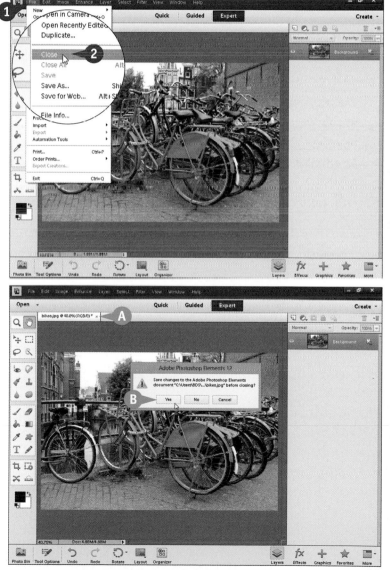

A You can also click ✕ to close a photo.

B If you have made any changes to the file and have not saved them, Photoshop Elements prompts you to do so before closing the file. Click **Yes** to save your work.

Note: See the section "Save a Photo" for more on how to save files.

After saving, if needed, Photoshop Elements closes the photo. The program remains open.

CHAPTER 3

Organizing Your Photos

Are you ready to organize your digital photos? You can catalog, view, and sort photo files by using the Organizer. A complement to the Editor in Photoshop Elements, the Organizer helps you manage your growing library of digital pictures by categorizing them in a variety of ways. This chapter shows you how to take advantage of the many photo-management features in the Organizer.

Introducing the Organizer 44

Open the Organizer. 46

Create a Catalog 48

View Photos in the Media Browser 50

View Photos in Full Screen 52

Display a Slide Show in Full Screen 54

View Photo Information 56

Add a Caption 58

Work with Albums 60

Find Photos 62

Rate Photos 64

View Versions of a Photo 66

Remove a Photo from the Organizer. 67

Introducing the Organizer

You can use the Organizer program to manage your growing library of digital photos. Photos you import or save in Photoshop Elements are automatically added to the Organizer catalog. In the Organizer, you can sort and filter your photo collection in different ways. You can associate your photos with people, places, or events. You can also group photos into albums and tag them with descriptive keywords.

Once you have found one or more photos that you want to edit, you can switch to the Editor workspace to cut and paste objects in your photo, adjust color and lighting, or apply special effects. You can switch back to the Organizer when you are done or when you need to find more photo content.

Virtual Browser

The Organizer acts as a virtual browser, enabling you to view *thumbnails,* or miniature versions, of your pictures. The thumbnails you see in the Organizer are merely pointers to the original file locations. The images remain intact in their original location unless you decide to delete them. The Organizer enables you to view your photos from one convenient window. See the section "View Photos in the Media Browser" to learn more.

Catalog

When you bring photo files into the Organizer, the program adds them to your catalog of images. Images are cataloged by date. You can keep all your photos in one catalog, or you can store them in separate catalogs. If you want to group your photos further, you can place them into albums or stacks. See the sections "Create a Catalog" and "Work with Albums" for more on these topics. For more on stacking photos, see Chapter 4.

Keyword Tags

You can use keyword tags to help you sort and track your photos. A *keyword tag* is a text identifier you assign to a photo. After you assign tags, you can search for photos that match certain tags and also sort your photos in tag order. You can assign any of the preset tags that come with the Organizer, or you can create your own. The Organizer's presets include tags for colors, photography, activities, and more. You can also assign multiple tags to the same photo. For more on keyword tags, see Chapter 4.

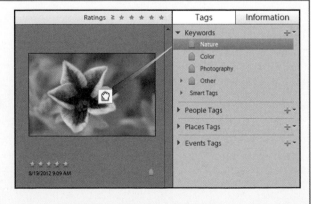

People, Places, and Events

An important way we categorize photos in our minds is by remembering the people in them, the places they were taken, and the events at which they were taken. Photoshop Elements 12 has improved tools for grouping photos in these three ways. You can automatically import your list of Facebook friends and match photos to names on that list. You can place photos on a geographic map. You can also organize photos by events based on the time they were taken.

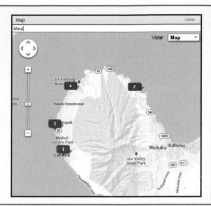

Find Photos

As your photo collection grows, being able to quickly find photos becomes critically important. Although filtering photos by album or keyword tag offers one way to find photos, the Organizer also includes full-featured searching tools. You can search your catalog by date, filename, visual similarity, or by the people, places, and events associated with your photos. You can apply ratings using a five-star system, and then view photos that meet a certain rating criteria. See the sections "Find Photos" and "Rate Photos" for more information.

Create and Share

Because it enables you to easily organize and find photos in your collection, using the Organizer is an important first step in completing various Photoshop Elements projects. For example, you can display your favorite photos in the Organizer and then create a custom slide show or photo book to distribute to friends and family. You can also select photos to share on social networks such as Facebook or Twitter and photo-sharing sites such as Flickr, or send your images to others via e-mail. See Chapter 16 for photo projects you can build in Photoshop Elements and for more about sharing.

Open the Organizer

You can organize and manage your digital photos in the Organizer in Photoshop Elements. The Organizer works alongside the Editor to help you keep track of your digital photos and other media. You can open the Organizer from the welcome screen that appears when you start up Photoshop Elements or switch to it from the Editor.

The main feature of the Organizer is the Media Browser, which features a grid of *thumbnails*, or miniature versions of your photos. You can select a thumbnail and then perform basic commands on it in the Organizer or open the image in the Editor to perform more complex operations.

Open the Organizer

From the Welcome Screen

1 Start Photoshop Elements.

Note: See Chapter 1 for more on starting Photoshop Elements.

The welcome screen appears.

2 Click **Organizer** to open the Organizer.

The Organizer opens.

To import photos into the Organizer workspace, see Chapter 2.

To create a new catalog with which to organize your photos, see the next section, "Create a Catalog."

From the Editor

 Start Photoshop Elements.

2 From the welcome screen that appears, click **Photo Editor** to open the Editor.

3 Click **Organizer**.

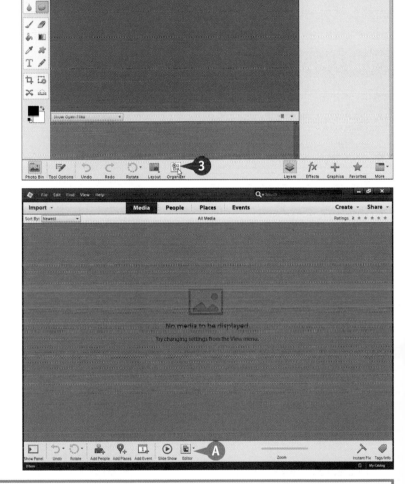

The Organizer opens.

Ⓐ To return to the Editor, click **Editor**.

TIP

How do I edit photos from within the Organizer?

The Organizer offers basic editing commands in the Instant Fix panel. The commands can save you from having to switch to the Editor to optimize your photos. To access them, click **Instant Fix** in the Organizer. The editing buttons appear (Ⓐ). Click a thumbnail in the Media Browser, and click an editing button to optimize the color or lighting in your photo, or to crop it, for example. In addition to those shown, the panel also includes Sharpen, Levels, and Smart Fix options.

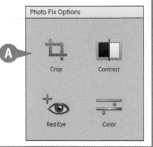

Create a Catalog

The photos you manage in the Organizer are stored in catalogs. You can keep your photos in one large catalog or separate them into smaller catalogs. When you start the Organizer, Photoshop Elements creates a default catalog for you called My Catalog.

You can organize your photos within a catalog into smaller groups called albums. See the section "Work with Albums" for more. You can also combine similar photos into stacks to save space when viewing your catalog. See Chapter 4 for details. Photoshop Elements 12 can open catalogs created in previous versions of Photoshop Elements and can convert them so you can use all the newest features of the Organizer.

Create a Catalog

1 In the Organizer, click **File**.

2 Click **Manage Catalogs**.

Ⓐ You can restore a catalog you have previously backed up by clicking **Restore Catalog**. See Chapter 16 for more on backing up photos.

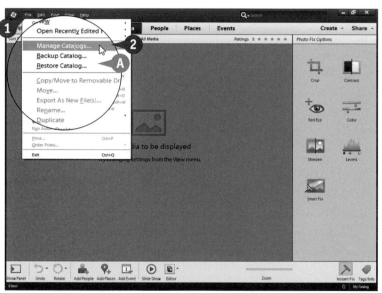

The Catalog Manager dialog box opens.

Photoshop Elements lists the available catalogs.

3 Click **New**.

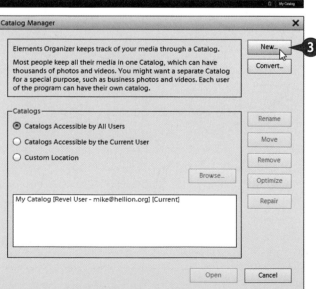

④ Type a name for the new catalog.

Ⓑ You can click this option to import free music (☐ changes to ☑), which Windows users can use in the backgrounds of slide shows.

⑤ Click **OK**.

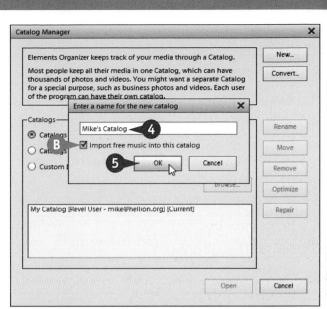

Ⓒ Photoshop Elements creates the new catalog and opens it.

Ⓓ Photoshop Elements displays the name of the current catalog.

Ⓔ The number of files in the catalog and the range of dates for the files appear here.

Ⓕ In this example, free music files have been imported.

Note: To add photos by importing, see Chapter 2.

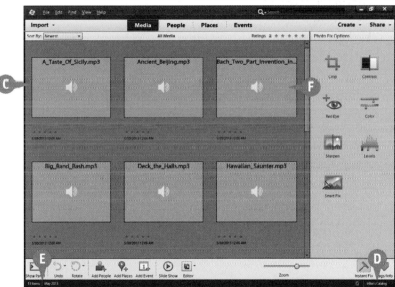

TIPS

How do I switch to a different catalog in the Organizer?
Open the Catalog Manager by following steps **1** and **2** in this section. Select the catalog that you want to open in the catalog list and then click **Open**. You can open only one catalog at a time in the Organizer.

How can I keep others from viewing the photos in the Organizer?
You can change the security settings of a catalog so that only the user currently logged into your computer can access it.

Open the Catalog Manager by following steps **1** and **2** in this section. From the list that appears, select the catalog that you want to protect and then click **Move**. A dialog box opens that enables you to change the accessibility of the catalog.

View Photos in the Media Browser

After you add photos to your catalog, you can view them by using the Organizer's Media Browser. The Media Browser displays thumbnails, or miniature versions, of your photos, along with details about those photos.

You can filter, sort, and change the size of the thumbnails. Shrinking the thumbnails enables you to view more of them at the same time, whereas enlarging the thumbnails lets you examine their details from within the Organizer. Filtering and sorting enables you to find specific photos from thousands very quickly. For more about sorting and filtering using keyword tags, see Chapter 4.

View Photos in the Media Browser

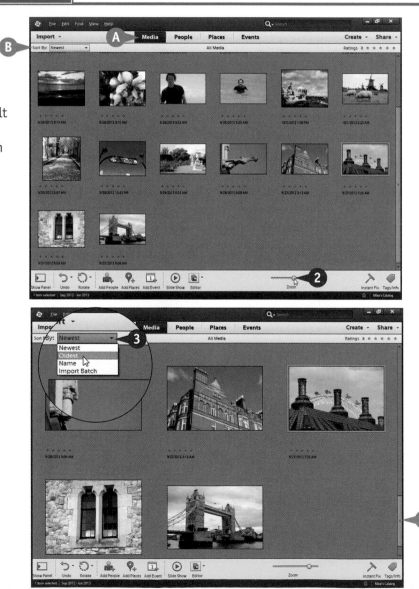

1 Open the Organizer.

The Media Browser displays the photos in the Organizer catalog.

A The Media Browser is the default view in the Organizer. You can click **Media** to switch to it from another view.

B Photos are sorted by their capture date from newest to oldest by default.

2 Click and drag the thumbnail size slider (🔘) to the right.

The thumbnails enlarge.

Dragging the slider (🔘) to the left decreases the size of the thumbnails.

C You can use the scroll bar to browse other available thumbnails in the Media Browser.

3 Click the **Sort By** 🔽 and then click **Oldest**.

The sorting order reverses in the Media Browser, with the oldest photos at the top.

D Use the scroll bar to scroll up to the beginning of the grid of photos.

4 Click the **Sort By** and then click **Import Batch**.

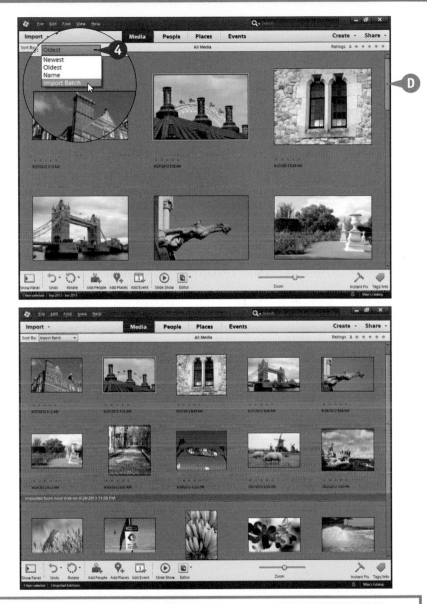

Photoshop Elements displays your photos in the order in which they were imported, with the most recent batch at the top.

TIP

How can I hide certain file types in the Media Browser?

The Media Browser can help you organize photos, video files, audio files, creative projects built in Photoshop Elements, and PDF files. You can filter the file types that appear in the Media Browser by clicking **View** and then **Media Types**. The shown media types are checked. Click a checked media type (**A**); Photoshop Elements hides the media type in the Media Browser.

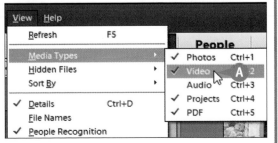

View Photos in Full Screen

You can switch to Full Screen mode in the Organizer to get a clearer view of your photos. Photoshop Elements expands the photos to fill the workspace and displays special panels for applying commands.

Full Screen mode is useful when you want to perform basic edits on a large version of your photo but do not want to switch to the Editor workspace. You can access a film strip in Full Screen mode that displays image thumbnails from your current catalog. This enables you to switch to another image.

View Photos in Full Screen

1 In the Organizer, click the photo you want to view in Full Screen.

2 Click **View**.

3 Click **Full Screen**.

Photoshop Elements opens the photo in Full Screen.

A A Quick Edit panel for performing image edits is shown.

B A Quick Organize panel for adding images to albums and applying keyword tags is shown.

C The panels automatically hide if not used. You can click the pin icon (🖈) to turn this hiding on and off.

D Controls for viewing different photos and managing panels appear here.

4 Click the **Next** button (▶) to go to the next photo in the Organizer, or press ➡.

Photoshop Elements displays
the next photo.

5 Click **Film Strip**.

E The Film Strip opens, displaying
thumbnail versions of your
images.

6 Click a thumbnail.

Photoshop Elements displays
the photo.

7 Click **Exit** or press the `Esc`
key to exit Full Screen mode.

TIP

How do I view detailed areas of my photos in Full Screen?

1 While in Full Screen mode, roll the mouse wheel forward or click with
a mouse or trackpad button.

A The image zooms in and displays the zoom percentage.

2 Click and drag the image with the mouse.

The image pans.

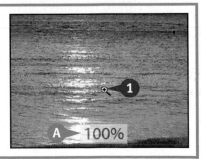

Display a Slide Show in Full Screen

You can play a slide show in Full Screen mode to cycle through large versions of your images, with background music and transition effects to accompany the slides. This enables you to display photos from a vacation or event on a monitor or, if your computer is hooked up to one, on a television screen. You can also send your slide show to others.

Buttons enable you to play or pause the slide show, or flip through the slides one at a time. See Chapter 16 for details. Note that although Mac users can view images in Full Screen, only Windows users can create slide shows.

Display a Slide Show in Full Screen

1 In the Organizer, display the images you want to view as a slide show in the Media Browser.

Ⓐ You can click **Show Panel** and then choose an album to display its photos as a slide show.

2 Click **Slide Show**.

Photoshop Elements displays the first image in Full Screen mode.

3 Click **Settings**.

The Full Screen View Options dialog box opens.

4 Click the ▼ to choose background music.

Ⓑ You can click **Browse** to browse for music on your computer to use as background music.

5 Click **OK** to close the dialog box.

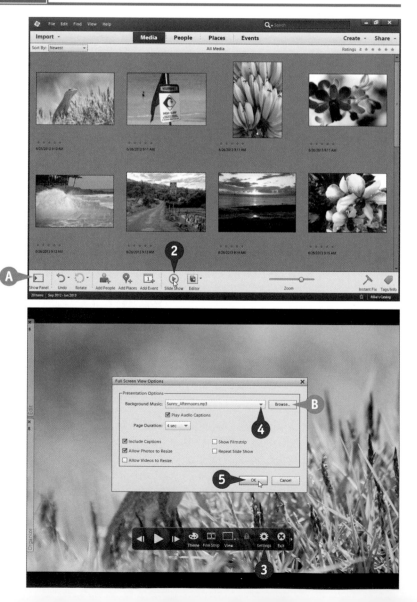

54

6 Click **Theme**.

The Select Transition dialog box opens.

7 Click a transition effect to display between slides in the slide show (○ changes to ◉).

C You can position your mouse pointer over an option to preview the option.

8 Click **OK** to close the dialog box.

9 Click the **Play** button (▶) or press Spacebar (▶ changes to ‖).

Photoshop Elements plays the slide show, cycling through the images at full screen.

You can click the **Pause** button (‖) to pause the slide show.

TIP

How can I customize my slide show?
Repeat steps **1** to **3** to open the Full Screen View Options dialog box. Click the **Page Duration** ▾ to determine how long a slide is shown, which can range from two to 10 seconds. Click **Include Captions** to show captions with your slides (☐ changes to ☑). See the section "Add a Caption" for more about captions. Clicking **Show Filmstrip** (☐ changes to ☑) displays thumbnails of all the slides at the bottom as the show plays. To loop your slides, click **Repeat Slide Show** (☐ changes to ☑). Click **OK** to save the settings.

View Photo Information

You can view the information associated with any photo in your catalog. The Information panel displays a photo's general information, which includes the filename, file size, image size, and location. Text boxes and links under general information enable you to edit this data.

You can also view any associated tags, file history, and metadata information. *Metadata* is detailed information about how a digital photo was taken and stored; it includes camera settings, such as exposure time and f-stop.

View Photo Information

1 In the Organizer, right-click a photo.

2 Click **Show File Info**.

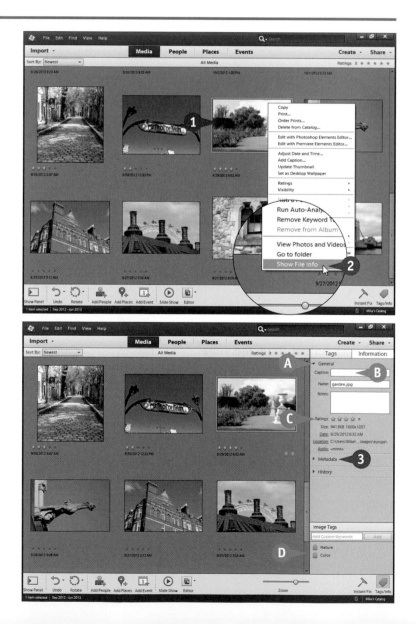

The Information panel opens.

A The General properties appear by default.

B You can add or edit a caption for the photo here.

C The rating, size, capture date, and other information for the photo are shown here.

D If you have assigned keyword tags to the photo, they appear here. See Chapter 4 for details.

3 Click **Metadata**.

The Metadata properties appear. This includes the camera model and settings if the photo came from a digital camera.

E You can click 田 to display the complete metadata for a photo.

4 Click **History**.

The History properties appear.

Photoshop Elements displays Organizer statistics for the photo, such as when the file was last modified and when it was imported.

5 Click **Tags/Info** to close the Information panel.

How do I change the photo's date and time?

1 Right-click the photo you want to edit.

2 Click **Adjust Date and Time**.

3 Click **Change to a specified date and time** (○ changes to ◉).

4 Click **OK**.

5 Set the new date and time.

6 Click **OK**.

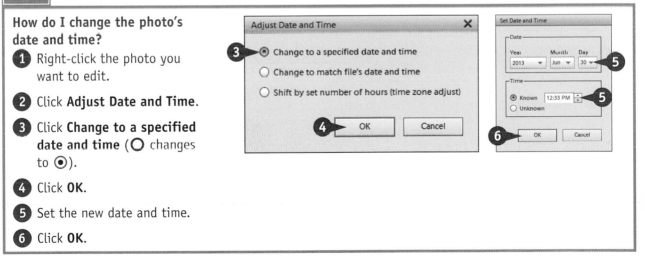

Add a Caption

In the Organizer, you can add captions to your photos to help you remember important information about the images you catalog. For example, you may add captions to your vacation pictures with details about the location or subject matter.

Captions appear below a photo when the image is viewed with details showing. You can display captions when viewing a slide show in the Organizer; see the section "Display a Slide Show in Full Screen." You can also include caption information with photos when you print them; see Chapter 16.

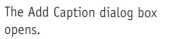

Add a Caption

① In the Organizer, right-click the photo you want to caption.

② Click **Add Caption**.

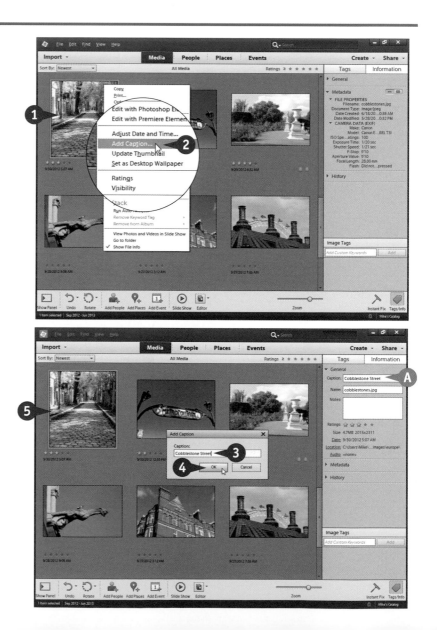

The Add Caption dialog box opens.

③ Type a caption for the photo.

④ Click **OK**.

Ⓐ The Organizer adds the caption to the photo. The caption is added to the metadata of the photo, which programs besides Photoshop Elements can access.

⑤ Double-click the image.

A large thumbnail of the
photo appears.

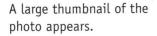 Click **View**.

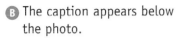 Click **Details**.

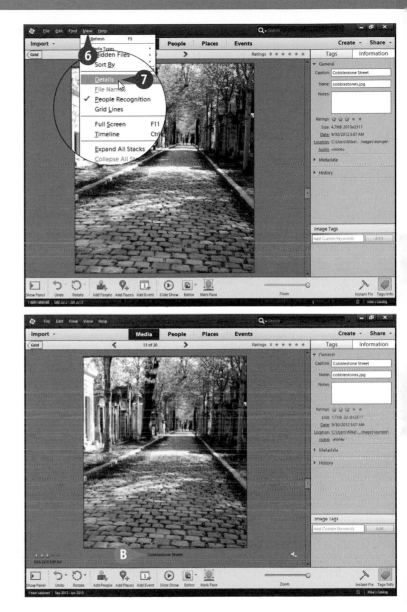

B The caption appears below
the photo.

TIPS

Are there other ways to add captions to my photos?
Yes. You can also add captions to your photos by using the Information panel. See the previous section, "View Photo Information," for more.

How do I edit a caption?
To edit a caption in the Media Browser, follow steps **5** to **7**, click the caption, and make your changes. You can delete the caption completely, type a new caption, or make changes to the existing caption text. Click outside the text box to save your changes.

Work with Albums

Albums are a way to organize your photos within an Organizer catalog. For example, you can take photos shot at a particular time or place and group them as an album. This makes it easier to find the photos later. Selecting an album to access a group of photos is often the first step in making a slide show or photo book.

You can also organize photos in a catalog by using keyword tags, or by defining people, places, or events. See Chapter 4 for more about these features.

Work with Albums

Create a New Album

1 In the Organizer, open the catalog within which you want to create an album.

Note: For more on catalogs, see the section "Create a Catalog."

2 Click **Show Panel** to access the Albums information in the Panel Bin. The button changes to read Hide Panel.

The Albums information appears.

3 Click the plus sign (⊞).

A The New Album panel opens.

4 Type a name for the album.

B You can assign the album to an album category.

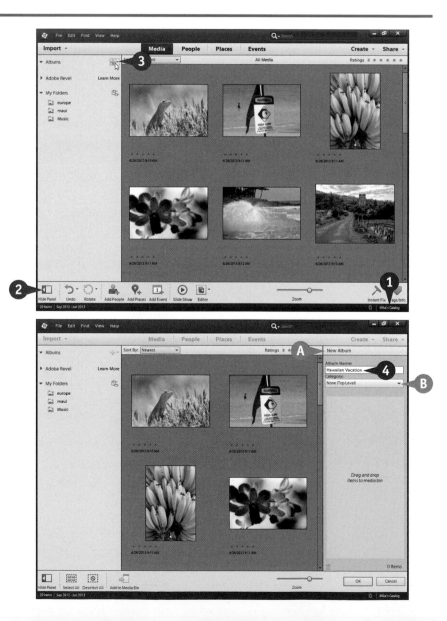

5 Click and drag a photo from the Media Browser to the Content list box.

The Organizer adds the photo to the album.

6 Repeat step **5** for all the photos you want to add to the album.

You can Ctrl +click (⌘ +click on a Mac) to select multiple photos and then click and drag to add them all to the album.

7 Click **OK** to close the Add New Album panel and save the album information.

View an Album

1 Click the album name in the list of albums.

The Organizer displays all the photos in the album.

C Photos assigned to an album are marked with an album icon (▣) in the photo details. Click **View** and then **Details** to view them.

D You can click **All Media** to return to the entire catalog.

E To delete an album, right-click the album name and select **Delete** in the menu that appears.

TIPS

How do I remove a photo from an album?
In the Organizer, right-click the album's name and then click **Edit**. Under the Content tab, click to select a photo to remove. Click the trash can icon (🗑). The Organizer removes the photo from the album.

How do I create an album using photos from an event?
Click **Events** to display the events you have defined. Double-click an event to display its photos. Press Ctrl +
A (⌘ +A on a Mac) to select all the photos. Then click the plus sign (➕) in the Albums panel to create your new album. For more about events, see Chapter 4.

Find Photos

The Organizer offers a variety of methods for finding particular photos in your catalog. You can search for photos by date, filename, tags, text, and more. This can be helpful as your catalogs in the Organizer grow to thousands of photos and span years.

In this example, you search for photos taken during a specific date range and by text. When you search by text, Photoshop Elements examines captions, keyword tags, album names, and other text associated with your Organizer catalog.

Find Photos

Find Photos by Date

1. In the Organizer, click **View**.

2. Click **Set Date Range**.

   The Set Date Range dialog box opens.

3. Select the start date for the date range you want to search.

4. Select the end date for the date range you want to search.

5. Click **OK**.

Ⓐ The Organizer displays any matching photos in the Media Browser.

Ⓑ A summary appears at the bottom of the Media Browser.

Note: You can reset the date search by clicking **View** and then **Clear Date Range**.

Find Photos by Text

① Type one or more keywords in the search box.

Photoshop Elements searches the filenames, captions, keyword tags, album names, and other text associated with your photos.

ⓒ Photoshop Elements displays photos associated with the text as you type.

If you type multiple keywords, photos must be associated with all the keywords to match.

② Click **Back**.

Photoshop Elements cancels the search.

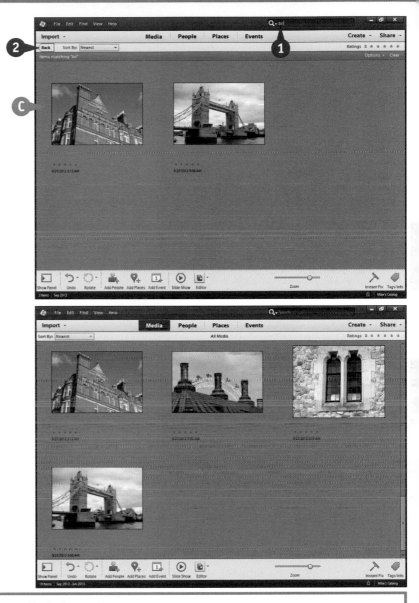

TIP

What other search methods can I use to find photos?

You can search the Organizer by way of the Find menu.

Search Option	Function
By Caption or Note	Looks for photos based on the text of the notes and captions you have added
By Filename	Searches the catalog for a particular filename
By History	Looks up a photo based on when it was printed or e-mailed or by other criteria
By Media Type	Searches for projects, photos, and audio or video files in your catalog

Rate Photos

You can add star ratings to your photos in the Organizer to distinguish which ones are interesting and suitable for editing or projects. Photoshop Elements enables you to give each photo a rating of from one to five stars. After you rate your photos, you can filter them by rating and then add those photos to an album or use them in a slide show.

To view the ratings along with your photo thumbnails in the Media Browser, you can turn on details for your photos.

Rate Photos

Apply a Rating

1 Click **View**.

2 Click **Details**.

Ⓐ The details for photos appear under the thumbnails.

3 Click a star rating icon (★) below a photo.

You can add a star rating from 1 to 5 by clicking the icons from left to right. After clicking a thumbnail to select it, you can also press a number key from **0** to **5**. Pressing **0** removes the rating.

Ⓑ Photoshop Elements assigns the rating and gold stars (★) appear.

You can also apply ratings in the Information panel. See the section "View Photo Information" for more.

Filter by Rating

1 Click the ⊡ and then choose a rating setting.

2 Click a star rating (⭐).

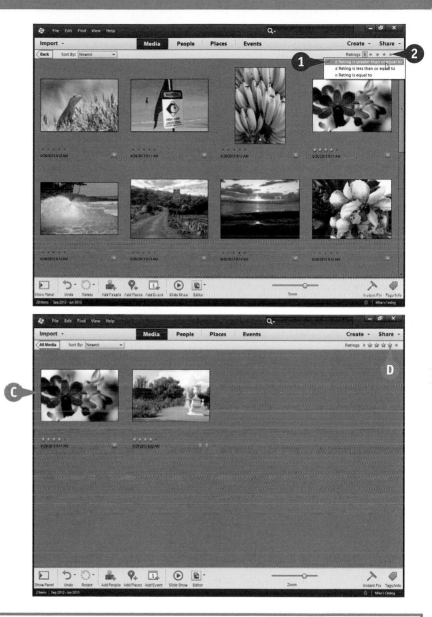

C Photoshop Elements displays photos that meet the rating criteria.

D You can click the star rating again to remove the rating filter.

How do I apply the same rating to multiple photos?

Ctrl +click (⌘+click on a Mac) to select the photos you want to rate. Apply a star rating to one of the selected photos. The rating is applied to all the selected photos.

Does the rating filter work in the different Organizer views?

Yes. For example, if the People view is selected and the rating filter is set to greater or equal to three stars, only people in a photo with a three-, four-, or five-star rating appear. This works similarly with the Places and Events views.

View Versions of a Photo

As you make edits to a photo in Photoshop Elements, the Organizer can keep track of the changes and keep the different versions grouped together. In the Organizer, photos grouped in a version set are marked with an icon. Having versions grouped together makes it easy to compare different effects applied to a photo or to access an original version of a photo before effects were applied.

To save an edited photo in a version set, you can click **Save in Version Set with Original** when saving. See Chapter 2 for more about saving photos.

View Versions of a Photo

1 Save a photo in Photoshop Elements in a version set. See Chapter 2 for details.

Ⓐ The version set is marked with an icon (▣).

2 Click ▶.

Ⓑ Photoshop Elements displays the photos in the version set.

Ⓒ You can click ◀ to collapse the version set.

By default, the most recent version appears on top of the collapsed set.

To display a different version on top of the set, you can right-click a version, click **Version Set** in the menu, and then click **Set as Top Item**.

Remove a Photo from the Organizer

You can remove a photo from the Organizer so that the photo no longer exists in your Organizer catalog and no longer appears in the Media Browser. You may want to remove a photo when you do not have any use for it or to make your catalog of photos less cluttered.

Removing a photo from the Organizer does not delete the photo file from your computer's hard drive, unless you specify that you also want this in the confirmation dialog box.

Remove a Photo from the Organizer

1 Right-click a photo.

2 Click **Delete from Catalog**.

The Confirm Deletion from Catalog dialog box appears.

A You can click this option to also delete the photo from your hard drive (☐ changes to ☑).

3 Click **OK**.

Photoshop Elements removes the photo from the Organizer catalog.

B You can click **Undo** to put the removed photo back in the catalog.

CHAPTER 4

Using Advanced Organizing Tools

Photoshop Elements includes advanced tools for managing images. For example, you can associate tags with photos to help you identify their content. You can group photos based on the people who are in them, the places they were taken, and other criteria.

Perform an Advanced Search 70

Work with Keyword Tags 72

Define People in Photos 76

Define Places 78

View Places 80

Define Events 82

Using Smart Events. 84

Work with People, Place, and Event Tags 86

Apply an Instant Fix 88

Stack Photos. 90

Find by Visual Similarity 92

Perform an Advanced Search

You can perform an advanced search to sort and filter your Organizer photos by various user-defined categories. This is useful if you want to go beyond searching by keyword and, for example, search for photos that feature a particular person but only if the photos were taken in a particular city.

In the advanced search, you can filter by keyword tags to only view photos associated with certain subjects. You can select people, places, and events that you have defined in the Organizer to limit your results further. The advanced search interface also enables you to choose sorting criteria and to filter by star rating.

Perform an Advanced Search

1 In the Organizer, click the search box 🔍 and select **Advanced Search**.

The Advanced Search pane opens.

2 Click the **Sort by** 🔽 and select a sort option.

3 Click here to specify a star rating filter. For details, see Chapter 3.

4 Click the Keywords check boxes to require photos to be tagged with one or more keywords (☐ changes to ☑).

Ⓐ You can click ▶ to expand keyword categories (▶ changes to 🔽).

For more about keyword tags, see the next section, "Work with Keyword Tags."

70

5 Click the People check boxes to require photos to be associated with people.

6 Click the Places check boxes to require photos to be associated with locations.

7 Click the Events check boxes to require photos to be associated with events.

See other sections in this chapter for more about defining people, places, and events.

If you select multiple categories by which to filter, each photo in the results will be associated with *all* selected categories.

Photoshop Elements displays the photos that meet the criteria.

B You can click ![] to collapse the category lists but keep the search selections intact.

C You can click ![] to cancel and close the advanced search.

D You can click **Clear** to clear the category selections.

TIP

How can I save an advanced search?

After you select an advanced search category, an Options menu appears above the selection results. Click **Options** from that menu. Click **Save Search Criteria as Saved Search**. The Create Saved Search dialog box appears. Type a name for the search (**A**) and click **OK**. To access a saved search, click the search box ![] and then click **Saved Searches**.

Saved Search
Name:
Good photos of Griffin in Maui ── **A**

Work with Keyword Tags

Keyword tags help you categorize and filter your digital photos. For example, you can create a tag called *car* and apply it to all your photos of cars. You can assign the Organizer's preset tags or use tags that you have created. You can also assign more than one tag to a photo. For example, a photo of an automobile could have a *car* tag as well as a *convertible* tag.

The Organizer comes with several generic tags already defined. You can assign tags to categories and subcategories. In addition to keyword tags, there are tags for people, places, and events. See the section "Work with People, Place, and Event Tags" for more.

Work with Keyword Tags

Create a Keyword Tag

1 In the Organizer, click **Tags/ Info**.

2 Click **Tags**.

3 Click the plus sign (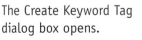).

The Create Keyword Tag dialog box opens.

4 Click the ▼ and choose a category for the new tag.

5 Type a name for the keyword tag.

Ⓐ You can add a note about the keyword tag here.

6 Click **OK**.

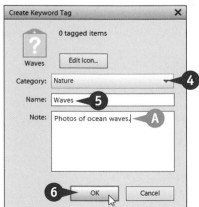

Assign Tags

1 Click and drag the tag from the Keyword Tags panel, and then drop it on the photo you want to tag.

B The Organizer assigns the keyword tag (▣). A keyword tag icon indicates that the photo has a tag assigned to it.

You can also drag a thumbnail image from the Media Browser to a keyword tag to assign a tag.

2 Type text for a tag in the Keyword Tags search box.

Photoshop Elements suggests tags with that text.

3 Click a tag in the list that appears.

4 Click a photo you want to tag.

You can `Ctrl`+click (`⌘`+click on a Mac) to select multiple photos.

5 Click **Add**.

C Photoshop Elements applies the tag (▣) to the selected photo.

TIP

How do I edit a keyword tag?

Right-click the keyword tag and then choose **Edit** (**A**). The Edit Keyword Tag dialog box opens. Type a new keyword tag name or make other edits to the tag and click **OK**. Photoshop Elements applies the changes. Any images that have the keyword tag applied are updated.

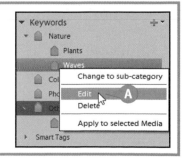

continued ▶   73

After you assign keyword tags, you can filter your catalog to show only those photos that have certain tags. For example, you can filter your photos to show only photos of people or events. You can also simultaneously filter multiple keyword tags.

To learn about how to quickly add tags to people in your photos by recognizing their faces, see the next section, "Define People in Photos." Another way to filter photos in your Organizer catalog is to place them into albums. See Chapter 3 for more about albums.

Work with Keyword Tags (continued)

Filter by Tags

1 Open the Tags panel if it is not already displayed.

2 Position your mouse pointer over the keyword tag you want to apply and click ▶.

Ⓐ You can click ▶ to expand a tag category.

Ⓑ You can click ▼ to collapse a tag category.

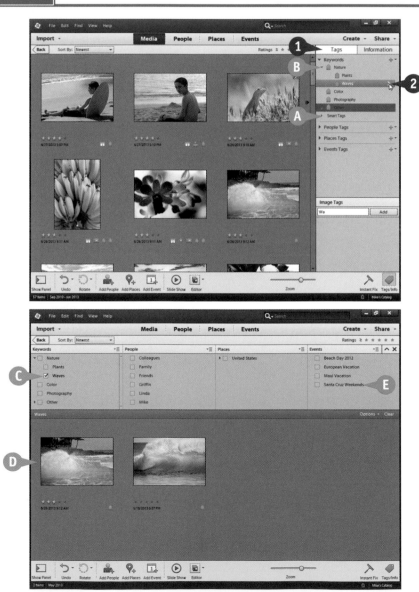

Ⓒ The advanced search panel opens, showing the selected tag.

Ⓓ The Organizer displays the photos that share the keyword tag.

Ⓔ To filter by multiple tags, click additional check boxes (☐ changes to ☑).

If you check multiple tags, only photos that have all the tags appear.

Remove a Tag from a Photo

1 Right-click the photo containing the tag you want to remove.

2 Click **Remove Keyword Tag**.

3 Click the keyword tag you want to remove.

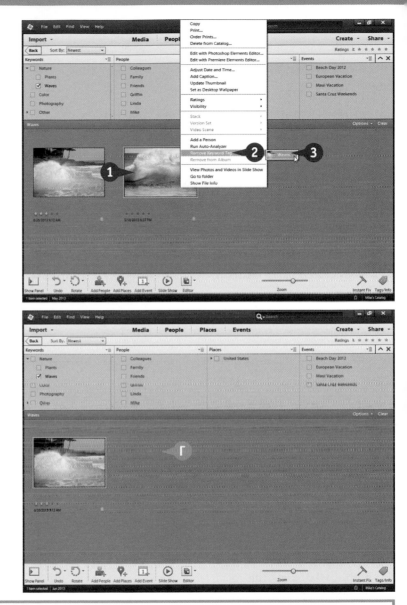

The Organizer removes the keyword tag from the photo.

F If a tag was filtering the Media Browser, the photo disappears.

TIP

How can I create a new keyword tag category?

Photoshop Elements comes with several predefined categories such as Nature and Color, but you can define your own. Click the ▼ next to ▦ ▾ and click **New Category** from the menu that appears. The Create Category dialog box opens. Type a name for the category (**A**). You can optionally specify a color and icon (**B**). Click **OK** to save the category.

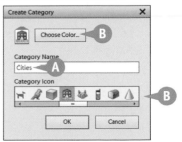

Define People in Photos

You can group your photos based on who is in them by defining people in the Organizer. First, the Organizer's face-recognition technology pinpoints the faces in your photos. Photoshop Elements automatically scans photos in the Organizer for the colors and structures characteristic of human faces. It then presents the faces from the photos for you to name.

Clicking **People** at the top of the Organizer presents you with a grid of stacked photos representing all the people you have named. You can double-click a stack to view the photos featuring the person.

Define People in Photos

1 In the Organizer, **Ctrl**+click (**⌘**+click on a Mac) to select the photos that have people in them.

If you do not select any photos, Photoshop Elements searches all the photos on display.

2 Click **Add People**.

Photoshop Elements searches for faces and displays the results in a People Recognition dialog box.

3 Click a face.

4 Type a name for the face.

5 Press **Enter**.

Photoshop Elements tags the face with the name.

6 Repeat steps **3** to **5** for the other faces.

7 Click **Save**.

Depending on how many photos you are analyzing, Photoshop Elements may present additional sets of faces to name or confirm. You can continue naming them and click **Save** or click **Cancel** to stop.

 Photoshop Elements adds people icons (◉) to the named photos. You can position your cursor over them to view the names.

You can right-click a people icon (◉) to untag a person from a photo.

⑧ Click **People**.

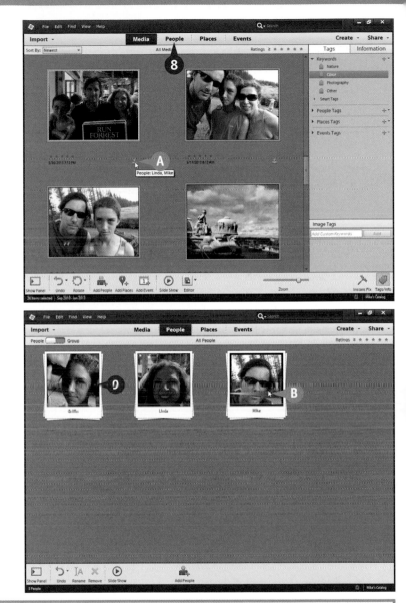

Photoshop Elements displays the people you have defined.

Ⓑ You can move your cursor across a thumbnail to preview the faces for a person.

⑨ Double-click a face to display the photos for that person.

Define Places

You can group your photos based on location by defining places in the Organizer. To define a place, you specify where on a world map a photo was taken. You click and drag a thumbnail for the photo onto a Google map.

How discretely you want to define a place is up to you. You can take a large batch of photos and quickly put them all at a single place on the map, for example at the center of a large park where they were all taken. Or you can place the individual photos at different places in the park one by one.

Define Places

1 In the Organizer, **Ctrl**+click (⌘+click on a Mac) to select the photos that you want to map to a place.

To map all the photos, do not make a selection.

2 Click **Add Places**.

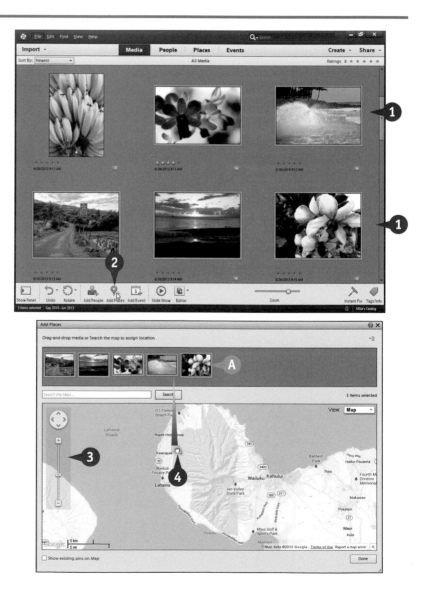

The Add Places dialog box appears.

3 Use the map controls to pan and zoom to the location where the photos were taken.

Ⓐ By default, all the thumbnails for the photos are selected.

4 Click and drag one of the selected thumbnails onto the map. This associates all the photos with a single place.

You can also click the thumbnails one at a time and then click and drag to locate each at a different place on the map.

Ⓑ Photoshop Elements displays an icon to mark the place.

⑤ Click ☑ to confirm the location.

Ⓒ You can click ⊘ or press Esc to cancel the placement.

⑥ Click **Done**.

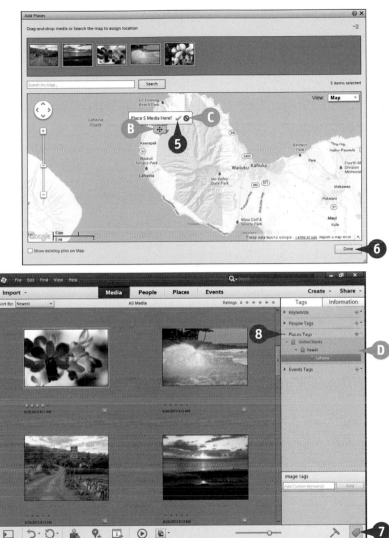

⑦ Click **Tags/Info** to view tags for your photos.

⑧ Click **Places Tags**.

Ⓓ Photoshop Elements automatically tags your selected photos based on the place.

For more about tags, see the section "Work with People, Place, and Event Tags."

To view a map showing where you have placed all your photos in the Organizer, see the next section, "View Places."

What happens if my photos have location information associated with them already?

Some cameras, such as iPhones and other cameraphones, can assign location information to a photo when you shoot it, a process known as *geo-tagging*. Photoshop Elements can read this information and suggest a location on the Add Places map. This is why you may see icons already on the map when you add your places.

How can I place the photos at a named location?

If you know the name of a location, such as a city or a landmark, you can type the name in the Add Places search box and click **Search**. Photoshop Elements tries to find the location and enables you to place your photos there.

View Places

As you define places by assigning locations to your photos, your map accumulates icons representing where your photos were taken. You can view this map to see all the places you have defined. You can click the icons to view the photos associated with a location. This is an easy way to see all the photos taken in a particular city or at a landmark.

You can use zoom and panning controls on the map to find photos that you have placed at certain locations. You can also search for places by keyword.

View Places

1 In the Organizer, click **Places**.

A map appears.

Ⓐ Icons on the map represent defined places with numbers representing the number of photos at a place.

2 Use the map controls to pan and zoom to find a location of interest.

Ⓑ You can also type a search term in the text field and press Enter to find locations.

3 Click a place icon on the map.

Ⓒ Photoshop Elements selects the photos associated with the place.

4 Click **Show Media**.

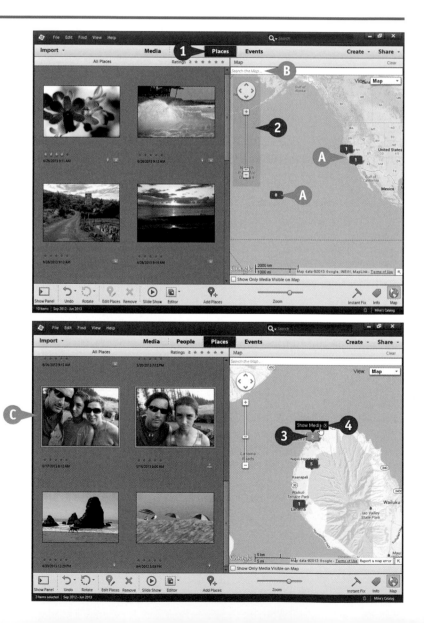

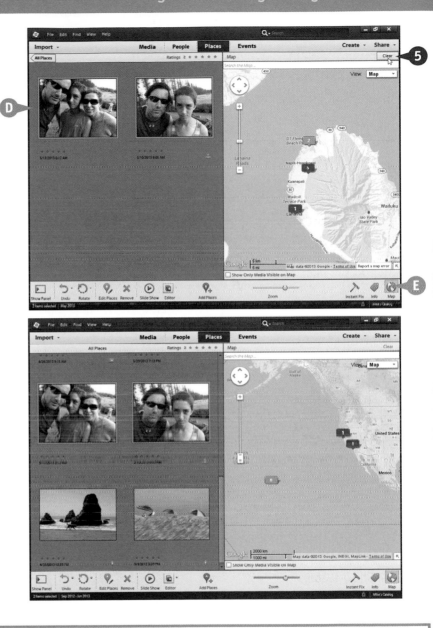

Ⓓ Photoshop Elements shows only the photos associated with the place.

Ⓔ You can click **Map** to toggle the map open and closed. Closing the map gives you a larger area for viewing photos.

❺ Click **Clear**.

Photoshop Elements shows all the photos again and returns to the default view on the map.

How can I move a photo to a different place?
If you want to change the location associated with a photo, you can select the photo and click **Edit Places** at the bottom of the Organizer workspace. The Edit Place dialog box appears, enabling you to click and drag the photo to a different map location.

How can I remove a photo from a place?
You can right-click the place icon (📍) for the photo and then click a Remove command from the menu that appears.

Define Events

You can group your photos into events to associate them with time periods. This can be useful for organizing photos taken on birthdays, holidays, and vacations. Creating an event can be an alternative to grouping photos in an album. See Chapter 3 for more about albums. You can view all of your defined events by clicking **Events** at the top of the Organizer.

You can filter your Organizer photos based on the events the photos are associated with. See the section "Perform an Advanced Search" for more.

Define Events

1 In the Organizer, **Ctrl**+click (**⌘**+click on a Mac) to select the photos for your event.

To find photos that were taken during a specific time period, see Chapter 3.

2 Click **Add Event**.

The Add New Event pane opens with your photos added.

A You can click and drag to add more photos to your event.

3 Type a name for the event.

Photoshop Elements sets a start and end date for your event based on the timestamps associated with the photos.

B You can click the calendar icon to change the dates.

4 Type a description for the event.

5 Click **Done**.

Ⓒ Photoshop Elements adds event icons (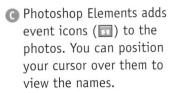) to the photos. You can position your cursor over them to view the names.

You can right-click an event icon (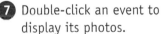) to remove a photo from an event.

6 Click **Events**.

Photoshop Elements displays the events you have defined.

Ⓓ You can move your cursor across a thumbnail to preview the photos for an event.

7 Double-click an event to display its photos.

Note: Every event you create has a tag associated with it. See the section "Work with People, Place, and Event Tags" for more.

TIPS

After saving an event, how do I add more photos to it?

Click **Events** to view the events you have defined, and then double-click the event to which you want to add photos. At the bottom of the Organizer workspace, you can click **Add Media** to add more photos.

How can I view my event photos as a slide show?

When viewing an event, click **Slide Show** at the bottom of the Organizer workspace. Photoshop Elements cycles through the event photos as a slide show. If you position your cursor over the slide show, a toolbar appears enabling you to change settings such as slide duration and background music. You can also use the slide show feature when viewing people and places.

Using Smart Events

Y ou can use the Smart Event feature to automatically group your photos based on time periods. This offers a convenient starting point for creating custom events. You can select one or more Smart Event groups and then name those photos as a custom event.

You can organize photos in the Smart Events interface by date, and Photoshop Elements groups photos taken on the same day. You can also organize photos by time. With the time setting, you can click and drag a slider to determine whether Photoshop Elements groups the photos into short or long time periods.

Using Smart Events

1 In the Organizer, click **Events**.

2 Click here to set the view to **Smart Events**.

Photoshop Elements displays your photos in groups based on the day the photos were taken.

A Groups are labeled with their date and the number of photos.

3 Click **Time** (O changes to ⊙).

Photoshop Elements displays your photos in groups based on time.

B You can click and drag the slider (▢) to determine the length of time used to create the groups.

Drag to the right to use shorter lengths of time. Drag to the left to use longer.

4 Ctrl +click (⌘+click on a Mac) to select the groups to define as a custom event.

5 Click **Name Event(s)**.

The Name Event dialog box opens.

6 Type a name for the event.

Photoshop Elements sets a start and end date for your event based on the timestamps associated with the photos.

C You can click the calendar icon to change the dates.

7 Type a description for the event.

8 Click **OK**.

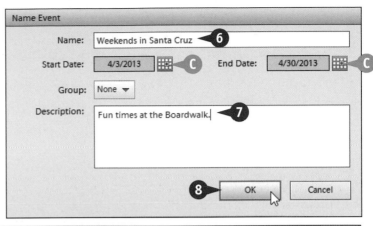

Photoshop Elements saves the event.

9 Click here to set the view to Events.

Photoshop Elements displays the events.

D The new event appears in the grid.

You can double-click the event to view its photos.

TIP

How can I filter my events by date?

1 In the Events view, click **Calendar** at the bottom of the Organizer workspace.

2 Click the ▼ and select a year.

A To filter by month, you can click a month. Months with events are highlighted.

B To filter by day, you can click a day. Days with events are highlighted.

Photoshop Elements displays the events for the selected time period.

Work with People, Place, and Event Tags

When you associate people, places, or events with your photos, descriptive tags are created that match those associations. This helps you easily view who is in your photos, where your photos were taken, and at what time your photos were taken using the Tags panel.

By filtering your photos using these tags, you can display just photos featuring your uncle, for example, by clicking the tag for his name, or just photos taken on a vacation by clicking that vacation location tag. For more about people, places, and events, see the other sections in this chapter.

Work with People, Place, and Event Tags

1 In the Organizer, click **Tags/Info**.

2 Click **Tags**.

3 Click **People Tags**.

People-related tags appear.

A Each person defined in your photos is associated with a tag.

B People tags are marked by a 🖼️.

4 Click **Places Tags**.

Place-related tags appear.

C Each place defined in your photos is associated with a hierarchical set of location tags.

D Place tags are marked by a 📍.

5 Click **Events Tags**.

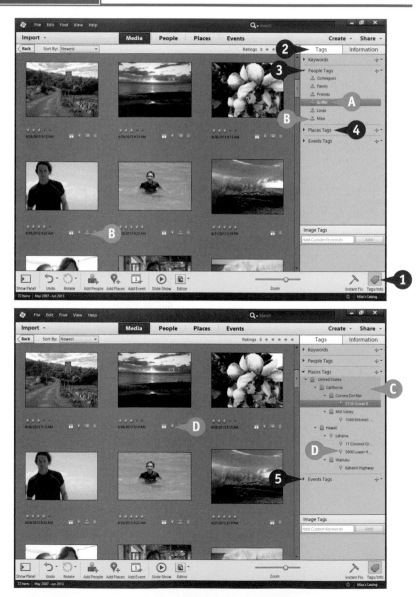

Event-related tags appear.

E Each event defined in your photos is associated with a tag.

F Event tags are marked by a 🔳.

6 Position your mouse over the tag you want to apply and click ▶.

G The advanced search panel opens showing the selected tag.

H The Organizer displays the photos that share the tag.

I You can filter by additional tags by clicking other check boxes in the search panel (☐ changes to ☑).

TIP

How do I create a place shortcut?

You can make a shortcut for a place tag to replace a long address with a more descriptive name. For example, you can replace the tag for "123 South Main Street" with "Home." In the Tags panel, right-click a place name and click **Rename**. A dialog box appears enabling you to rename the place with shortcut text.

Apply an Instant Fix

You can optimize color, lighting, and other aspects of your photos in the Organizer using the Instant Fix tools. This can be convenient when you want to make simple changes to your photos in the Organizer but do not want to switch to the Editor.

Most of the fixes available are automatic fixes requiring a single click of a button. To make more complex adjustments to your photos, see the chapters later in this book. After you apply a fix, the updated photo is saved in an Organizer version set with the original photo. See Chapter 3 for more about version sets.

Apply an Instant Fix

1 In the Organizer, click the photo you want to fix.

2 Click **Instant Fix**.

The Photo Fix Options panel opens.

3 Click an instant fix, such as **Crop**.

The Crop Photo dialog box appears.

4 Click and drag the edges of the crop tool to define the area of the photo you want to keep.

Ⓐ You can click the 🔽 to select various ways to constrain the crop tool.

5 Click **Done**.

Ⓑ You can click **Cancel** to exit the tool without cropping.

C Photoshop Elements crops the photo.

6 Click another instant fix command.

D The Red Eye command searches for people in the photo and attempts to correct any red eye caused by flash.

Other commands make color and lighting adjustments to the photo.

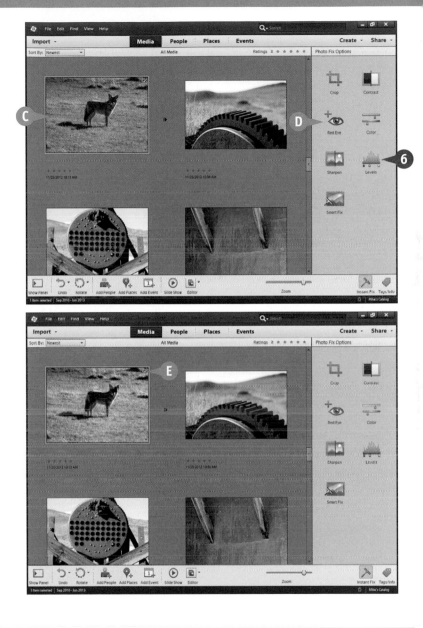

Photoshop Elements applies the command.

E The edited version of the photo is placed in a version set with the original photo. Version sets are marked with a 🖼 icon.

Note: For more on version sets, see Chapter 3.

TIPS

How do I rotate a photo in the Organizer?
You can click to select a photo and then click **Rotate** at the bottom of the Organizer workspace to rotate the photo counterclockwise. You can click the Rotate button's 🔽 to access a clockwise button.

How do I undo Instant Fix changes?
You can click **Undo** at the bottom of the Organizer workspace. If you performed multiple changes in the Instant Fix panel, you must click **Undo** multiple times to undo them.

Stack Photos

In the Organizer, you can group similar photos into stacks. This can help you conserve space in the Organizer workspace because stacks can be collapsed so that only the top photo on the stack appears. Stacks are organized similarly to version sets, which are covered in Chapter 3.

Stacks can be based on any measure of similarity that you choose. For example, you can stack photos of the same scene or group of people, or photos that have similar lighting, exposure, or colors. In addition to manually stacking your photos, you can have Photoshop Elements suggest stacks based on photographic similarity.

Stack Photos

Create a Stack

1. In the Organizer, **Ctrl**+click (⌘+click on a Mac) to select the photos you want to stack.

2. Right-click one of the selected photos.

3. Click **Stack**.

4. Click **Stack Selected Photos**.

Ⓐ You can click **Automatically Suggest Photo Stacks** to have Photoshop Elements suggest stacks based on photographic similarity.

Ⓑ Photoshop Elements creates a stack for the selected photos. The photo that you right-clicked is placed on top of the stack and is shown here.

5. Click the stack button (▶) to expand.

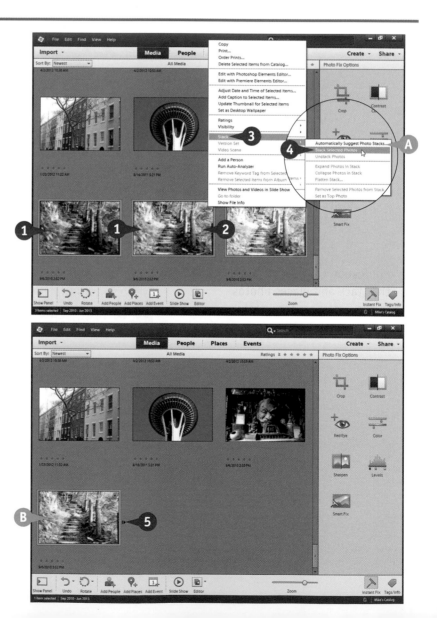

The stack expands to show its contents.

C You can click here to collapse the stack (◀).

Unstack Photos

1 Right-click a photo in a stack. If the stack is collapsed, right-click the top photo.

2 Click **Stack**.

3 Click **Unstack Photos**.

Photoshop Elements removes the stack and places photos in the Organizer separately.

How do I automatically stack photos as I import them?

1 Click **Import**, and then click **From Files and Folders**.

2 In the dialog box that opens, click **Automatically Suggest Photo Stacks** (☐ changes to ☑).

When you import the photos, Photoshop Elements suggests groups of photos to be stacked based on their photographic similarity.

Find by Visual Similarity

You can search for photos that contain similar colors and shapes. This can be useful for tracking down specific images in a large catalog or collecting similar images for a collage or other art project.

Photos can be considered alike if they have a common appearance, even if they contain very different subject matter. For example, a photo of a yellow flower might be matched with a photo of a yellow hat. You can fine-tune results by specifying whether to favor the colors or shapes in the images. You can also search based on multiple images.

Find by Visual Similarity

1 Click a photo to search by.

You can **Ctrl**+click (**⌘**+click on a Mac) to select multiple photos.

2 Click **Find**.

3 Click **By Visual Searches**.

4 Click **Visually similar photos and videos**.

Note: You can click **Objects appearing in photos** to search for images containing similar objects.

Ⓐ If a dialog box appears asking if you want to index your photos, click **OK, Start Indexing**. Indexing improves the tool's accuracy.

Photoshop Elements displays photos ordered by visual similarity to the selected photo. More similar photos are at the top.

5 To adjust the search, click and drag the slider (▢) to the left to favor color or to the right to favor shape.

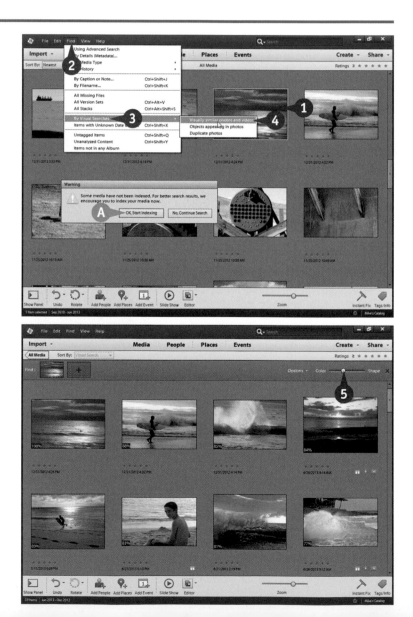

Photoshop Elements refreshes the results based on the adjustment.

6 Click and drag a different photo to the empty box to search by it as well.

Photoshop Elements refreshes the results based on similarity to both selected photos.

B You can click **All Media** to clear the search.

TIP

How do I organize photos with the same content?
You can search for duplicate photos in your catalog and organize them into stacks. Click **Find**, **By Visual Searches**, and then **Duplicate photos**. In the Visual Similarity Photo Search dialog box, Photoshop Elements groups photos with duplicate content (**A**). Click **Stack** to merge a group into a stack (**B**). For more about stacks, see the section "Stack Photos."

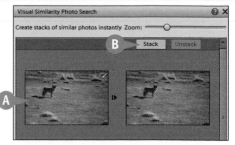

CHAPTER 5

Applying Basic Image Edits

Are you ready to start working with images? This chapter shows you how to fine-tune your workspace to best arrange your open images. You also discover how to change the on-screen image size, set a print size, and crop your images. Quick mode is also introduced.

Manage Open Images. 96

Magnify with the Zoom Tool 100

Adjust the Image View 102

Change the On-Screen Image Size. 104

Change the Image Print Size 106

Change the Image Canvas Size 108

Work in Quick Mode 110

Apply an Effect in Quick Mode 112

Add a Frame in Quick Mode. 113

Crop an Image 114

Rotate an Image 116

Undo Changes to an Image 118

Revert an Image 119

Manage Open Images

ach image you open in Photoshop Elements appears in its own window, and you can have multiple windows open at the same time. In Expert mode, tabs at the top of each window enable you to switch between images. Each tab lists the name of the image file, the current magnification, and the image mode.

Viewing one image at a time gives you the maximum space for viewing and editing an image. You can also use the Photo Bin or Window menu to switch between different open images. This switching works in all three modes — Quick, Guided, and Expert.

Manage Open Images

Using Tabs

1 In the Editor, click **Expert**.

2 Open two or more images.

Note: For more on opening the Editor, see Chapter 1. For more on opening image files, see Chapter 2.

Ⓐ The active or current image appears here.

Ⓑ Each open image has its own tab, which displays its filename and magnification.

3 Click a tab for the image you want to view.

Ⓒ The image appears as the active image. You can make changes to the active image by applying commands and effects.

Using the Photo Bin

Ⓓ By default, the Photo Bin displays smaller versions, or *thumbnails*, of the images.

Note: See the tip for more on how to display other images in the Photo Bin.

Ⓔ If the Photo Bin is closed, you can click **Photo Bin** to open it.

1 Double-click a thumbnail.

F The image appears as the active image.

Using the Window Menu

1 Click **Window**.

2 Click an image filename.

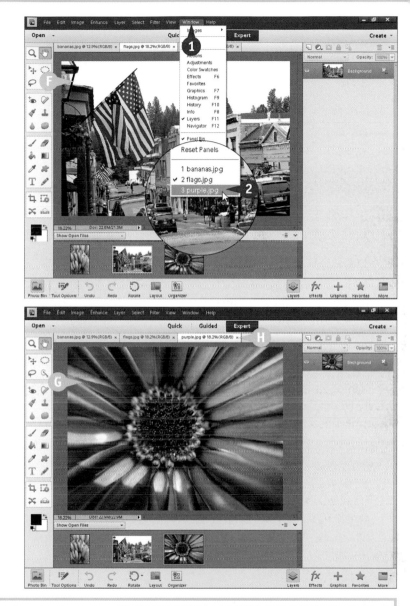

G The image appears as the active image.

H You can click ☒ to close an image.

How do I display images from the Organizer in the Photo Bin?

You can display images from the Photoshop Elements Organizer in the Editor. Click the ▼ and then click this option (**A**) to display images that you have selected in the Organizer. You can also click an album name (**B**) to display images from an Organizer album. See Chapter 3 for more on the Organizer and creating albums.

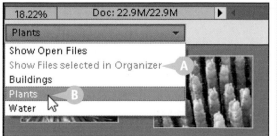

continued ▶ 97

Manage Open Images (continued)

You can view multiple image windows at the same time by choosing a layout. Layouts enable you to display images as a grid, in columns, or in rows. Viewing more than one image window at a time can be helpful when comparing images.

When viewing multiple images at once, only one of the windows is active. You can choose the active window by clicking its tab, clicking inside the window, or selecting the image from the Photo Bin or the Window menu. When you apply commands in Photoshop Elements, the commands act on the active image.

Manage Open Images (continued)

Using Layouts

1 Click **Layout**.

Photoshop Elements displays a menu of layouts.

Ⓐ You can click **All Grid**, **All Column**, or **All Row** to display all open images all at once as a grid, in vertical columns, or in horizontal rows, respectively.

2 Click a layout.

Photoshop Elements displays multiple windows, each with a different image.

③ Click **Layout**.

Ⓑ You can click **Column and Rows** or **Rows and Column** to display three images at a time.

④ Click a layout.

Photoshop Elements displays multiple windows at one time, each with a different image.

Ⓒ If you have more open images than windows, you can click tabs to switch between images.

TIP

Where else can I find commands for controlling image windows?
With the Hand tool (🖑) selected, click **Scroll All Windows** (☐ changes to ☑) in the Tool Options panel. When you scroll or drag in one window, all open images scroll in the same way. If you are comparing several photos on-screen, click **Window**, **Images**, and then **Match Zoom** to view each open window at the same zoom percentage. Click **Window**, **Images**, and then **Match Location** to view the same area in each open window. With the Zoom tool (🔍) selected, click **Zoom All Windows** (☐ changes to ☑) in the Tool Options panel to make the tool affect all windows. See the next section, "Magnify with the Zoom Tool," for more on magnification.

Magnify with the Zoom Tool

You can change the magnification of an image with the Zoom tool. This enables you to view small details in an image or view an image at full size. Magnifying has no effect on the size of the actual saved image.

Zooming in on an image can be helpful when you are making detailed selections with a selection tool, searching for imperfections, or aligning layers precisely with one another. For more about making selections, see Chapter 6. For details about layers, see Chapter 8. You can also adjust the magnification of an image to an exact percentage using the field in the lower left corner of the image window.

Magnify with the Zoom Tool

Increase Magnification

1 In the Editor, click the **Zoom** tool (Q).

You can also press Z.

Note: For more on opening the Editor, see Chapter 1.

2 Click the image.

Photoshop Elements increases the magnification of the image. By default, the Zoom tool zooms in when you click the image.

The current magnification shows in the image title bar and the Tool Options panel.

The Tool Options panel is available only in Expert mode.

Ⓐ You can specify an exact magnification by clicking and dragging the slider (Ⓞ) in the Tool Options panel or by typing a percentage in the lower left corner of the image window.

Decrease Magnification

1 Click the **Zoom Out** button ().

You can also press and hold **Alt** (**Option** on a Mac) to zoom out.

2 Click the image.

Photoshop Elements decreases the magnification of the image.

Magnify a Detail

1 Click the **Zoom In** button (🔍).

2 Click and drag with the zoom tool mouse pointer (⊕) to select the detail.

The area appears enlarged on-screen.

The more you zoom in, the larger the pixels appear and the less you see of the image's content.

TIP

How do I quickly return an image to 100% magnification?

Here are seven ways to return an image to 100% magnification:

1 Double-click the **Zoom** tool (🔍).

2 Click **1:1** in the Tool Options panel.

3 Click **View** and then **Actual Pixels** from the menu.

4 Click and drag the **Zoom** slider (◻) in the Tool Options panel all the way to the right.

5 Type **100%** in the lower left corner of the image window.

6 Right-click the image and select **Actual Pixels**.

7 Press **Alt**+**Ctrl**+**0** (**Option**+**⌘**+**0** on a Mac).

Adjust the Image View

You can move an image within the window by using the Hand tool or scroll bars. The Hand tool helps you navigate to an exact area in the image by dragging freely in two dimensions. The scroll bars enable you to pan an image vertically or horizontally.

Using the Hand tool is helpful when you are working with a high-resolution image and want to examine details throughout the image at high magnification. The tool is also useful when you have a low-resolution monitor, leaving a smaller area for the Photoshop Elements workspace.

Adjust the Image View

Using the Hand Tool

1 In the Editor, click **Expert**.

Note: For more on opening the Editor, see Chapter 1.

2 Click the **Hand** tool (🖐).

You can also press **H**.

Note: For the Hand tool (🖐) to have an effect, the image must be larger than the image window.

3 Click and drag inside the image window.

The view of the image shifts inside the window.

Using the Scroll Bars

1 On a PC, click and hold one of the window's scroll bar buttons (▲, ▼, ◀, or ▶).

The image scrolls in the direction you select — in this example, down.

Note: On a Mac with OS X Lion or Mountain Lion, you can scroll by clicking and dragging scroll bars.

How can I quickly adjust the image window to see the entire image at its largest possible magnification on-screen?

The following are five ways to magnify the image to its largest possible size:

1 Double-click the **Hand** tool (✋).

2 Click **Fit Screen** on the Tool Options panel.

3 Click **View** and then **Fit on Screen** from the menu.

4 Right-click the image and select **Fit on Screen**.

5 Press Ctrl+0 (⌘+0 on a Mac).

Change the On-Screen Image Size

You can change the on-screen size of an image you are working with in Photoshop Elements to make it better fit the confines of your monitor when viewed at the same magnification. Shrinking an image can also lower its file size and make it easier to share via e-mail or on the web.

When you change an image's on-screen size, you need to resample it. *Resampling* is the process of increasing or decreasing the number of pixels in an image. Enlarging or shrinking an image too much can cause a noticeable decrease in image quality, which you can see by examining details using the Zoom tool.

Change the On-Screen Image Size

1 In the Editor, click **Image**.

Note: For more on opening the Editor, see Chapter 1.

2 Click **Resize**.

3 Click **Image Size**.

The Image Size dialog box opens, listing the width and height of the image in pixels.

You can also press Alt + Ctrl + I (Option + ⌘ + I on a Mac) to open the Image Size dialog box.

Ⓐ To resize by a certain percentage, click the ▼ and change the units to **percent**.

4 Click **Resample Image** (☐ changes to ☑).

Note: Of the options in the Resample Image menu, Bicubic Smoother is often better for enlarging, whereas Bicubic Sharper is better for shrinking.

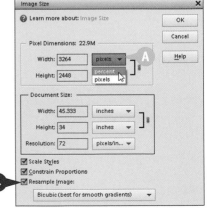

5 Type a size or percentage for a dimension.

Ⓑ You can click **Constrain Proportions** (□ changes to ☑) to cause the other dimension to change proportionally.

6 Click **OK**.

Ⓒ You can restore the original dialog box settings without exiting the dialog box by pressing and holding Alt (Option on a Mac) and clicking **Cancel**, which changes to Reset.

Photoshop Elements resizes the image.

In this example, the image decreases to 50 percent of the original size.

Note: You can also resize a photo by executing an action. For more about actions, see Chapter 15.

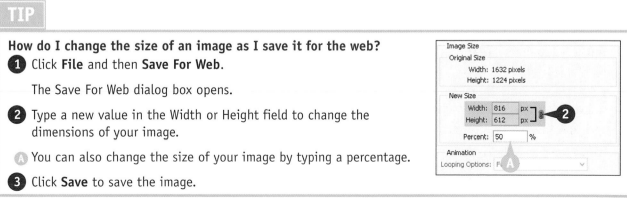

TIP

How do I change the size of an image as I save it for the web?

1 Click **File** and then **Save For Web**.

The Save For Web dialog box opens.

2 Type a new value in the Width or Height field to change the dimensions of your image.

Ⓐ You can also change the size of your image by typing a percentage.

3 Click **Save** to save the image.

Change the Image Print Size

You can change the printed size of an image to determine how it appears on paper. Print size is sometimes called *document size* in Photoshop Elements. If you change the print size of an image with the resampling option checked, Photoshop Elements adjusts the number of pixels in the image but keeps the resolution the same. If the resampling option is unchecked, the resolution changes but not the number of pixels.

Photoshop Elements also gives you resizing options when you print your image. You can either print it at actual size, or you can choose from a list of common photo print sizes. For more about printing, see Chapter 16.

Change the Image Print Size

1 In the Editor, click **Image**.

Note: For more on opening the Editor, see Chapter 1.

2 Click **Resize**.

3 Click **Image Size**.

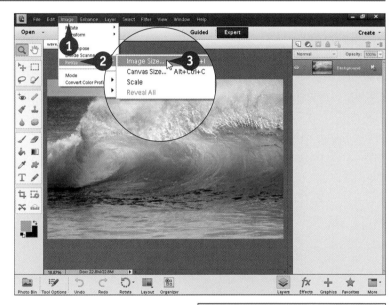

The Image Size dialog box opens, listing the current width and height of the printed image.

Ⓐ You can click the ▼ to change the unit of measurement.

Ⓑ If you click the **Resample Image** check box, Photoshop Elements adjusts the number of pixels in the image to resize. Otherwise, it adjusts the resolution.

Note: To determine the printed size of an image, you can divide the pixel dimensions by the resolution. If you have an image with a width of 480 pixels and a resolution of 120 pixels per inch, the printed width is 4 inches.

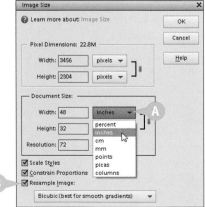

4 Type a size or percentage for a dimension.

C You can click **Constrain Proportions** (☐ changes to ☑) to cause the other dimension to change proportionally.

5 Click **OK**.

D You can restore the original dialog box settings by pressing and holding **Alt** (**Option** on a Mac) and clicking **Cancel**, which changes to Reset.

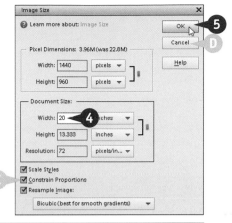

Photoshop Elements resizes the image.

Note: Changing the size of an image, especially enlarging, can add blur. To sharpen a resized image, see Chapter 9.

TIP

How do I preview an image's printed size?

1 Click **File**.

2 Click **Print**.

A The Print Preview dialog box shows how the image will print on the page.

B To select other dimensions, click the ▼ and choose a print size.

3 Click **Print** to print the image.

Note: For more on printing, see Chapter 16.

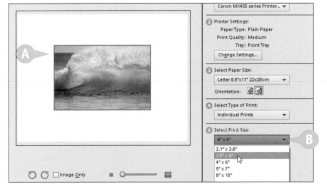

Change the Image Canvas Size

You can alter the canvas size of an image to change its rectangular proportions or add space around its borders. The canvas is the area on which an image sits. Changing the canvas size is one way to crop an image or add *matting*, which is space, around an image.

Photoshop Elements warns you when you decrease the dimensions of the image canvas because this deletes part of the image. You might want to increase the canvas size if you are making a collage of images and want the images to overlap one another. Increasing the canvas gives you space to add other images.

Change the Image Canvas Size

1. In the Editor, click **Image**.

Note: For more on opening the Editor, see Chapter 1.

2. Click **Resize**.

3. Click **Canvas Size**.

The Canvas Size dialog box opens, listing the current dimensions of the canvas.

Ⓐ You can click the ▼ to change the unit of measurement.

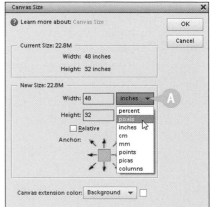

4 Type the new canvas dimensions.

Ⓑ You can click an arrow () to determine in which directions Photoshop Elements changes the canvas size. Clicking the square in the middle of the arrows crops the image equally on opposite sides.

5 Click **OK**.

Note: If you decrease a dimension, Photoshop Elements displays a dialog box asking whether you want to proceed. Click **Proceed**.

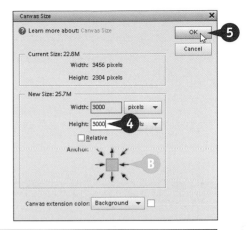

Photoshop Elements changes the image's canvas size.

In this example, because the width is increased, Photoshop Elements creates new canvas space on the sides of the image.

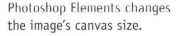

TIP

How do I specify the matte color around my canvas?

1 In the Canvas Size dialog box, click the ▼ to specify the matte color.

Ⓐ You can click the color box or select **Other** to select a custom color.

Ⓑ The color appears when you enlarge a dimension of your image.

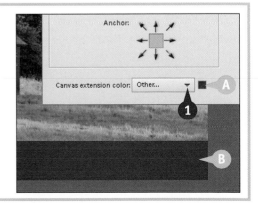

Work in Quick Mode

In Quick mode, you can enhance your photos in a simple, less-cluttered interface that gives you access to the most commonly used tools for performing image edits. The Zoom and Hand tools enable you to view details in your photo. A selection of lighting and color correction tools on the right-hand panel enable you to adjust the appearance of your photo.

Other modes in Photoshop Elements include Guided mode, which provides step-by-step instructions for enhancing your photos, and Expert mode, which gives you access to the entire complement of editing features.

Work in Quick Mode

View Details

1 In the Editor, click **Quick** to enter Quick mode.

Note: For more on opening the Editor, see Chapter 1.

2 Click the **Zoom** tool ().

Note: For more about the Zoom tool, see the section "Magnify with the Zoom Tool."

3 Click a detail in the image window.

Photoshop Elements zooms the image and enlarges the detail.

Ⓐ After zooming, you can click the **Hand** tool (🖐) to move your image within the image window.

Select an Object

1 Click the **Quick Selection** tool (🖎).

2 Click and drag over an object in your image.

For best results, select an object that contrasts with its background.

Ⓑ Photoshop Elements selects the object.

Note: For more about making selections, see Chapter 6.

Make an Adjustment

① Click a tool in the right panel.

The tool displays settings for adjusting aspects of your photo.

② Make changes to the settings to enhance the photo.

If you have selected an object, the changes affect only the selected object.

Ⓒ Photoshop Elements applies the changes.

This example uses the Hue setting in the Color tool to shift the colors in the selected object.

Ⓓ To undo the changes, click the **Reset** button (🔲).

Ⓔ For access to more tools, click **Expert** to enter Expert mode.

Note: To save your changes, see Chapter 2.

TIP

How do I add text in Quick mode?
Click the **Horizontal Type** tool (🔲). Specify the format and style of your text in the Tool Options panel. Click in the image and then type your text (Ⓐ). Click ✓ or press Enter. See Chapter 14 for more about adding text.

Apply an Effect in Quick Mode

You can apply a variety of effects in Quick mode to automatically change the colors in your image. These one-click effects can boost saturation to give your photo a stunning appearance or remove color to make your photo look old-fashioned. You open the Effects panel to access these features. Thumbnails in the Effects panel give you a preview of each effect. For more about applying special effects to your images, see Chapter 13.

Apply an Effect in Quick Mode

1 In the Editor, click **Quick** to enter Quick mode.

Note: For more on opening the Editor, see Chapter 1.

2 Click **Effects**.

The Effects panel opens, listing example effects.

3 Click an effect.

In this example, the Red Noir effect is applied, which desaturates all colors in your image except red.

Photoshop Elements applies the effect to your image.

A To remove the effect, click the **Reset** button (🖼).

You can apply similar effects using filters in Expert mode. See Chapter 13 for details.

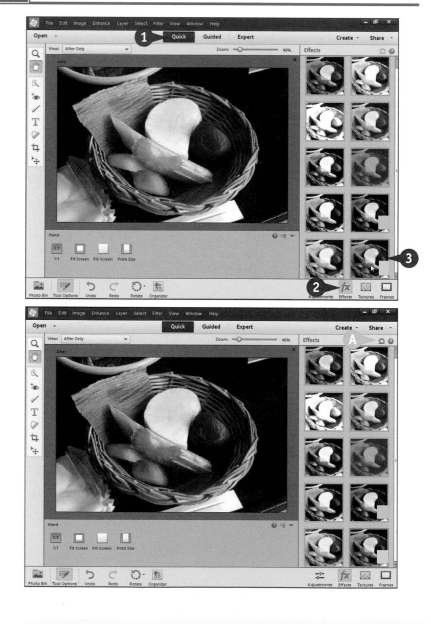

Add a Frame in Quick Mode

You can add surrounding decoration to a photo by adding a frame. Quick mode offers a variety of frame styles to add elegance or whimsy to your imaging project.

The frame effects are applied to the image as layers. If you switch to Expert mode and view the Layers panel after adding a frame, you can temporarily turn off the frame by hiding the frame layers.

Add a Frame in Quick Mode

1 In the Editor, click **Quick** to enter Quick mode.

Note: For more on opening the Editor, see Chapter 1.

2 Click **Frames**.

The Frames panel opens, listing border designs.

3 Click a frame.

In this example, the 35mm frame is applied, which adds camera-film decoration.

Photoshop Elements applies the frame to your image.

A To remove the frame, click the **Reset** button ().

Crop an Image

You can use the Crop tool to quickly remove unneeded space on the top, bottom, and sides of an image. Cropping is a great way to edit out unwanted background elements or reposition a subject in your photo. You can also rotate the cropping boundary prior to cropping, which enables you to align elements of your image while you are cropping.

You can also crop an image by changing its canvas size. See the section "Change the Image Canvas Size" for more on setting a new canvas size. Another way is by selecting an area with a selection tool, clicking **Image**, and then clicking **Crop**. See Chapter 6 for more on making selections.

Crop an Image

① In the Editor, click **Expert**.

Note: For more on opening the Editor, see Chapter 1.

② Click the **Crop** tool (⌗).

③ Click and drag to select the area of the image you want to keep.

Another way to crop an image is by changing its canvas size; you do this by clicking **Image**, **Resize**, and **Canvas Size** and then typing new dimensions for the image.

Ⓐ You can set specific dimensions for a crop by using the Width and Height boxes in the Tool Options panel.

④ Click and drag the side and corner handles (◻) to adjust the size of the cropping boundary.

You can click and drag inside the cropping boundary to move it without adjusting its size.

You can click and drag outside the cropping boundary to rotate the tool prior to executing the crop.

114

5 Click ✅ or press **Enter** to accept the crop.

You can also double-click inside the crop area to crop the photo.

B To exit without cropping, click 🚫 or press **Esc**.

Photoshop Elements crops the image, deleting the pixels outside the cropping boundary.

How do I crop my image into an interesting shape?

Click the **Crop** tool (▦) and then click the **Cookie Cutter** tool (▦) in the Tool Options panel. Click the 🔽 and then click a shape for the crop (Ⓐ). You can click the 🔽 to access additional shapes (Ⓑ). Adjust the cropping boundary and then perform the crop similar to using the regular Crop tool. Photoshop Elements crops the selected content as a shape. Unlike with the Crop tool, the dimensions of the image canvas remain unchanged.

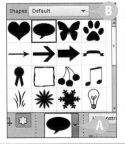

Rotate an Image

You can rotate an image to turn it within the image canvas. If you import or scan a horizontal image vertically, you can rotate it so that it appears in the correct orientation. You can also flip a photo to change the direction of the subject matter. Flipping it horizontally, for example, creates a mirror image of the photo.

Rotating an image can add blank space around the sides. You can crop the image to remove this extra space. Note that rotating an image by something other than 90-degree multiples can decrease image quality slightly.

Rotate an Image

Rotate 90 Degrees

1 In the Editor, click **Expert**.

Note: For more on opening the Editor, see Chapter 1.

2 Click **Image**.

3 Click **Rotate**.

4 Click **90° Left** or **90° Right** to rotate an image.

Ⓐ To change subject direction, click **Flip Horizontal** or **Flip Vertical**.

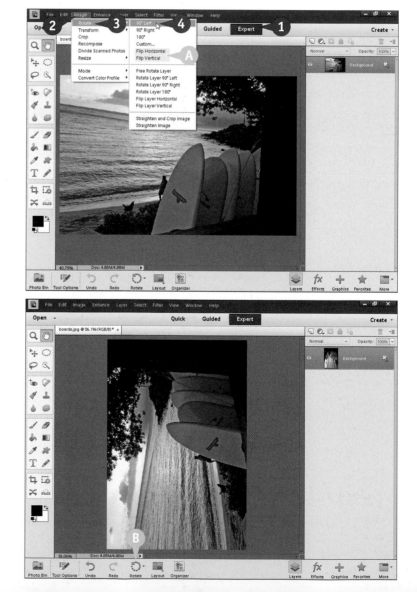

Photoshop Elements rotates the image.

Ⓑ You can also click **Rotate** to rotate your photo counterclockwise in increments of 90 degrees.

Rotate Precisely

1 Click **Image**.

2 Click **Rotate**.

3 Click **Custom**.

The Rotate Canvas dialog box opens.

4 Type an angle from −359.99 to 359.99.

5 Click a direction to rotate (○ changes to ⊙).

6 Click **OK**.

Photoshop Elements rotates the image to your exact specifications.

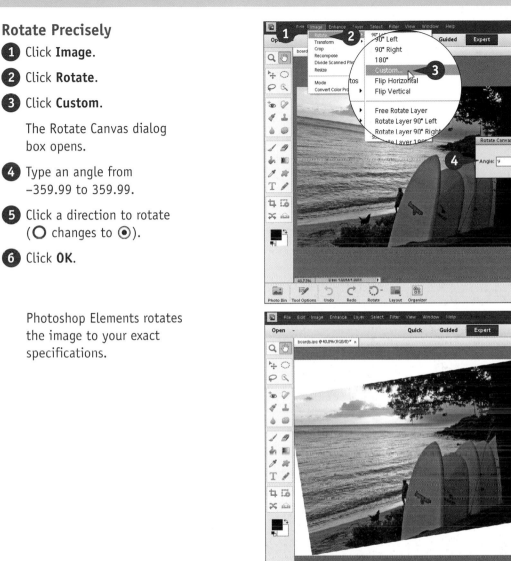

How can I use the Straighten tool?

The Straighten tool (🔲) enables you to fix a tilted image by clicking and dragging. Select the tool (Ⓐ) and then click and drag to define the line that you want to be horizontal (Ⓑ). This will typically be the horizon in an outdoor image. Photoshop Elements straightens the image.

Undo Changes to an Image

You can undo commands by using the History panel. This enables you to correct mistakes or change your mind about operations you have performed on your image. The History panel lists recently executed commands, with the most recent command at the bottom. In the Preferences dialog box, you can control how many commands Photoshop Elements remembers in the History panel. To change preferences in Photoshop Elements, see Chapter 1.

To undo just a single command, you can click **Undo**, located at the bottom of the Editor workspace, or press Ctrl+Z (⌘+Z on a Mac).

Undo Changes to an Image

① In the Editor, click **Expert**.

Note: For more on opening the Editor, see Chapter 1.

② Click **Window**.

③ Click **History**.

The History panel opens, listing recently executed commands.

④ Click the **History** slider (▢) and then drag it upward.

Ⓐ Alternatively, you can click a previous command in the History panel.

Photoshop Elements undoes the previous commands.

Ⓑ You can click and drag the slider down to redo the commands.

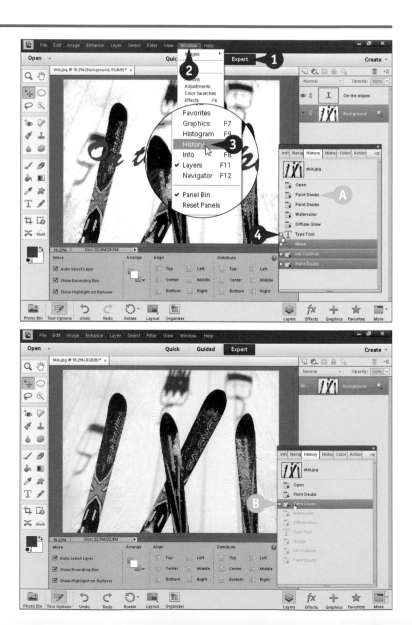

118

Revert an Image

You can revert an image to the previously saved state. This enables you to start your image editing over. After you revert an image, you can still change your mind and switch back to the unreverted state by clicking **Edit** and then **Undo Revert**.

An alternative to reverting all at once is undoing commands. The Undo History panel enables you to roll back your image-editing work by undoing a set number of commands. See the previous section, "Undo Changes to an Image," for details.

Revert an Image

1 In the Editor, click **Edit**.

Note: For more on opening the Editor, see Chapter 1.

2 Click **Revert**.

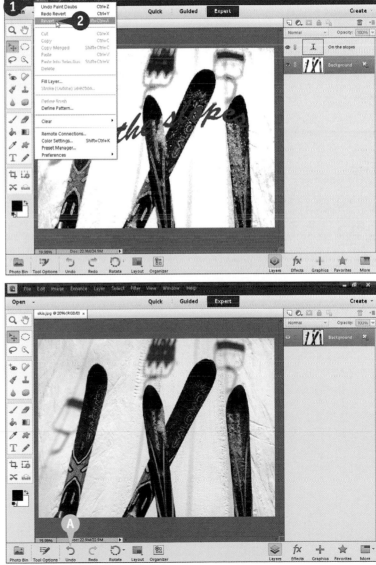

Photoshop Elements reverts the image to its previously saved state.

A To return to the unreverted state, click **Undo**.

CHAPTER 6

Making Selections

Do you want to move, color, or transform parts of your image independently from the rest of the image? The first step is to make a selection. This chapter shows you how to use the Photoshop Elements selection tools to isolate portions of your images for editing. You can use different tools to select objects in your image or areas of similar color. You can even save your selections for loading later.

Select an Area with the Marquee 122

Select an Area with the Lasso. 124

Select an Area with the Magic Wand. 128

Select an Area with the Quick Selection Tool 130

Select an Area with the Selection Brush. 132

Save and Load a Selection 134

Invert a Selection 136

Deselect a Selection 137

Select an Area with the Marquee

You can select parts of an image for editing by using a marquee. You can then make changes to the selected area by using other Photoshop Elements commands.

Two marquee tools are available: the Rectangular Marquee enables you to select rectangular shapes, including squares, and the Elliptical Marquee enables you to select elliptical shapes, including circles. You click and drag diagonally in your image to apply both tools. You can also use settings in the Tool Options panel to define specific dimensions for your marquees such as a fixed size or ratio.

Select an Area with the Marquee

Select with the Rectangular Marquee

1 In the Editor, click **Expert**.

Note: For more on opening the Editor, see Chapter 1.

2 Click the **Rectangular Marquee** tool (⬚) or press M.

3 Click and drag diagonally inside the image window.

You can press and hold **Shift** while you click and drag to create a square selection.

A Photoshop Elements selects a rectangular portion of your image.

You can reposition selections by pressing the arrow keys: ⬆, ⬇, ⬅, and ➡. You can also click and drag inside the selection while a marquee tool is active.

B You can deselect a selection by clicking **Select** and then **Deselect**, pressing Ctrl+D (⌘+D on a Mac), or by clicking outside the selection area.

Select with the Elliptical Marquee

1 Click the **Rectangular Marquee** tool ([ ]). Pressing **M** also toggles between the Rectangular and Elliptical marquee tools.

C If the Tool Options panel is not open, click here to open it.

2 Click the **Elliptical Marquee** tool ([ ]).

3 Click and drag diagonally inside the image window.

You can press and hold **Shift** while you click and drag to create a circular selection, or you can press and hold **Shift**+**Alt** (**Shift**+**Option** on a Mac) to draw the circle directly out from the center.

D Photoshop Elements selects an elliptical portion of your image.

You can reposition selections by pressing the arrow keys: **↑**, **↓**, **←**, and **→**.

E You can deselect a selection by clicking **Select** and then **Deselect**, pressing **Ctrl**+**D** (**⌘**+**D** on a Mac), or by clicking outside the selection area.

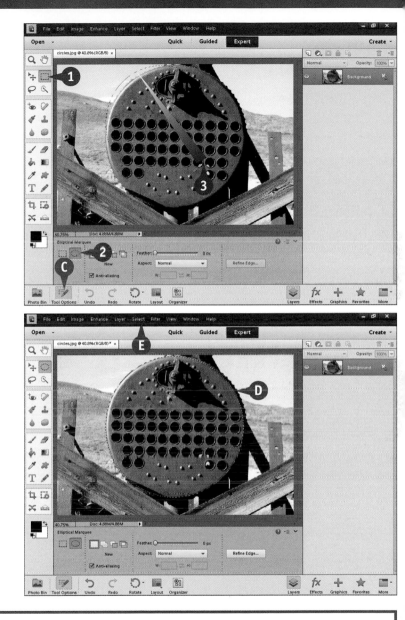

TIP

How do I customize the marquee tools?

You can customize the marquee tools ([ ] and [ ]) by using the boxes and menus in the Tool Options panel. Marquee options appear only when you click a marquee tool.

- **Feather:** Typing a value softens and blends selection edges that you move, cut, or copy.
- **Aspect:** Selecting an option from the Mode list defines the operation of the marquee tool as Normal (no restrictions), Fixed Ratio, or a Fixed Size.
- **Width and Height:** Entering values enables you to set an exact width and height for a selection.

Select an Area with the Lasso

You can outline irregularly shaped selections with the lasso tools. You can then make changes to the selected area by using other Photoshop Elements commands. You can use three types of lasso tools: the regular Lasso, the Polygonal Lasso, and the Magnetic Lasso. What lasso you use depends on the objects in your image that you want to select.

You can use the regular Lasso tool to create freehand selections. The Polygonal Lasso tool enables you to easily create a selection composed of many straight lines. The Magnetic Lasso tool automatically applies a selection border to edges as you drag.

Select an Area with the Lasso

Select with the Regular Lasso

1 In the Editor, click **Expert**.

Note: For more on opening the Editor, see Chapter 1.

2 Click the **Lasso** tool (⊘).

3 Click and drag with your mouse pointer (⊘) to make a selection.

Ⓐ To accurately trace a complicated edge, you can initially magnify that part of the image with the Zoom tool (🔍).

Note: See Chapter 5 for more on the Zoom tool.

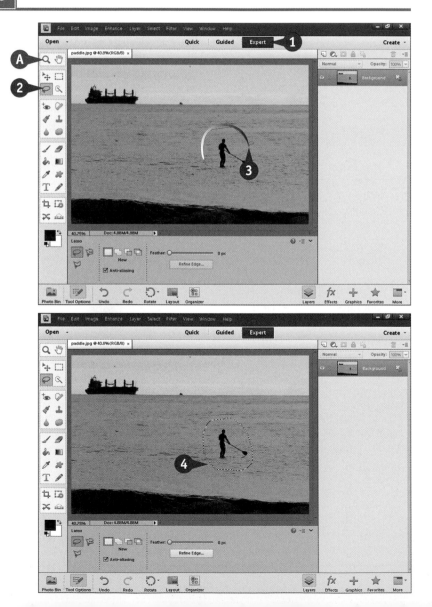

4 Drag to the beginning point and then release the mouse button.

Photoshop Elements completes the selection.

If you release the mouse button before completing the selection, Photoshop Elements completes the selection for you with a straight line.

Select with the Polygonal Lasso

1 Click the **Lasso** tool (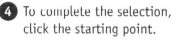).

B If the Tool Options panel is not open, click here to open it.

2 Click the **Polygonal Lasso** tool (📐).

3 Click multiple times along the border of the area you want to select.

4 To complete the selection, click the starting point.

You can also double-click anywhere in the image. Photoshop Elements adds a final straight line that connects to the starting point.

Photoshop Elements completes the selection.

TIPS

How do I select all the pixels in my image?

For a single-layer image, you can use the Select All command to select everything in your image. Click **Select** and then click **All.** You can also press Ctrl+A (⌘+A on a Mac). You can select all the pixels to perform an action on the entire image, such as copying the image. For multilayer images, Select All selects all the pixels in the currently selected layer.

What if my selection is not as precise as I want it to be?

You can deselect your selection by clicking **Select** and then **Deselect.** You can then try to fix your selection. Or you can switch to the Magnetic Lasso tool (📐). You can also add to or subtract from a selection. For details, see Chapter 7.

Select an Area with the Lasso (continued)

You can quickly and easily select elements of your image that have well-defined edges by using the Magnetic Lasso tool. The Magnetic Lasso works best when the element you are trying to select contrasts sharply with its background; a bird in flight against a clear blue sky would be a good candidate for the tool.

As you drag the Magnetic Lasso along an edge, Photoshop Elements places anchor points along the edge that fix the selection outline. You can press **Backspace** (**Delete** on a Mac) to remove the anchor points as you draw the selection.

Select an Area with the Lasso (continued)

Select with the Magnetic Lasso

1 In the Editor, click **Expert**.

A If the Tool Options panel is not open, click here to open it.

2 Click the **Lasso** tool (🔎).

Note: For more on opening the Editor, see Chapter 1.

3 Click the **Magnetic Lasso** tool (🧲).

4 Click the edge of the object you want to select.

This creates a beginning anchor point, which is a fixed point on the lasso path.

5 Drag your mouse pointer (🖱) along the edge of the object.

The Magnetic Lasso's path snaps to the edge of the element as you drag.

To help guide the lasso, you can click to add anchor points as you go along the path.

You can press **Delete** to remove the most recently added anchor point. This enables you to restructure the incorrect lasso path.

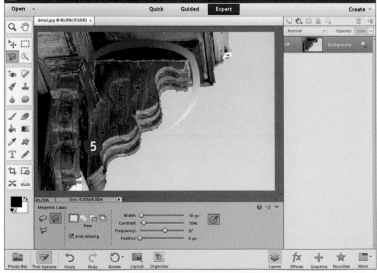

6 Click the beginning anchor point to finish your selection.

Alternatively, you can double-click anywhere in the image and Photoshop Elements completes the selection for you with a straight line.

The path is complete, and the object is selected.

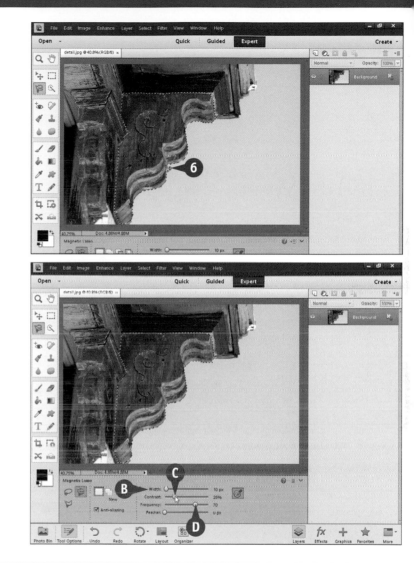

Adjust the Precision of the Magnetic Lasso Tool

You can adjust the Magnetic Lasso tool's precision with different settings.

B The Width determines the pixels that the lasso considers when creating a selection.

C The Contrast determines how much contrast is required for the lasso to consider something an edge.

D The Frequency determines how often anchor points appear.

How can I select just the content of an object in a layer?
Select the layer whose content you want to select. Use a Lasso tool to draw a selection around the object (**A**). Hold down Ctrl (⌘ on a Mac) and press ⬆. Photoshop Elements snaps the selection to the edge of the object (**B**).

Select an Area with the Magic Wand

You can select groups of similarly colored pixels with the Magic Wand tool. You may find this useful if you want to remove an object from a background. The tool is especially handy for selecting a clear sky, a green lawn, or white sand at a beach.

By specifying an appropriate tolerance value, you can control how similar a pixel needs to be for Photoshop Elements to select it. The tolerance value for the tool can range from 0 to 255, with smaller numbers causing the tool to select a narrower range of colors.

Select an Area with the Magic Wand

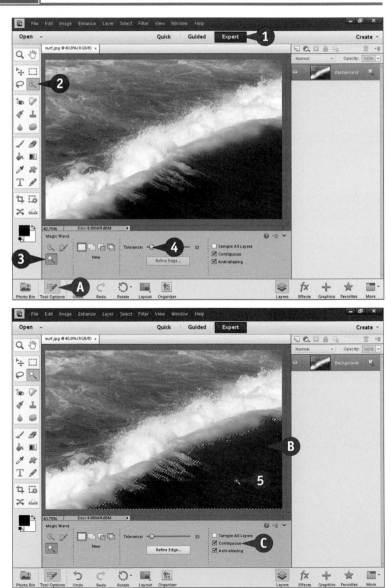

1 In the Editor, click **Expert**.

Note: For more on opening the Editor, see Chapter 1.

2 Click the **Quick Selection** tool (⬚).

A If the Tool Options panel is not open, click here to open it.

3 Click the **Magic Wand** tool (⬚).

The mouse pointer (⬚) changes to a magic wand (⬚).

4 Click and drag the **Tolerance** slider (⬚) to select a value from 0 to 255. You can also click the value and type in a number. The default value of 32 often produces good results.

To select a narrow range of colors, type a small number; to select a wide range of colors, type a large number.

5 Click the area you want to select inside the image.

B Photoshop Elements selects the pixel you clicked, plus any similarly colored pixels near it.

C To select all the similar pixels in the image, not just the contiguous pixels, click **Contiguous** (☑ changes to ☐). See the tip for more.

D This example shows a higher tolerance value, resulting in a greater number of similarly colored pixels selected in the image.

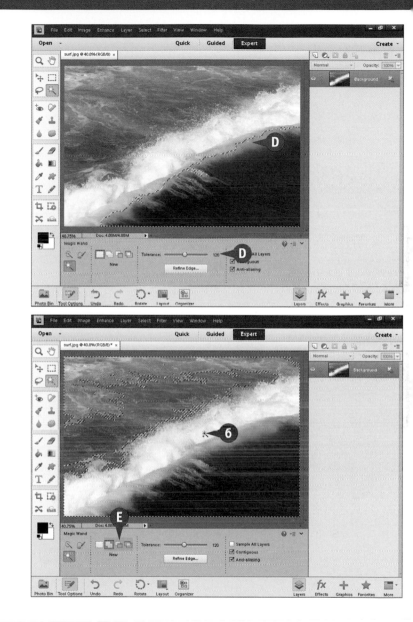

6 To add to your selection, press **Shift** and then click elsewhere in the image.

Photoshop Elements adds to your selection.

E You can also click one of three selection buttons in the Tool Options panel to add to or subtract from the selection.

Note: For more details on adding to or subtracting from a selection, see Chapter 7.

TIP

How can I ensure that the Magic Wand tool selects all the instances of a color in an image?
You can click **Contiguous** (☑ changes to ☐) in the Tool Options panel so the Magic Wand tool selects similar colors, even when they are not contiguous with the pixel you click with the tool. This can be useful when objects intersect the solid-color areas of your image. You can also click **Sample All Layers** (☐ changes to ☑) to select similar colors in all layers in the image, not just in the currently selected layer.

Select an Area with the Quick Selection Tool

You can paint selections onto your images with the Quick Selection tool. The tool automatically expands the area you paint to include similar colors and textures. You can control the size and hardness of the tool, similar to how you work with the Brush tool. This determines how much area the tool selects and the softness of the selection edges.

To paint a selection onto your image without automatically selecting similar, nearby colors, you can use the Selection Brush tool. See the next section, "Select an Area with the Selection Brush," for details.

Select an Area with the Quick Selection Tool

1 In the Editor, click **Expert**.

Note: For more on opening the Editor, see Chapter 1.

2 Click the **Quick Selection** tool ().

A If the Tool Options panel is not open, click here to open it.

3 Click **Brush Settings** to open the Brush menu.

B The Brush Settings menu opens.

In the Brush Settings menu, you can specify the tool's size and other characteristics. Decreasing the tool's hardness causes it to partially select pixels at the perimeter.

4 Click and drag inside the object you want to select.

C Photoshop Elements selects parts of the object based on its coloring and the contrast of its edges.

D After you make a selection, the Add to Selection button () becomes active.

5 Click and drag to select more of the object.

Note: You can select an object and apply color and tonal adjustments at the same time with the Smart Brush. See Chapter 12 for more.

E Photoshop Elements adds to the selection.

F The Quick Selection tool is also available in Quick mode.

TIP

How can I adjust my selection?
In the Tool Options panel, click **Refine Edge** to open the Refine Edge dialog box. Increase **Smooth** to lessen the sharpness of any corners. Increase **Feather** to make the edges partially transparent. Use **Shift Edge** to decrease or increase the selection slightly.

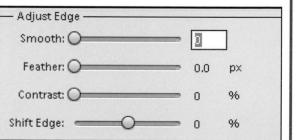

Select an Area with the Selection Brush

Using the Selection Brush, you can select objects in your image by painting over them. By customizing the size and hardness of the brush, you can accurately select objects with curved or undefined edges. Painting on a selection with the Selection Brush tool can often be faster than using a lasso tool if the object being selected has smooth edges and no sharp corners.

The Selection Brush differs from the Quick Selection tool in that it selects only the area you paint over and does not automatically select similar pixels. For more information, see the previous section, "Select an Area with the Quick Selection Tool."

Select an Area with the Selection Brush

Select with the Selection Brush

1 In the Editor, click **Expert**.

Note: For more on opening the Editor, see Chapter 1.

2 Click the **Quick Selection** tool ( ).

A If the Tool Options panel is not open, click here to open it.

3 Click the **Selection Brush** tool ( ).

4 Click and drag the slider ( ) to specify a size for the tool.

5 Click and drag the slider ( ) to specify a hardness from 0% to 100%.

A smaller value produces a softer selection edge.

6 Click the and then click **Selection**.

7 Click and drag to paint a selection.

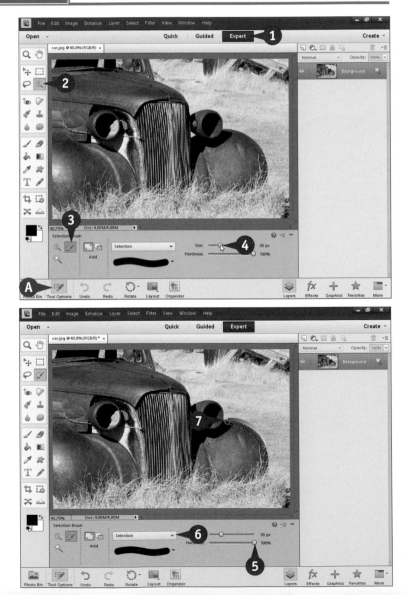

⑧ Click and drag multiple times to paint a selection over the area you want to select.

Photoshop Elements creates a selection.

You can change the brush settings as you paint to select different types of edges in your object.

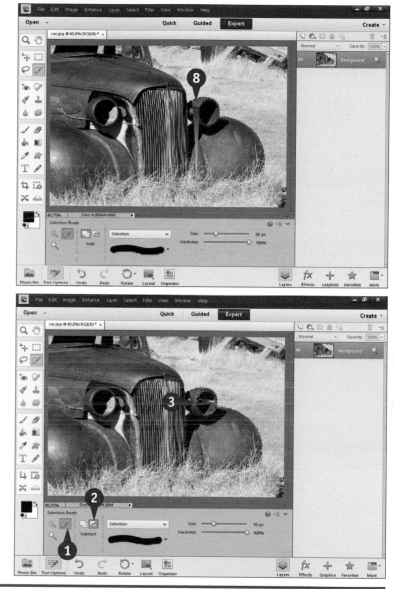

Deselect with the Selection Brush

① Click the **Selection Brush** tool (⬚).

② Click the **Subtract from Selection** button (⬚).

③ Click and drag where you want to remove the selection area.

Photoshop Elements removes the selection.

TIP

How do I paint a mask with the Selection Brush?

Click the ⬇ in the Tool Options panel and then select **Mask**. Click and drag to define the mask (**A**). By default, the masked area appears as a see-through red color called a *rubylith*. To turn a painted mask into a selection, click the ⬇ in the Tool Options panel and then click **Selection**.

Save and Load a Selection

You can save a selected area in your image to reuse later. This can be useful if you anticipate future edits to the same part of your image and have complicated and difficult-to-select objects in your image. You can load the saved selection instead of having to reselect it.

If you save your image project as a Photoshop file, any stored selections are saved with the image and are available if you close the image and open it again. See Chapter 16 for more about saving image files. See the previous sections in this chapter to learn about choosing the appropriate tool for selecting areas in your image.

Save and Load a Selection

Save a Selection

1 In the Editor, click **Expert**.

Note: For more on opening the Editor, see Chapter 1.

2 Make a selection by using one or more of the selection tools.

3 Click **Select**.

4 Click **Save Selection**.

The Save Selection dialog box opens.

5 Make sure New is chosen in the Selection field.

New is the default setting.

6 Type a name for the selection.

7 Click **OK**.

Photoshop Elements saves the selection.

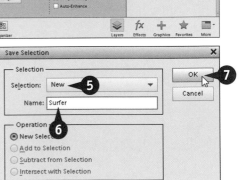

Load a Selection

 Click **Select**.

 Click **Load Selection**.

Note: See the previous subsection, "Save a Selection," to learn how to save your selection.

The Load Selection dialog box opens.

3 Click the ⬇ and then choose the saved selection you want to load.

4 Click **OK**.

A The selection appears in the image.

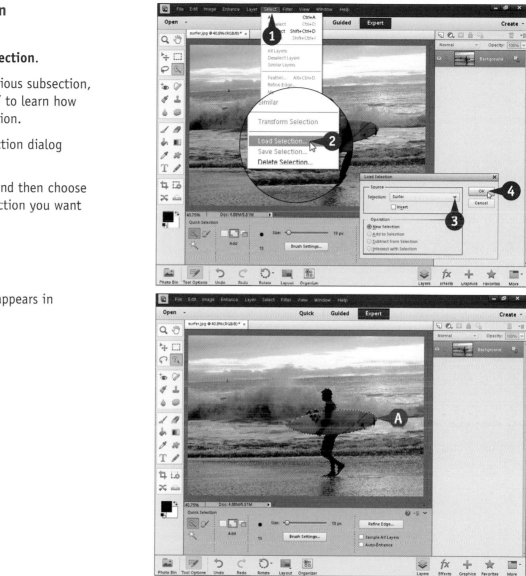

TIP

How can I modify a saved selection?
You can modify a saved selection by making a new selection in your image window, completing steps **3** and **4** in the subsection "Save a Selection" to open the Save Selection dialog box, and then choosing the selection you want to modify from the Selection menu. Clicking **Intersect with Selection** (○ changes to ◉) keeps any area where the new selection and the saved selection overlap. Click **OK** to modify your saved selection.

Invert a Selection

You can invert a selection to deselect what is currently selected and select everything else. This is useful when you want to select the background around an object. You can select the object with one of the Photoshop Elements selection tools and then perform the Invert command to switch the selection to the background.

The inverted selection has the same characteristics as your initial selection. For example, if the initial selection has a feathered edge, the inverted result will also have a feathered edge. For more information about selecting objects, see the other sections in this chapter.

Invert a Selection

 In the Editor, click **Expert**.

 Make a selection by using one of the selection tools.

Note: For more on the various selection tools, see the previous sections in this chapter. For more on opening the Editor, see Chapter 1.

 Click **Select**.

 Click **Inverse**.

 Photoshop Elements inverts the selection.

Note: You can also press Shift + Ctrl + I (Shift + ⌘ + I on a Mac) to invert a selection.

Deselect a Selection

Y ou can deselect a selection when you are done manipulating what is inside of it or if you make a mistake and want to try selecting again.

If you want to keep your selection but temporarily hide it, you can use the Hide command, which is located under the View menu. You can undo a deselect command that you have just performed by clicking **Edit** and then **Undo Deselect**. This is useful if you want to reselect an object after accidentally deselecting it.

Deselect a Selection

1 In the Editor, click **Expert**.

2 Make a selection by using one or more of the selection tools.

Note: For more on the various selection tools, see the previous sections in this chapter. For more on opening the Editor, see Chapter 1.

In this example, a sign is selected.

3 Click **Select**.

4 Click **Deselect**.

Photoshop Elements deselects the selection.

Note: You can also press Ctrl + D or Esc (⌘ + D on a Mac) to deselect a selection.

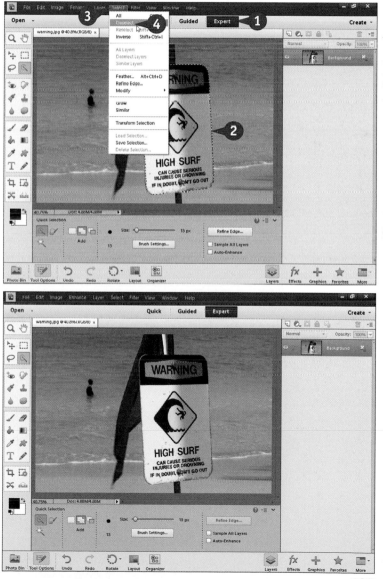

CHAPTER 7

Manipulating Selections

Making a selection in Photoshop Elements isolates a specific area of your image. This chapter shows you how to move, stretch, erase, and manipulate your selection in a variety of ways. You can use these techniques to rearrange people and objects in your image, enlarge elements to give them prominence, or delete things altogether.

Add to or Subtract from a Selection 140

Move a Selection 142

Apply the Content-Aware Move Tool 144

Duplicate a Selection 146

Delete a Selection 147

Rotate a Selection 148

Scale a Selection 149

Skew or Distort a Selection 150

Refine the Edge of a Selection 152

Feather the Border of a Selection 154

Add to or Subtract from a Selection

You can add to or subtract from your selection by using various selection tool options. Adding enables you to select a large object in your image by making multiple selections. By subtracting, you can fix a selection that includes extraneous pixels.

Most selection tools have add and subtract settings in the Tool Options panel. You can also create a selection using one selection tool and then add to or subtract from the selection using other tools. See Chapter 6 to learn how to choose the appropriate tool for selecting elements in your photo.

Add to or Subtract from a Selection

Add to Your Selection

① In the Editor, click **Expert**.

Note: For more on opening the Editor, see Chapter 1.

② Make a selection with a selection tool.

③ Click a selection tool.

This example uses the Magnetic Lasso tool (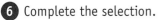).

④ Click the **Add to Selection** button (□).

⑤ Select the area you want to add.

⑥ Complete the selection.

In this example, the starting point is clicked to complete the selection.

Photoshop Elements adds to the selection.

You can enlarge the selection further by repeating steps **3** to **6**.

You can also add to a selection by pressing `Shift` as you select an area.

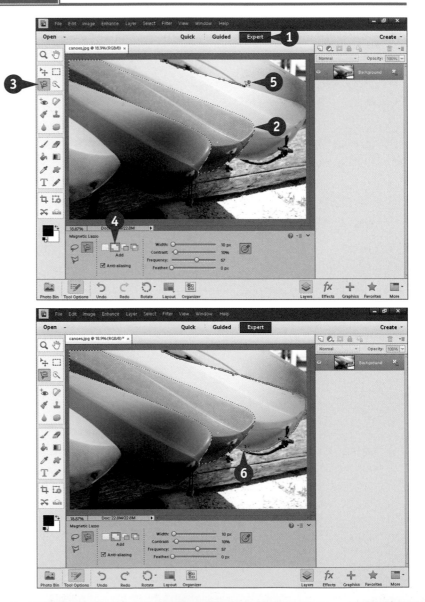

Subtract from Your Selection

1 Make a selection with a selection tool.

2 Click a selection tool.

This example uses the Quick Selection tool (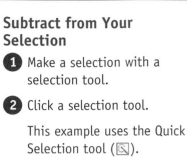).

3 Click the **Subtract from Selection** button (□).

4 Select the area you want to subtract.

A Photoshop Elements deselects, or subtracts, the selected area.

You can subtract other parts of the selection by repeating steps **2** to **4**.

You can also subtract from a selection by pressing Alt (Option on a Mac) as you select an area.

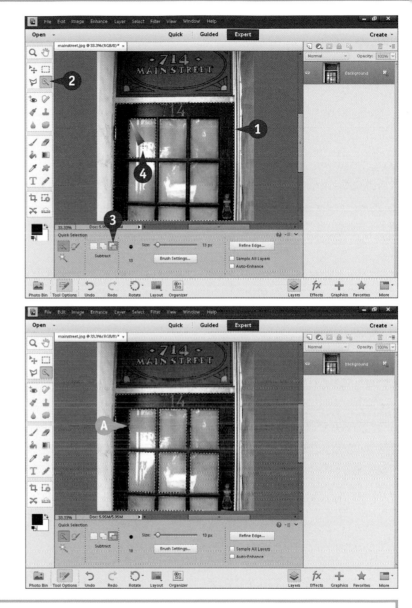

What is an intersection?
An intersection is the area where two selections overlap. For example, two rectangular selections created with the Rectangular Marquee tool might overlap to define a smaller rectangle. You can select this intersection when drawing the second selection by first clicking the **Intersect with Selection** button (□) in the Tool Options panel.

Can I move the selection marquee without moving the item selected?
Yes. Use any of the selection tools to select an area and then press an arrow key — ↑, ↓, ←, → — to move the selection in 1-pixel increments. Press and hold Shift while pressing an arrow key to move the selection in 10-pixel increments.

Move a Selection

You can rearrange elements of your image by moving selections with the Move tool. This enables you to change the composition of your image to emphasize or de-emphasize certain elements. You can move elements of your image either in the default Background layer or in other layers you create for your image.

If you move elements in the Background layer, Photoshop Elements fills the original location with the current background color. If you move elements in another layer, Photoshop Elements makes the original location transparent, revealing any underlying layers. See Chapter 8 for more on layers.

Move a Selection

Move a Selection in the Background

1 In the Editor, click **Expert**.

2 Click **Layers** to display the Layers panel.

Note: For more on opening the Editor or opening panels, see Chapter 1.

3 Click the Background layer.

Note: A newly imported image has only a Background layer. See Chapter 8 for more on using layers.

4 Make a selection.

Note: For more on selecting elements, see Chapter 6.

5 Click the **Move** tool ().

6 Click inside the selection and then drag.

A Photoshop Elements fills the original location of the selection with the current background color.

B In this example, white is the default background color.

If you press **Alt** (**Option** on a Mac) while you drag, a copy of the selection is created.

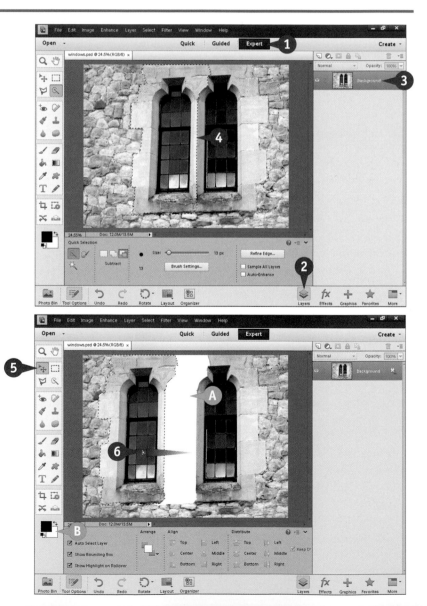

Move a Selection in a Layer

1 Click a layer in the Layers panel.

Note: See Chapter 8 for more on layers.

2 Make a selection with a selection tool.

Note: See Chapter 6 for more on making selections.

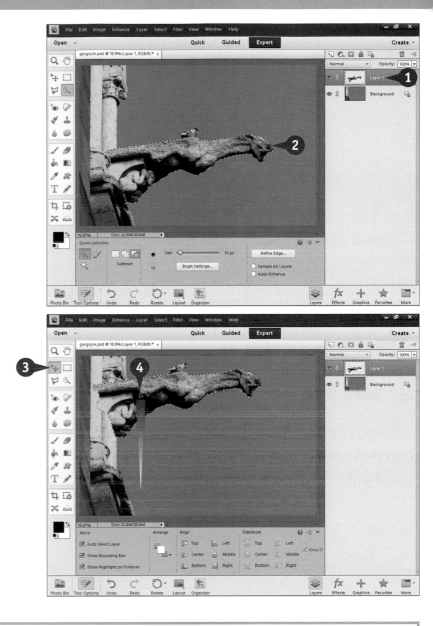

3 Click the **Move** tool ().

4 Click inside the selection and then drag.

Photoshop Elements moves the selection and fills the original location of the selection with transparent pixels.

Note: Unlike the Background — the opaque default layer in Photoshop Elements — other layers can include transparent pixels.

TIPS

How do I move a selection in a straight line?
Press and hold Shift while you drag with the Move tool (⊹). Doing so constrains the movement of your selection horizontally, vertically, or diagonally, depending on the direction you drag.

How do I move several layers at a time?
You can link the layers you want to move, select one of the linked layers, and then move them all with the Move tool. For more, see Chapter 8. You can also Ctrl +click (⌘+click on a Mac) to select multiple layers in the Layers panel. Using the Move tool moves the selected layers.

Apply the Content-Aware Move Tool

You can move an object in your image and have Photoshop Elements automatically fill in the space where the object was originally with surrounding content with the Content-Aware Move tool. Photoshop Elements takes into account the colors and textures around the object when filling in the original location. This is in contrast to using the Move tool, which fills the original space with the current background color or transparent pixels. See the previous section, "Move a Selection," for details. For best results with the Content-Aware Move tool, select an object in an area of continuous color and texture.

Apply the Content-Aware Move Tool

1 In the Editor, click **Expert**.

Note: For more on opening the Editor, see Chapter 1.

2 Click the **Content-Aware Move** tool (![icon]).

A Make sure the Mode is set to Move (○ changes to ⊙).

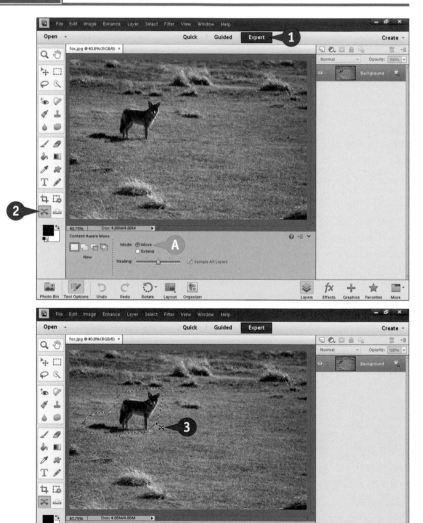

3 Click and drag to select the object you want to move.

Note: The Content-Aware Move tool works similarly to the Lasso tool. See Chapter 6 for details.

Note: Alternatively, you can first select with a selection tool and then click the Content-Aware Move tool.

④ Click inside the selection and drag to another location in your image.

⑤ Release the mouse button.

Ⓑ Photoshop Elements copies the object to the new location.

Ⓒ The original location is filled with surrounding content.

TIP

How can I extend an object in my image?
You can use the Content-Aware Move tool to extend objects such as buildings and fences. With the Content-Aware Move tool (◪) selected, set the Mode to **Extend** (○ changes to ◉). Select an object, click and drag the selection (Ⓐ), and then release the mouse button. Photoshop Elements extends the object, making color and texture adjustments based on the content near the selection.

Duplicate a Selection

You can copy a selection and make a duplicate of it somewhere else in the image. You may use this technique to retouch an element in your photo by placing good content over bad. When you perform the copy using the Move tool and **Alt** (**Option** on a Mac), Photoshop Elements keeps the duplicate in the same layer as the original.

You can also use the Copy and Paste commands to duplicate content in your image. This places the duplicate content in a new layer, which you can then freely move and transform independent of the rest of the image. For more on using the Copy and Paste commands with layers, see Chapter 8.

Duplicate a Selection

1 In the Editor, click **Expert**.

2 Make a selection with a selection tool.

Note: For more on opening the Editor, see Chapter 1. For more on using selection tools, see Chapter 6.

3 Click the **Move** tool ().

A box with handles on the sides and corners surrounds the selection.

A You can also click **Copy** and **Paste** in the Edit menu to copy and paste selections or press **Ctrl**+**J** (**⌘**+**J** on a Mac).

4 Press **Alt** (**Option** on a Mac) while you click and drag the selection.

5 Release the mouse button to drop the selection into place.

Photoshop Elements creates a duplicate of the selection and then places it in the new location.

6 Press **Esc** to deselect the selection.

Delete a Selection

You can delete a selection to remove unwanted elements from an image. If you are working in the Background layer, Photoshop Elements turns deleted pixels the current background color. For more about specifying the background color, see Chapter 12. If you are working in a layer other than the Background layer, deleting a selection turns the selected pixels transparent, and layers below it show through.

Delete a Selection

1 In the Editor, click **Expert**.

2 Make a selection with a selection tool.

Note: For more on opening the Editor, see Chapter 1. For more on using selection tools, see Chapter 6.

3 Press Delete.

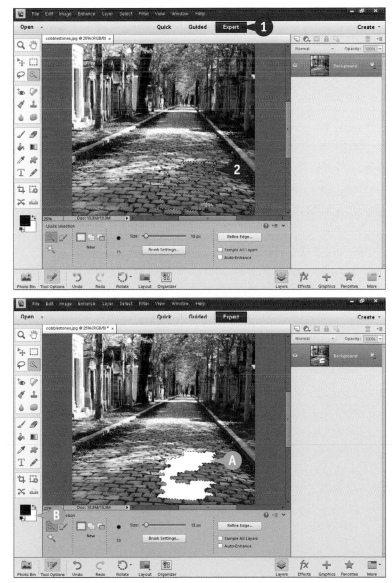

A Photoshop Elements deletes the contents of the selection.

B If you are working in the Background layer, the original location fills with the background color — in this example, white.

If you are working in a layer other than the Background layer, deleting a selection turns the selected pixels transparent, and layers below it show through.

Note: Another way to remove content from your image is to place that content in a layer and then hide the layer. You can reveal the layer to make the content reappear. For more about hiding layers, see Chapter 8.

Rotate a Selection

You can rotate a selection to tilt an element or turn it upside down in your image. You may rotate an element to create a better composition or to correct the appearance of an element. The Free Rotate Selection command, located under the Image menu's Rotate submenu, enables you to rotate a selection an arbitrary amount. Other rotate commands let you rotate a selection a fixed number of degrees.

When you rotate a selection in the Background layer, Photoshop Elements replaces the exposed areas that the rotation creates with the current background color. If you rotate a selection in another layer, the underlying layers appear in the exposed areas. See Chapter 8 for more on layers.

Rotate a Selection

1 In the Editor, click **Expert**.

2 Make a selection with a selection tool.

In this example, content in a layer is selected.

Note: See Chapter 6 for more on using selection tools. See Chapter 8 for more on layers.

3 Click **Image**.

4 Click **Rotate**.

5 Click **Free Rotate Selection**.

A box with handles on the sides and corners surrounds the selection.

6 Click and drag outside the selection.

A You can precisely rotate your selection by typing percentage values in the W and H fields in the Tool Options panel.

The selection rotates.

7 Click ☑ or press Enter to commit the rotation.

B You can click ⊘ or press Esc to cancel.

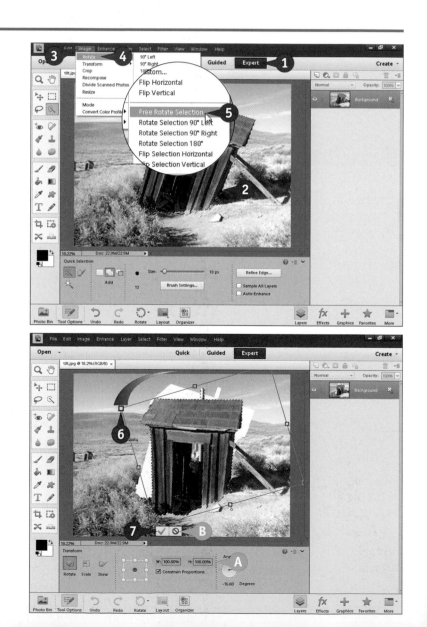

Scale a Selection

You can scale a selection to make it larger or smaller. Scaling enables you to adjust or emphasize parts of your image. When you scale a selection in the Background layer, Photoshop Elements replaces the exposed areas that scaling to a smaller size creates with the current background color. If you scale a selection in another layer, the underlying layers appear in the exposed areas.

Scaling image content to a much larger size can decrease the quality of the content, making it blurry. You can correct blurriness using the Sharpen filter. See Chapter 9 for details.

Scale a Selection

① In the Editor, click **Expert**.

② Make a selection with a selection tool.

In this example, content in a layer is selected.

Note: See Chapter 6 for more on using selection tools. See Chapter 8 for more on layers.

③ Click **Image**.

④ Click **Resize**.

⑤ Click **Scale**.

A box with handles on the sides and corners surrounds the selection.

⑥ Click and drag a handle to scale the selection.

Drag a corner handle to scale both the horizontal and vertical dimensions.

Ⓐ You can precisely scale your selection by typing percentage values in the W and H fields in the Tool Options panel.

Ⓑ With Constrain Proportions selected, the height and width change proportionally.

⑦ Click ☑ or press Enter to apply the scale effect.

Ⓒ You can click ☒ or press Esc to cancel.

Skew or Distort a Selection

You can transform a selection by using the Skew or Distort commands. This enables you to stretch elements in your image into interesting shapes. You can also use skewing and distortion to make changes to perspective in your image. You can make an object appear as if it recedes into the distance.

When you skew or distort a selection in the Background layer, Photoshop Elements replaces the exposed areas that the skewing or distorting creates with the current background color. If you skew or distort a selection in another layer, the underlying layers appear in the exposed areas.

Skew or Distort a Selection

Skew a Selection

1 In the Editor, click **Expert**.

2 Make a selection with a selection tool.

Note: For more on opening the Editor, see Chapter 1. See Chapter 6 for more on using selection tools.

3 Click **Image**.

4 Click **Transform**.

5 Click **Skew**.

A rectangular box with handles on the sides and corners surrounds the selection.

6 Click and drag a handle.

Photoshop Elements skews the selection.

Because the Skew command works along a single axis, you can drag either horizontally or vertically.

7 Click ☑ or press **Enter** to apply the skewing.

Ⓐ You can click ◎ or press **Esc** to cancel.

Distort a Selection

1 Make a selection with a selection tool.

Note: See Chapter 6 for more on using selection tools.

2 Click **Image**.

3 Click **Transform**.

4 Click **Distort**.

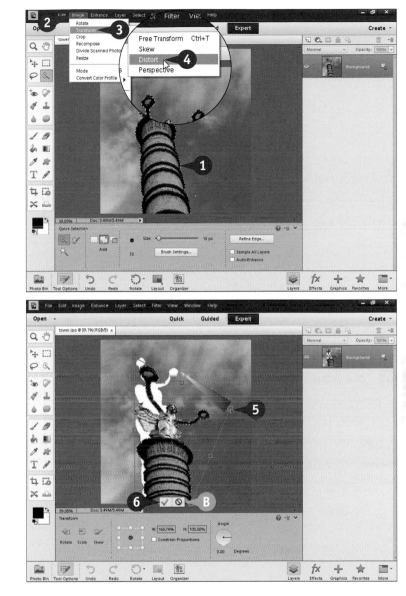

A rectangular box with handles on the sides and corners surrounds the selection.

5 Click and drag a handle.

Photoshop Elements distorts the selection. The Distort command works independently of the selection's axes; you can drag a handle both vertically and horizontally.

Note: You can precisely distort your selection by typing percentage values in the W and H fields in the Tool Options panel.

6 Click ☑ or press Enter to apply the distortion.

Ⓑ You can click ⊘ or press Esc to cancel.

TIP

How can I perform several transforming effects in a row on a selection?
Click **Image**, **Transform**, and then **Free Transform**. If the Tool Options panel is not open, click **Tool Options** to open it. For each transformation effect you want to apply, select a transformation type — Rotate, Scale, or Skew — in the Tool Options panel and then click and drag a handle on the box that surrounds the selection. Click ☑ or press Enter to apply the effects.

Refine the Edge of a Selection

You can open the Refine Edge dialog box to make a variety of adjustments to the edge of your selection. For example, you can shift the edge in or out or smooth any sharp angles along an edge. Smoothing can be useful if you have made a selection using the Polygonal Lasso tool, which can create pointy edges.

For more on feathering an edge by using the Refine Edge dialog box, see the next section, "Feather the Border of a Selection."

Refine the Edge of a Selection

1 In the Editor, click **Expert**.

2 Make a selection with a selection tool.

Note: For more on opening the Editor, see Chapter 1. For more on using selection tools, see Chapter 6.

A If the Tool Options panel is not open, click here to open it.

3 Click **Refine Edge**.

The Refine Edge dialog box opens.

4 Click and drag the **Smooth** slider (○) to determine the smoothness of the edge.

5 Click and drag the **Feather** slider (○) to determine the softness of the edge.

B Photoshop Elements shows a preview of the effects.

6 Click and drag the **Shift Edge** slider () to move the selection edge in or out from the selected object.

Drag to the left to move the edge in.

Drag to the right to move the edge out.

7 Click **OK**.

C Photoshop Elements adjusts the selection.

TIPS

How do I place my selection into a new layer?
Open the Refine Edge dialog box and make your adjustments. In the Output To menu, select **New Layer**. Photoshop Elements creates a new layer containing your selection. Other output options include sending the selection to a layer mask or a new document. For more on layers, see Chapter 8.

How can I easily apply the same settings to future selections?
In the Refine Edge dialog box, click **Remember Settings** (☐ changes to ☑). The next time you open the Refine Edge dialog box, the previous settings appear. Click **OK** to apply them.

Feather the Border of a Selection

You can feather a selection's border to create soft edges. You can use this technique with other layers to create a blending effect between the selected area and any underlying layers. Soft edges around content can add a sentimental or romantic feel to your image.

To create a soft edge around an object, you must first select the object, feather the selection border, and then delete the part of the image that surrounds your selection. You can change the final effect achieved by changing the applied background color.

Feather the Border of a Selection

Feather a Selection

① In the Editor, click **Expert**.

② Make a selection with a selection tool.

Note: For more on opening the Editor, see Chapter 1. For more on using selection tools, see Chapter 6.

Ⓐ If the Tool Options panel is not open, click here to open it.

③ Click **Refine Edge**.

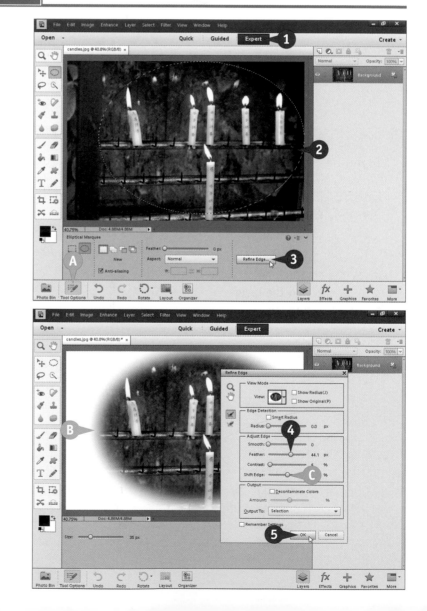

The Refine Edge dialog box opens.

④ Click and drag the **Feather** slider (Ⓞ) to determine the softness of the edge.

Ⓑ Photoshop Elements shows a preview of the feathering.

Ⓒ You can click and drag the **Shift Edge** slider (Ⓞ) to adjust the selection inward or outward.

⑤ Click **OK**.

Delete the Surrounding Background

 Click **Select**.

② Click **Inverse**.

You can also press Shift+ Ctrl+I (Shift+⌘+I on a Mac) to apply the Inverse command.

The selection inverts but remains feathered.

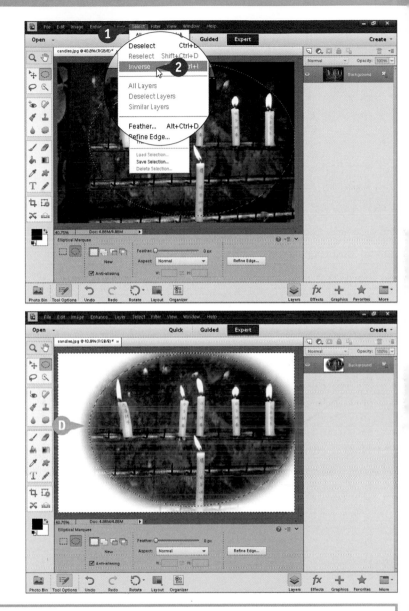

③ Press Delete.

Ⓓ If you are working with the Background layer, the deleted area fills with the current background color.

If you are working with a layer other than the Background layer, the deleted area becomes transparent, and the layers below show through.

You can now see the effect of the feathering.

TIPS

How do I feather my selection into a colored background?

You can add a solid-color fill layer behind your photo and then blend the feathered selection into the new layer. The layer containing the selection appears on top of the solid-color fill layer, and the feathering technique creates a softened blend between the two layers. For more on layers, see Chapter 8.

What happens if I feather a selection and then apply a command to it?

The command is applied only partially to pixels near the edge of the selection. If you remove color from a selection by using the Hue/Saturation command, color at the feathered edge of the selection is only partially removed. For more on Hue/Saturation, see Chapter 10.

CHAPTER 8

Using Layers

You can separate the elements in your image so you can move and transform them independently of one another. You can accomplish this by placing them in different layers. To change what layer elements are visible, you can rearrange the stacking order of layers or adjust their opacity. You can also add special layers known as adjustment layers to control the lighting, color, and other aspects of your image.

Introducing Layers 158

Create and Add to a Layer 160

Hide a Layer 162

Move a Layer 163

Duplicate a Layer 164

Delete a Layer 165

Reorder Layers 166

Change the Opacity of a Layer 168

Link Layers 169

Merge Layers 170

Rename a Layer 171

Create a Fill Layer 172

Create an Adjustment Layer 174

Blend Layers 176

Add a Layer Mask 178

Edit a Layer Mask 180

Introducing Layers

A Photoshop Elements image can consist of multiple layers, with each layer containing different objects, adjustments, or fills in the image. This enables you to edit and adjust parts of the image independently. You can select different layers in an image or change their stacking order using the Layers panel.

When you open a digital camera photo or a newly scanned image in Photoshop Elements, it exists as a single layer known as the Background layer. You can add new layers on top of the Background layer as you work.

Layer Independence

Layered Photoshop Elements files act like several images combined into one. Each layer of an image has its own set of pixels that you can move and transform independently of the pixels in other layers. The content of a layer can take up the entire image canvas or include just a small object within a larger image. If you want, you can select every distinct object in your image in its own layer. An image can have dozens or even hundreds of layers.

Apply Commands to Layers

Most Photoshop Elements commands affect only the layers that you select in the Layers panel. For example, if you click and drag by using the **Move** tool (⬚), the selected layers move, but the other layers stay in place. If you apply a color adjustment, only colors in the selected layer change. Putting content into layers offers a useful way to isolate the effects that you apply to your image projects. For example, by placing a fish in its own layer, you can change the color of the fish without changing the colors of the other sea creatures in your image.

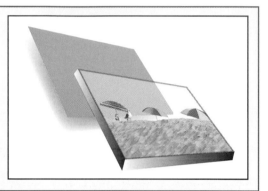

Manipulate Layers

You can combine, duplicate, and hide layers in an image and also shuffle their order. You can also link particular layers so they move in unison, or you can blend content from different layers in creative ways. You manage all of this in the Layers panel.

Transparency

Layers can have transparent areas, where the elements in the layers below show through. When you perform a cut or erase command on a layer, the affected pixels become transparent. You can also make a layer partially transparent by decreasing its opacity.

Adjustment Layers

Adjustment layers are special layers that contain information about color or tonal adjustments. An adjustment layer affects the appearance of the pixels in all the layers below it. You can increase or decrease an adjustment layer's intensity to get precisely the effect you want.

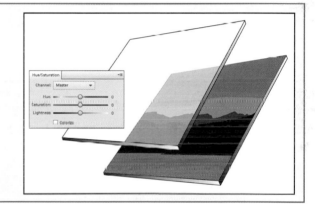

Save Layered Files

You can save multilayered images only in the Photoshop, PDF, and TIFF file formats. To save a layered image in another file format — for example, PNG, BMP, GIF, or JPEG — you must combine the image's layers into a single layer, a process known as *flattening*. For more on saving files, see Chapter 16.

Create and Add to a Layer

To keep elements in your image independent of one another, you can create separate layers and add objects to them. Typically, you copy and paste elements from one part of your image, or from a different image, and paste them to place them into new layers.

When you create a new layer, the layer appears in a list in the Layers panel. Layers higher in the list appear above and can cover layers lower in the list. To rearrange layers that you have created, see the section "Reorder Layers." To get rid of layers in your image, see the section "Delete a Layer."

Create and Add to a Layer

Create a Layer

1. In the Editor, click **Expert**.

2. Click **Layers** to open the Layers panel.

Note: For more on opening the Editor or panels, see Chapter 1.

3. Click the layer above which you want to add the new layer.

4. In the Layers panel, click the **Create a New Layer** icon (⬚).

Note: Alternatively, you can click **Layer**, **New**, and then **Layer**.

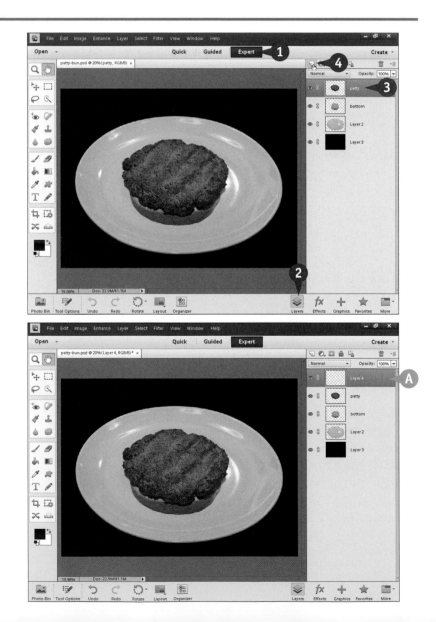

A. Photoshop Elements creates a new, transparent layer.

Note: To change the name of a layer, see the section "Rename a Layer."

Copy and Paste into a Layer

Note: This example shows how to add content to the new layer by copying and pasting from another image file.

 Open another image.

 Using a selection tool, select the content you want to copy into the other image.

Note: See Chapter 1 for more on opening an image. See Chapter 6 for more on selection tools.

3 Click **Edit**.

4 Click **Copy**.

5 Click the tab for the image window where you created the new layer in the previous subsection, "Create a Layer," named patty-bun in this example.

Note: See Chapter 1 for more on using tabs to select open images.

6 Click the new layer in the Layers panel.

7 Click **Edit**.

8 Click **Paste**.

B The selected content from the other image appears in the new layer.

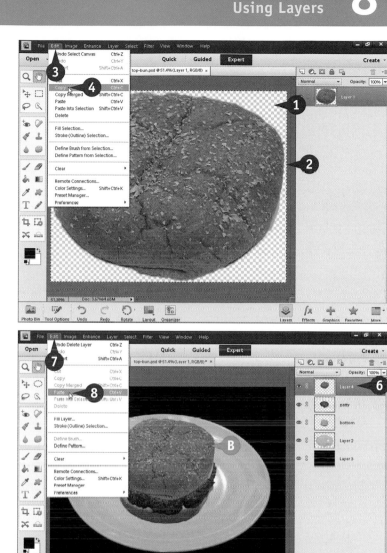

TIPS

What is the Background layer?

The Background layer is the default bottom layer. It appears when you create a new image that has a nontransparent background color or when you import an image from a scanner or digital camera. You can create new layers on top of a Background layer but not below it. Unlike other layers, a Background layer cannot contain transparent pixels.

How do I turn the Background layer into a regular layer?

If you have the Background layer selected, you can click **Layer**, **New**, and then **Layer from Background** to turn it into a regular layer. You can press Ctrl + J (⌘ + J on a Mac) to create an editable copy of the Background layer.

161

Hide a Layer

You can hide a layer to temporarily remove elements in that layer from view. Hiding a layer can be useful if you want to view or edit objects that appear in layers underneath.

Hidden layers do not appear when you print or use the Save for Web command.

You can remove a layer altogether by deleting it. See the section "Delete a Layer" for details. Hiding a layer is different from deleting a layer because you can always make a hidden layer visible again by clicking the visibility icon in the Layers panel.

Hide a Layer

① In the Editor, click **Expert**.

② Click **Layers** to open the Layers panel.

Note: For more on opening the Editor or panels, see Chapter 1.

③ Click a layer.

④ Click the visibility icon (👁) for the layer.

The icon changes to 👁, and Photoshop Elements hides the layer.

To show one layer and hide all the others, you can press Alt (Option on a Mac) and then click the visibility icon (👁) for the layer you want to show.

Note: You can also delete a layer. See the section "Delete a Layer" for more.

162

Move a Layer

You can use the Move tool to reposition the elements in one layer without moving those in others. You determine what layer elements move by selecting a layer in the Layers panel. Then you click and drag with the Move tool inside your image.

If you make a selection with a selection tool before using the Move tool, Photoshop Elements moves only the selected objects in the layer. For more on selection tools, see Chapter 6. To undo a move, click **Undo** or press Ctrl+Z (⌘+Z on a Mac). For more on undoing moves, see Chapter 5.

Move a Layer

1 In the Editor, click **Expert**.

2 Click **Layers** to open the Layers panel.

Note: For more on opening the Editor or panels, see Chapter 1.

3 Click a layer.

4 Click the **Move** tool ().

5 Click and drag inside the window.

Content in the selected layer moves.

Content in the other layers does not move.

Note: To move several layers at the same time, see the section "Link Layers."

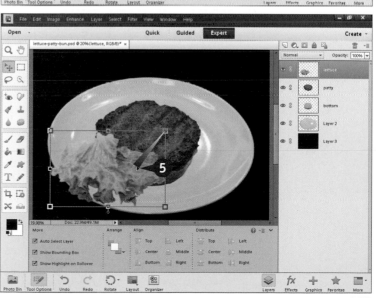

Duplicate a Layer

By duplicating a layer, you can manipulate elements in an image while keeping a copy of their original state. Duplicating a layer creates a new layer. You can repeat the duplicate command to create many copies of objects in your image, and then use the Move command to arrange the copies. For more, see the previous section, "Move a Layer."

When you duplicate a layer, the elements in that layer appear in the same position as in the original layer. Unless you change the position of elements in one of the two layers, one layer covers the content in the other layer.

Duplicate a Layer

1 In the Editor, click **Expert**.

2 Click **Layers** to open the Layers panel.

Note: For more on opening the Editor or panels, see Chapter 1.

3 Click a layer.

4 Click and drag the layer to the **Create a New Layer** icon (⬒).

Note: Alternatively, you can click **Layer** and then **Duplicate Layer**; a dialog box opens, asking you to name the layer you want to duplicate.

You can also press Ctrl+J (⌘+J on a Mac) to duplicate a selected layer in the Layers panel.

Note: If you have selected an area of the layer, only the selected area will be duplicated.

Ⓐ Photoshop Elements duplicates the selected layer.

Note: To rename the duplicate layer, see the section "Rename a Layer."

Ⓑ You can test that Photoshop Elements has duplicated the layer by selecting the new layer, clicking the **Move** tool (⊹), and clicking and dragging the layer.

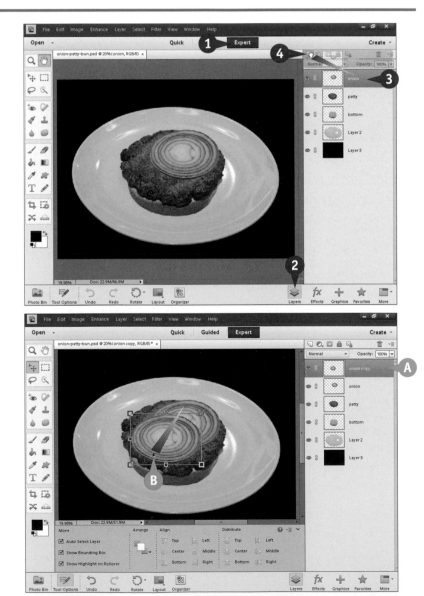

164

Delete a Layer

You can delete a layer when you no longer have a use for its contents. After deleting a layer, the layer no longer appears in the Layers panel and its content disappears from your image.

An alternative to deleting a layer is to hide it. Hiding a layer keeps the layer content in your image but does not display it in the image window. For more details, see the section "Hide a Layer."

To undo the deletion of a layer, you can click **Undo** in the taskbar or press `Ctrl`+`Z` (`⌘`+`Z` on a Mac). For more about undoing commands, see Chapter 5.

Delete a Layer

1 In the Editor, click **Expert**.

2 Click **Layers** to open the Layers panel.

Note: For more on opening the Editor or panels, see Chapter 1.

3 Click a layer.

4 Click and drag the layer to the trash can icon (🗑).

Note: Alternatively, you can click **Layer** and then **Delete Layer**, or you can select a layer and then click the trash can icon (🗑). In both cases, a confirmation dialog box opens.

Photoshop Elements deletes the selected layer, and the content in the layer disappears from the image window.

Note: You can also hide a layer. See the section "Hide a Layer" for more.

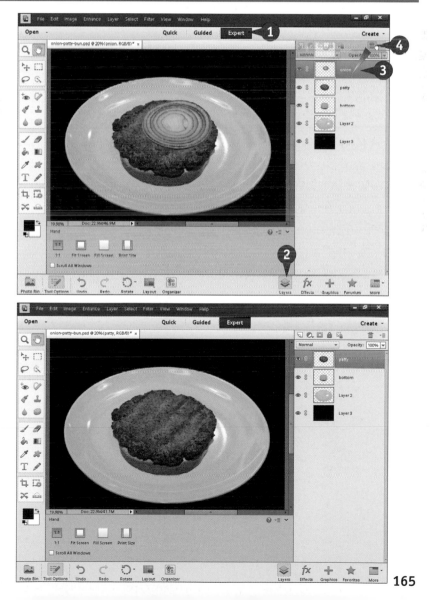

Reorder Layers

Layers listed in the Layers panel overlap one another depending on their stacking order. Layers higher in the list appear above layers lower in the list. You can change the stacking order of layers to move elements up or down in your image.

You can move a layer up in the Layers panel to display objects currently covered by content in layers above. If you have a layer in your image that you want to use as a background, you can move it down in the Layers panel to make it appear behind everything else.

Reorder Layers

Using the Layers Panel

1 In the Editor, click **Expert**.

2 Click **Layers** to open the Layers panel.

Note: For more on opening the Editor or panels, see Chapter 1.

3 Click a layer.

4 Click and drag the layer to change its arrangement in the stack.

A The layer assumes its new position in the stack.

B In this example, the cheese layer moves up in the stack.

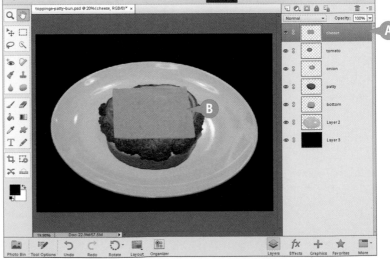

Using the Arrange Commands

1 Click a layer.

2 Click **Layer**.

3 Click **Arrange**.

4 Click the command for how you want to move the layer.

You can choose Bring to Front, Bring Forward, Send Backward, Send to Back, or Reverse.

Note: Reverse is available only if more than one layer is selected. You can Ctrl +click (⌘+click on a Mac) in the Layers panel to select multiple layers.

In this example, Bring Forward is chosen.

C The layer assumes its new position in the stack.

D In this example, the tomato layer moves to the top of the stack.

Note: You cannot move a layer in back of the default Background layer unless you rename the Background layer first.

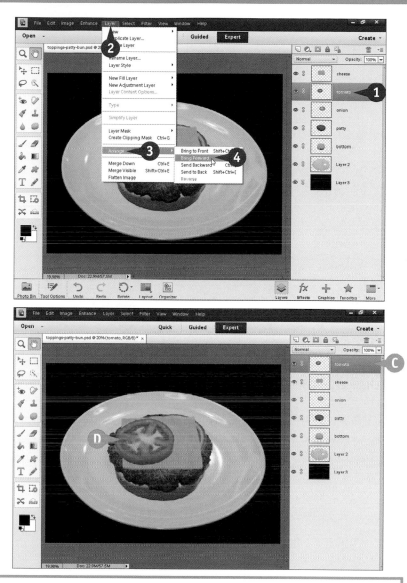

TIP

Are there shortcuts for changing the order of layers?

You can shift layers forward and backward in the stack by pressing the following shortcut keys:

Move	Shortcut (Windows)	Shortcut (Mac)
Forward one step	Ctrl +]	⌘ +]
Backward one step	Ctrl + [	⌘ + [
To the very front	Shift + Ctrl +]	Shift + ⌘ +]
To the very back	Shift + Ctrl + [	Shift + ⌘ + [

Change the Opacity of a Layer

You can adjust the opacity of a layer to let elements in the layers below show through. Opacity is the opposite of transparency — decreasing the opacity of a layer increases its transparency.

Layers can have opacities from 0 to 100 percent. A layer with an opacity of 100 percent is completely visible and obscures content below it. A layer with an opacity of 0 percent is completely transparent and is not visible in your image. Another way to make a layer disappear in your image is to hide it. For details, see the section "Hide a Layer."

Change the Opacity of a Layer

1 In the Editor, click **Expert**.

2 Click **Layers** to open the Layers panel.

Note: For more on opening the Editor or panels, see Chapter 1.

3 Click the layer whose opacity you want to change.

Note: You cannot change the opacity of the Background layer.

Ⓐ The default opacity is 100%, which is completely opaque.

4 Type a new value in the Opacity field.

Ⓑ You can also click the ▼ and then drag the selection slider (◯).

A layer's opacity can range from 0% to 100%.

Ⓒ The layer changes in opacity.

Changing the opacity of a layer also affects any layer styles applied to the layer. For more on layer styles, see Chapter 15.

Link Layers

Linking causes different layers to move in unison when you drag them with the Move tool. You can link layers when you want to keep elements of an image aligned with one another but do not want to merge their layers. Keeping layers unmerged allows you to apply effects to each layer independently.

See the next section, "Merge Layers," for more on merging. For more on moving a layer, see the section "Move a Layer." When you select a layer in the Layers panel, a link icon indicates any other layers linked to that layer.

Link Layers

1 In the Editor, click **Expert**.

2 Click **Layers** to open the Layers panel.

Note: For more on opening the Editor or panels, see Chapter 1.

3 Click one of the layers you want to link.

4 Press Ctrl (⌘ on a Mac) and then click one or more other layers that you want to link.

5 Click the **Link Layers** button (⬚) in the Layers panel.

Ⓐ The linking icon (⬚) next to each linked layer turns orange.

Ⓑ To see that Photoshop Elements has linked the layers, select one of the layers, click the **Move** tool (⊞), and then click and drag the layer.

Merge Layers

Merging layers lets you permanently combine information from two or more separate layers. The different layers become a single layer in the Layers panel. After merging layers, you can no longer move them independently of one another.

For more on moving a layer, see the section "Move a Layer." To move content in multiple layers in unison without merging the layers, you can link the layers. For details, see the previous section, "Link Layers." To undo a merge, you can click **Edit** and then **Undo** or press Ctrl+Z (⌘+Z on a Mac).

Merge Layers

1 In the Editor, click **Expert**.

2 Click **Layers** to open the Layers panel.

3 Place the two layers you want to merge next to each other.

4 Click the topmost of the two layers.

5 Click **Layer**.

6 Click **Merge Down**.

You can merge all the layers together by clicking **Flatten Image** or just the visible layers by clicking **Merge Visible**.

You can also Ctrl+click (⌘+click on a Mac) to select multiple layers in the Layers panel and then click **Merge Selected** to merge them.

Ⓐ The two layers merge.

Photoshop Elements keeps the name of the lower layer.

In this example, the tomato layer has merged with the onion layer.

You can also press Ctrl+Shift+E (⌘+Shift+E on a Mac) to merge all visible layers, or Ctrl+Shift+Alt+E (⌘+Shift+Option+E on a Mac) to merge the visible layers into a new layer without eliminating the existing layers.

Rename a Layer

You can rename a layer to give it a name that describes its content. For example, in a multilayered image of flowers, you can give one layer the name "red rose" and another the name "white lily."

When you create a new layer in the Layers panel, Photoshop Elements gives it the generic name "Layer 1." When you duplicate a layer in the Layers panel, the duplicate layer has the same name as the original layer with a "copy" suffix. After you create or duplicate a layer, you can rename it.

Rename a Layer

1 In the Editor, click **Expert**.

2 Click **Layers** to open the Layers panel.

Note: For more on opening the Editor or panels, see Chapter 1.

3 Click a layer.

4 Click **Layer**.

5 Click **Rename Layer**.

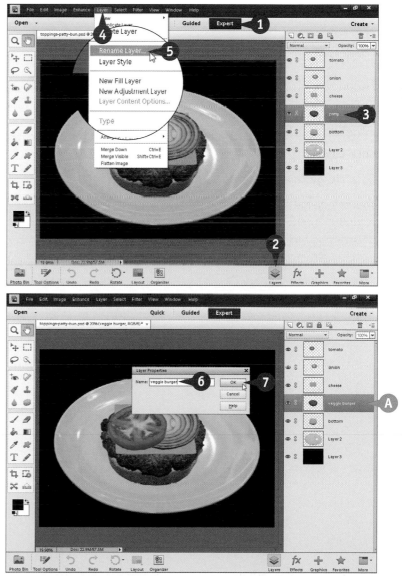

The Layer Properties dialog box opens.

6 Type a new name for the layer.

7 Click **OK**.

Ⓐ The name of the layer changes in the Layers panel.

You can also double-click the name of the layer in the Layers panel to edit the name.

Create a Fill Layer

You can create a solid fill layer to place an opaque layer of color throughout your image. You can use fill layers behind layers containing objects to create all kinds of color effects in your photos.

When you create a solid fill layer, a Color Picker dialog box appears, enabling you to select a color for the fill layer. The dialog box also enables you to select a blend mode and opacity. For more about these settings, see the sections "Blend Layers" and "Change the Opacity of a Layer."

You can rearrange the stacking order of a fill layer just as you can any other layer. For more information, see the section "Reorder Layers."

Create a Fill Layer

 In the Editor, click **Expert**.

2 Click **Layers** to open the Layers panel.

Note: For more on opening the Editor or panels, see Chapter 1.

3 Click the layer above which you want the solid color layer to appear.

4 Click **Layer**.

5 Click **New Fill Layer**.

6 Click **Solid Color**.

The New Layer dialog box opens.

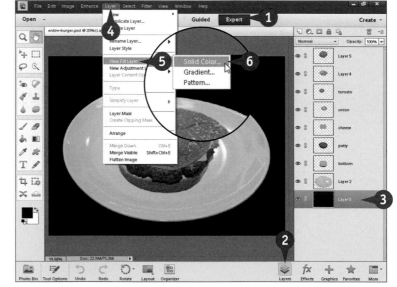

7 Type a name for the layer or use the default name.

A You can specify a type of blend or opacity setting for the layer.

Note: See the sections "Blend Layers" or "Change the Opacity of a Layer" for more.

8 Click **OK**.

The Color Picker dialog box opens.

9 To change the range of colors that appears in the window, click and drag the slider (■).

10 To select a fill color, click in the color window.

11 Click **OK**.

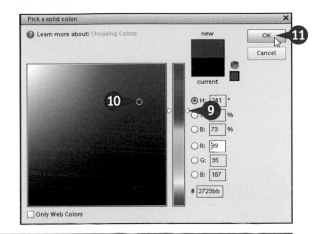

B Photoshop Elements creates a new layer filled with a solid color.

In this example, a solid blue layer appears below the Layer 2 layer.

TIPS

How do I add solid color to just part of a layer?
To add color to a specific part of a layer, make a selection with a selection tool before creating the solid fill layer, and then apply a color fill as outlined in steps **4** to **11** in this section. Photoshop Elements adds color only inside the selection.

What other types of fill layers can I add?
In the New Fill Layer menu, you can create gradient fill layers, which apply bands of colors instead of a solid fill. Or you can create a pattern fill layer, which applies a repeating pattern as a fill instead of a solid color. You can select from a variety of preset patterns and gradient effects.

Create an Adjustment Layer

Adjustment layers enable you to store color and tonal changes in a layer instead of having them permanently applied to your image. The information in an adjustment layer is applied to the pixels in the layers below it.

You can change the opacity of an adjustment layer to lessen its effect, or hide an adjustment layer to turn the changes off. Adjustment layers are handy for testing editing techniques, colors, or brightness settings. For more about the effects you can apply with adjustment layers, such as levels and curves adjustments, see Chapter 10.

Create an Adjustment Layer

1 In the Editor, click **Expert**.

2 Click **Layers** to open the Layers panel.

Note: For more on opening the Editor or panels, see Chapter 1.

3 Click the layer you want to appear below the adjustment layer.

4 Click **Layer**.

5 Click **New Adjustment Layer**.

6 Click an adjustment command.

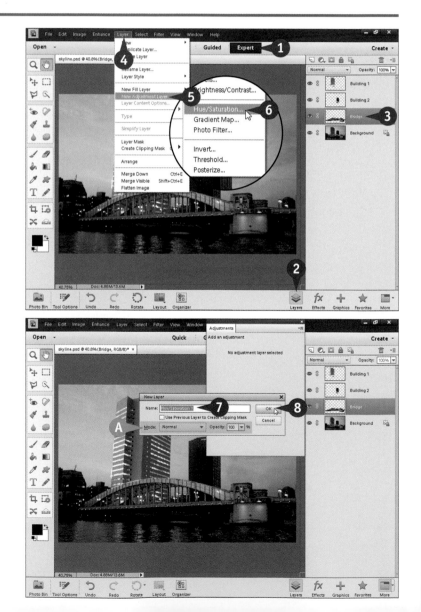

The Adjustments panel for the selected command and New Layer dialog box open.

7 Type a name for the adjustment layer or use the default name.

Ⓐ You can specify a type of blend or opacity setting for the layer.

Note: See the sections "Blend Layers" or "Change the Opacity of a Layer" for more.

8 Click **OK**.

B Photoshop Elements adds an adjustment layer to the image.

The panel for the adjustment command remains open.

Note: Depending on the type of adjustment layer you create, different settings appear.

In this example, an adjustment layer is created that changes the hue and saturation.

9 Click and drag the sliders (◉) or type values to adjust the settings.

You can see the adjustments take effect in the workspace.

C Photoshop Elements applies the effect to the layers below the adjustment layer.

You can double-click the adjustment layer to make changes to the settings.

TIPS

How do I apply an adjustment layer to only part of my image canvas?
Make a selection with a selection tool before creating the adjustment layer. Photoshop Elements applies an adjustment layer to the selected content by creating a layer mask. See the section "Add a Layer Mask" for more about masks. You can experiment with edits to the adjustment layer; any changes you make to the selection affect the underlying layers. See Chapter 6 for more on the kinds of selections you can make with selection tools in Photoshop Elements.

Is there a shortcut for creating an adjustment layer?
Yes. You can click the **Create Adjustment Layer** icon (◉) in the Layers panel and then click the type of adjustment layer you want to create.

Blend Layers

You can use the blending modes in Photoshop Elements to specify how pixels in a layer should blend with the layers below. You can blend layers to create visual effects in your photos. In this section, two photos are combined in one image file as two separate layers, and then the layers are blended together. To copy a photo into a layer, see the section "Create and Add to a Layer."

When you create a new layer, the default blending mode is Normal, which applies no special blending to the layer. If you make changes to the blending mode, switching back to Normal removes any blending effects.

Blend Layers

Blend a Regular Layer

1 In the Editor, click **Expert**.

2 Click **Layers** to open the Layers panel.

Note: For more on opening the Editor or panels, see Chapter 1.

3 Click the layer that you want to blend.

4 Click the and choose a blending mode.

Photoshop Elements blends the selected layer with the layers below it.

This example blends a rooftop image with the image of a flower by using the Hard Light mode.

Blend an Adjustment Layer

1 Open the Layers panel.

Note: For more on opening panels, see Chapter 1.

2 Click an adjustment layer that you want to blend.

3 Click the ▼ and choose a blending mode.

Photoshop Elements blends the selected layer with the layers below it.

This example shows the Exclusion mode applied to a Hue and Saturation adjustment layer, which creates a photonegative effect where the layers overlap.

What effects do some of the different blending modes have?
- **Multiply**: Darkens the colors where the selected layer overlaps layers below it.
- **Screen**: The opposite of Multiply. It lightens colors where layers overlap.
- **Color**: Takes the selected layer's colors and blends them with the light and dark details in the layers below it.
- **Luminosity**: The opposite of Color. It takes the selected layer's light and dark details and mixes them with the colors below it.

Add a Layer Mask

You can apply a layer mask to a layer to precisely control what pixels in the layer are shown and what pixels are hidden. You define the mask by applying colors using Photoshop Elements tools. A white color in the mask defines what in the layer is visible. Applying black to the layer mask with a brush or other tool specifies what parts of the layer are hidden. You can also apply shades of gray to partially show content in the layer.

When you add a layer mask to a layer, Photoshop Elements adds a mask icon next to the regular layer icon in the Layers panel.

Add a Layer Mask

1 In the Editor, click **Expert**.

2 Click **Layers** to open the Layers panel.

Note: For details about opening the Editor or panels, see Chapter 1.

3 Click to select the layer to which you want to apply the mask.

4 Click the **Add Layer Mask** icon (▣).

Note: You can alternatively click **Layer**, **Layer Mask**, and then **Reveal All** or **Hide All**. This creates an all white or all black layer mask, respectively.

Ⓐ Photoshop Elements adds a layer mask icon to the layer.

The new layer mask is completely white, which means none of the layer is hidden by the mask.

Ⓑ The foreground and background colors change to black and white, respectively.

5 Click the **Brush** tool (✐) or press B.

6 Set the brush size and shape using the settings in the Tool Options panel.

178

Note: For more about using the Brush tool, see Chapter 12.

7 Click and drag on the part of the layer you want to hide.

C The brush applies a black color to the mask.

D Photoshop Elements hides the pixels where the mask is black in color.

8 Click the foreground color box and select a shade of gray in the Color Picker that appears.

Note: See Chapter 12 for more about selecting colors.

9 Click and drag on the part of the layer you want to partially hide.

E The brush applies a gray color to the mask.

F Photoshop Elements turns the masked pixels partially transparent.

Darker gray colors result in the layer's content being more obscured.

TIPS

How do I paint colors onto layer content that has a mask?

To apply color normally to a layer that has a layer mask, click the regular layer icon in the Layers panel, and then apply color with the Brush or other tool. If the layer mask icon is selected instead of the regular layer icon, the painted colors are applied to the mask.

After I have my layer mask exactly how I want it, how do I apply it permanently to the layer?

Right-click the layer mask icon in the Layers panel and select **Apply Layer Mask** from the menu that appears. Photoshop Elements applies the mask to the layer, permanently removing the pixels that have been hidden by the mask. The layer mask is removed from the layer.

Edit a Layer Mask

A layer mask offers a convenient way for editing images because it hides pixels in your image instead of deleting them. You can reveal pixels that were previously hidden, or hide more pixels, by editing the colors in the mask.

To unhide a masked part of an image, you can paint a white color on the mask using the Brush tool. To hide more of your layer, you can paint on the mask using a black color. By zooming in to edges in your image, you can carefully edit the mask and display just the layer content that you want shown.

Edit a Layer Mask

1 Add a layer mask to a layer in your image.

Note: See the previous section, "Add a Layer Mask," for details.

2 Click the layer mask icon for the layer you want to edit.

3 Click the foreground color box and set it to white using the Color Picker that appears.

Note: See Chapter 12 for more on setting the foreground color.

4 Click to select the **Brush** tool (⟋) or press **B**.

5 Click and drag on the hidden part of the layer you want to appear.

(A) The brush applies a white color to the mask.

(B) Photoshop Elements reveals the pixels where the mask is painted white.

6 Click the **Zoom** tool (🔍).

7 Click the **Zoom In** tool (🔍).

8 Click to magnify the part of the masked layer that you want to edit.

9 Click the **Brush** tool (🖌) or press B.

10 Click the foreground color box and set it to black using the Color Picker that appears.

11 Click and drag on the visible part of the layer that you want hidden.

The brush applies a black color to the mask and hides content in that area of the mask.

Note: When applying colors to the layer mask, remember that white reveals and black conceals.

TIP

Are there other ways to view the layer masks that I apply?
With the masked layer selected in the Layers panel, press \, which is located above Enter (Return) on most keyboards. Photoshop Elements displays the mask as a transparent red color, called a rubylith, over your image. To turn off the rubylith, press \ again. You can display the mask as a black-and-white image by pressing and holding Alt (Option on a Mac) and clicking the layer mask icon for the layer. To turn off the black-and-white view, click the regular layer icon. You can edit your mask while in the rubylith or black-and-white modes by painting on the mask.

Enhancing and Retouching Photos

Do you need to fix a photo fast? This chapter offers you techniques for retouching your digital photos, including correcting color issues, making flaws disappear, and combining elements from different photos.

Quickly Fix a Photo. 184

Remove Red Eye 186

Retouch with the Clone Stamp Tool 188

Remove a Spot. 190

Sharpen an Image 192

Merge Group Shots 194

Recompose a Photo 196

Create a Photo Panorama 198

Fix Keystone Distortion. 200

Quickly Fix a Photo

You can use the Quick mode in Photoshop Elements to make fast corrections to your photos in one convenient window. You can adjust lighting, contrast, color, and focus as well as compare Before and After views of your adjustments.

The Quick mode pane consists of a variety of easy-to-use tools. The Smart Fix tool automatically corrects lighting, color, and contrast; the Exposure and Levels tools fix lighting problems; the Color and Balance tools fix color problems; and the Sharpen tool sharpens photos.

Quickly Fix a Photo

1 In the Editor, click **Quick**.

Note: For more on opening the Editor, see Chapter 1.

A Quick mode opens with various retouching tools available.

B You can zoom, pan, select objects, and perform other basic functions using these tools.

2 Click the ▼ and then a view mode.

The After Only view shows the results of your changes.

The Before Only view shows the original unedited photo.

The Before and After views show both the original image and the image with changes applied.

3 Click **Smart Fix**.

The Smart Fix tool opens.

4 Click and drag the slider ().

C You can also click a thumbnail.

D Photoshop Elements makes immediate adjustments to the lighting, contrast, and colors in the image.

E You can click the reset thumbnail to return to the original settings.

5 Click another tool.

6 Click and drag the slider () or click a thumbnail to adjust the setting.

In this example, the Vibrance setting is increased to brighten the colors in the image.

When you are happy with your results, you can save your image. See Chapter 2 for details.

F To access more-complex editing tools, click **Expert**. For more information on Expert mode tools, see the other sections in this chapter.

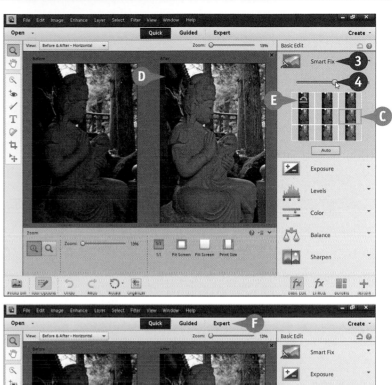

TIPS

Must I always use Quick mode to correct brightness, color, focus, and rotation problems?

No. You can make these corrections by using other tools in Photoshop Elements. The Enhance menu contains these same corrections, some of which open dialog boxes that enable you to fine-tune the adjustment.

How can I improve the look of teeth in Quick mode?

You can use the Whiten Teeth tool (▨). Click and drag the tool over a smile; it selects the teeth and whitens them all at once. The result is similar to using the Quick Selection tool (see Chapter 6) to select the teeth and then applying the Dodge tool (see Chapter 10) to lighten them and the Sponge tool (see Chapter 10) to remove any colorcast.

Remove Red Eye

You can use the Red Eye Removal tool to remove the red eye color that a camera flash can cause. Red eye is a common problem in snapshots taken indoors with a flash. The light from the flash reflects off the back of the subject's eyes, creating the red eye appearance. Using the Red Eye Removal tool, you can edit the eye to change its color without changing image details. You can experience a similar problem with animals, but their eyes can turn yellow, blue, or green. See the tip for details about how to fix that.

Remove Red Eye

1 In the Editor, click **Quick**.

Quick mode opens.

Note: For more on opening the Editor, see Chapter 1.

2 Click the **Red Eye Removal** tool (🔴).

Note: You can also access the tool in Expert mode.

3 Click and drag the slider (◎) to control the size of the area to correct.

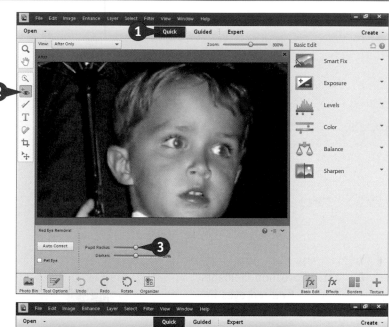

4 Click and drag the slider (◎) to the darkness setting you want.

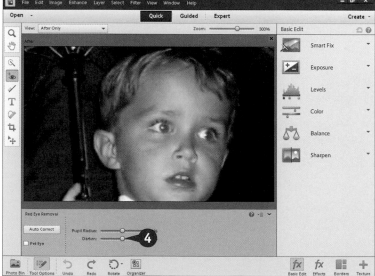

5 Click the eye you want to fix.

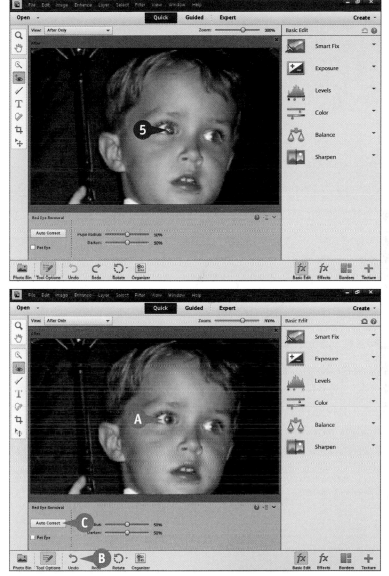

6 Release the mouse button.

Ⓐ Photoshop Elements repairs the color.

Ⓑ If you need to change the settings, you can click **Undo** to undo the color change.

Ⓒ You can also click **Auto Correct**; Photoshop Elements attempts to find red eyes in the photo and correct them automatically.

TIP

My pet photos have a yellow, blue, or green eye problem. How do I fix this?
Click the **Red Eye Removal** tool () and click **Pet Eye** in the Tool Options panel (☐ changes to ☑). You can then use the tool to remove the colors that can sometimes appear in non-human eyes (**Ⓐ**).

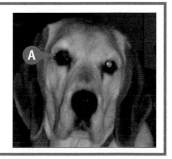

Retouch with the Clone Stamp Tool

You can clean up small flaws or erase elements in your image with the Clone Stamp tool. The tool copies information from one area of an image to another. For example, you can use the Clone Stamp tool to remove unwanted blemishes of all kinds by cloning an area near the flaw and then stamping over it.

You can adjust the opacity of the tool to copy information partially to the new location. Lowering the opacity and then copying from multiple areas in an image can sometimes be the best way to cleanly erase an unwanted object.

Retouch with the Clone Stamp Tool

1 In the Editor, click **Expert**.

Note: For more on opening the Editor, see Chapter 1.

2 Click the **Clone Stamp** tool (🔲).

3 Click the 🔽 to choose a brush size and type.

Ⓐ You can also click and drag the slider (⊙) to change the brush size.

You can change the brush size while using the tool by pressing [and].

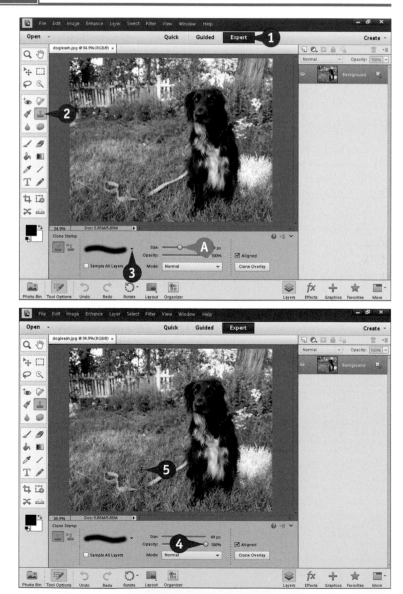

4 Click and drag the slider (⊙) to choose an opacity, which determines whether the tool covers an area completely or partially.

100% covers the area completely.

5 Press and hold Alt (Option on a Mac) and then click the area of the image from which you want to copy.

In this example, the Clone Stamp is used to remove the leash from the dog.

6 Click and drag the area of the photo that you want to correct.

Photoshop Elements copies the cloned area to where you click and drag.

7 Continue clicking new areas to clone and dragging over the area as many times as needed to achieve the desired effect.

Note: Short strokes can often produce better results than long strokes because they help avoid cloning from unintended areas.

B You can click **Undo** to undo the tool's effects.

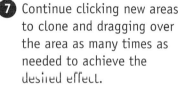

TIPS

How can I make the Clone Stamp's effects look seamless?
To erase elements from your image with the Clone Stamp without leaving a trace, try the following:

- Clone between areas of similar color and texture.
- To apply the stamp more subtly, lower its opacity.
- Use a soft-edged brush shape.

What can I do with the Pattern Stamp?
You can use the Pattern Stamp tool (🖿), which shares space in the Tool Options panel with the Clone Stamp tool (🖿), to paint repeating patterns on your images. You can select a pattern, brush style, and brush size, and then stamp the pattern on your photo by clicking and dragging.

Remove a Spot

You can use the Spot Healing Brush to quickly repair flaws or remove small objects in a photo. The tool works well on small spots or blemishes on both solid and textured backgrounds. You can adjust the brush size so that it covers the feature you want to remove.

The tool's Proximity Match setting analyzes pixels surrounding the selected area and replaces the area with a patch of similar pixels. The Create Texture setting replaces the area with a blend of surrounding pixels. The Content Aware setting, which is often the most useful, is similar to Proximity Match but can also recognize patterns within the surrounding pixels and keep them intact.

Remove a Spot

1 In the Editor, click **Expert**.

Note: For more on opening the Editor, see Chapter 1.

2 Click the **Spot Healing Brush** tool (⬚).

3 Click the ▼ to choose a brush size and type that will cover the spot.

Ⓐ You can also set a brush size by clicking and dragging the slider (◯).

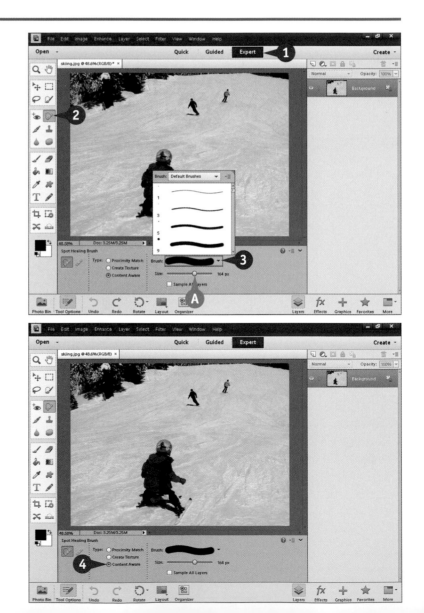

4 Click the type of healing effect you want to apply (◯ changes to ◉).

The Content Aware setting will attempt to recognize the area around the clicked image and copy it seamlessly.

5 Click the spot you want to correct.

You may have to click and drag across the spot to get the desired effect.

B Photoshop Elements replaces the selected area with pixels similar to those nearby.

C You can click **Undo** to undo the change.

TIP

How do I correct larger areas of a photo?
You can use the Healing Brush. Click the **Spot Healing Brush** tool (⬚) and then, in the Tool Options panel, click the **Healing Brush** tool (⬚). Press and hold **Alt** (**Option** on a Mac) and then click the area you want to copy from (**A**). Click and drag over the problem area to blend the cloned pixels into the new area (**B**).

Sharpen an Image

You can use the Adjust Sharpness dialog box to sharpen an image suffering from focus problems. The tool enables you to control the amount of sharpening you apply.

To apply sharpening to just part of your image, for example to the main feature of your image, you can first select that part with a selection tool. To use the selection tools, see Chapter 6. Photoshop Elements also lets you to perform the opposite of sharpening by applying a blur filter. The blur filter is covered in Chapter 13.

Sharpen an Image

1 In the Editor, click **Expert**.

Note: For more on opening the Editor, see Chapter 1.

2 Click **Enhance**.

3 Click **Adjust Sharpness**.

The Adjust Sharpness dialog box opens.

A A preview area displays the filter's effect.

B You can click **Preview** to preview the effect in the main window (☐ changes to ☑).

4 Click minus or plus (⊟ or ⊞) to zoom out or in. It is best to preview a sharpened image at 100% magnification.

5 Click and drag the sliders (◎) to control the amount of sharpening you apply to the image.

C Amount controls the overall amount of sharpening.

D Radius controls how far from any high-contrast edges sharpening is applied. A higher radius setting applies sharpening farther from edges in your image.

You can type values for the amount and radius settings.

E You can click the ▼ to remove a specific type of blur in the image. The default is Gaussian Blur, which applies sharpening across the image. Lens Blur concentrates the sharpening on details, whereas Motion Blur removes blur caused by camera or subject motion.

Note: Increasing sharpening too much can add unwanted noise to your image. Added noise can be desirable; see Chapter 13 for more about adding noise using a filter.

6 Click **OK**.

Photoshop Elements applies the enhancement.

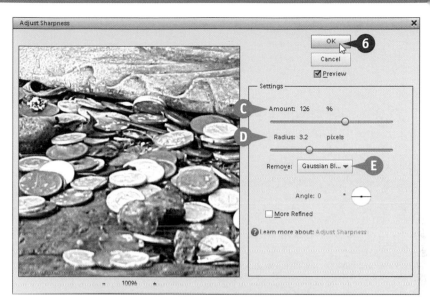

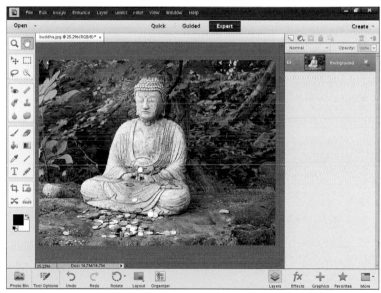

TIPS

When should I apply sharpening?
Sharpening an image after you resize it can be a good idea because changing an image's size, especially enlarging, can add blurring. Although the tool cannot make an unfocused image completely clear, it can sharpen slightly blurred images or blurring caused by applying other filters. Applying sharpening as a final step is best.

How can I sharpen an image in Quick mode?
You can quickly sharpen an image in Quick mode by opening the Sharpen tool in the right panel and then clicking and dragging the slider (🔘) or clicking a thumbnail image. You can also access the Adjust Sharpness dialog box in Quick mode, which lets you apply more-complex sharpening effects.

Merge Group Shots

You can take several photos of groups of people and then merge them so the good parts of the different versions are combined into a single optimized photo. This can help when some people have their eyes closed or are not smiling in photos. To merge content between the photos, you paint over the good areas of the source photo to add those areas to another photo.

The Group Shot tool works best when the different photos have similar backgrounds. This allows Photoshop Elements to align the different photos and place the different parts in the correct places.

Merge Group Shots

1 In the Editor, open multiple versions of the same group photo.

Note: For more on opening the Editor, see Chapter 1.

2 **Ctrl**+click (⌘+click on a Mac) to select the photos in the Photo Bin.

3 Click **Enhance**.

4 Click **Photomerge**.

5 Click **Photomerge Group Shot**.

Photoshop Elements opens the photos in the Photomerge Group Shot tool.

6 In the Photo Bin, click and drag the photo that you want to fix to the Final window.

7 Click to select the source photo you want to copy from.

Ⓐ The photo to select from appears in the Source window.

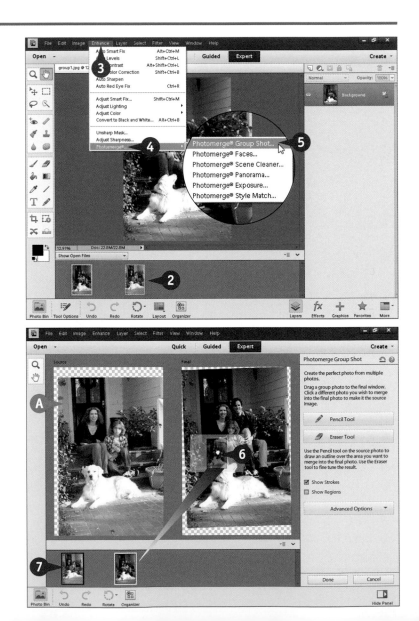

8 Click the **Pencil** tool.

9 Click and drag to apply brushstrokes in the Source window to define the area you want replaced in the Final window.

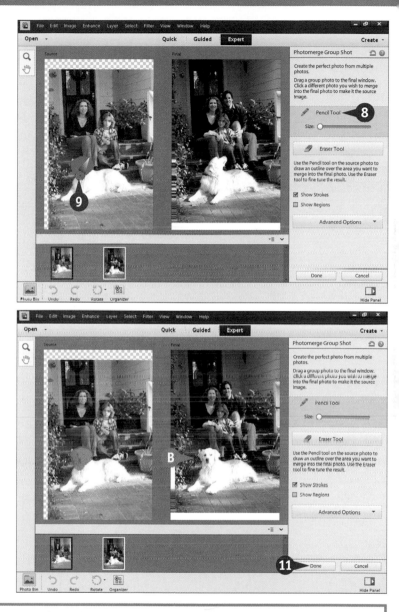

B Photoshop Elements merges the defined area into the similar area in the Final window.

You can click **Undo** to undo the change.

10 Repeat steps **8** and **9** to replace different areas of the final photo.

You can select other photos in the Photo Bin to replace more areas.

11 Click **Done** to exit the Photomerge Group Shot tool.

TIPS

How can I remove elements that I do not want in a large scene?

You can use the Scene Cleaner tool to remove extraneous people and objects. Take different versions of the scene and choose the areas you want to fix. The tool paints over the areas using unobstructed areas from the alternate versions. Click **Enhance**, **Photomerge**, and then **Photomerge Scene Cleaner** to access it.

How can I swap facial features between people in a scene?

The Photomerge Faces tool enables you to put the eyes, nose, or mouth from one face onto another. Align the faces you want to copy between in the tool and then paint over the features to swap. To access the Faces tool, click **Enhance**, **Photomerge**, and then **Photomerge Faces**.

Recompose a Photo

You can recompose a photo to change its size while keeping important objects within it intact. Recomposition is an alternative to cropping for when you want to reduce an image's size without trimming or deleting certain subject matter. For more on using the Crop tool, see Chapter 5.

Before you apply the Recomposition tool, you designate areas of your photo that you want kept unchanged by painting over them. You also paint over areas that you would prefer to eliminate. Photoshop Elements can then intelligently rearrange the correct areas of the photo as you resize.

Recompose a Photo

1 In the Editor, click **Expert**.

Note: For more on opening the Editor, see Chapter 1.

2 Click the **Recompose** tool ( ).

3 Click the **Mark for Protection** button ( ).

4 Click and drag the slider ( ) to specify a brush size.

5 Click and drag over the objects you want to keep unchanged.

6 Click the **Mark for Removal** button ().

7 Click and drag the slider (◯) to specify a brush size.

8 Click and drag over the areas that can be deleted.

9 Click and drag the side and corner handles to recompose the image.

Photoshop Elements rearranges content in the image, keeping the protected objects intact.

10 Click ☑ or press **Enter** to commit the changes.

Ⓐ You can fix misaligned edges in the recomposed image using the Spot Healing Brush tool (🖌) or Clone Stamp tool (🖊).

TIP

How do I edit my selections when using the Recompose tool?
You can click **Erase Highlights Marked for Protection** (🖌) or **Erase Highlights Marked for Removal** (🖌). Click and drag to erase coloring that marks protected (Ⓐ) or deletable areas (Ⓑ), respectively.

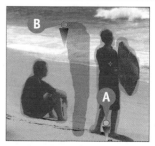

Create a Photo Panorama

You can use the Photomerge feature in Photoshop Elements to stitch several sequential images together into a single panoramic image. This enables you to capture more scenery than is usually possible in a regular photograph.

Photoshop Elements automatically merges the edges of your images together by taking into account the type of lens used and the geometry of the scenery. You can specify a merging technique or have the program choose it automatically with the Auto setting. Photoshop Elements fills in any extra space on the sides of the resulting panoramic image.

Create a Photo Panorama

1 In the Editor, click **Enhance**.

Note: For more on opening the Editor, see Chapter 1.

2 Click **Photomerge**.

3 Click **Photomerge Panorama**.

The Photomerge dialog box opens.

4 Click **Auto** (⚪ changes to ⦿).

With the Auto setting, Photoshop Elements evaluates the images and attempts to choose the best method for stitching your photos together.

5 Click **Browse**.

The Open dialog box opens.

6 Click the ⌄ to choose the folder that contains the images you want to merge.

7 Ctrl +click (⌘+click on a Mac) the images you want to merge into a panoramic image.

8 Click **OK**.

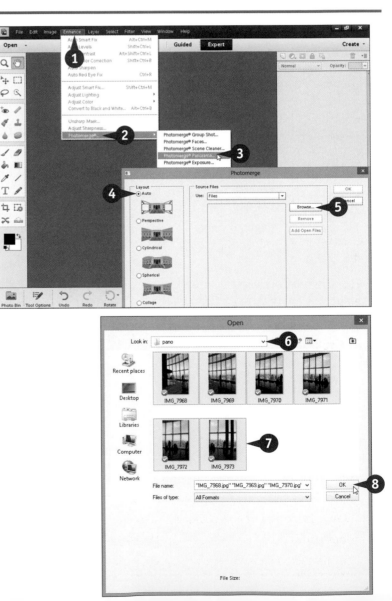

Ⓐ The filenames of the images appear in the Source Files list.

⑨ Click **OK** to build the panoramic image.

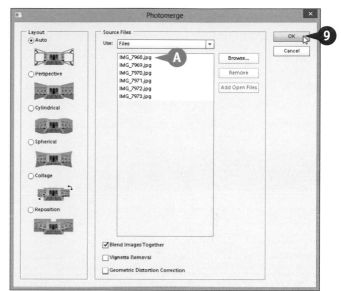

Photoshop Elements merges the images into a single panoramic image.

Ⓑ Parts of each original image appear in separate layers in the Layers panel.

Note: For more on layers, see Chapter 8.

Ⓒ The stitching process can leave empty areas along the edges of the panorama.

⑩ In the Clean Edges dialog box that appears, click **Yes** to automatically fill in the edges.

TIP

How can I create photos that merge successfully?

To merge photos successfully, you need to align and overlap the photos as you shoot them. Some hints:

- Use a tripod to keep your photos level with one another.
- Experiment with the different layout modes in the Photomerge dialog box.
- Do not use lenses that distort your photos, such as fisheye, and do not change zoom settings.
- Shoot your photos so they overlap 15–30%.
- Use the same exposure settings on your camera for your photos for consistent lighting.

Fix Keystone Distortion

You can use the camera distortion tools in Photoshop Elements to fix keystone effects. *Keystoning* can occur when taking pictures with the camera tilted horizontally or vertically, which can cause rectangular objects — such as tall buildings — to appear trapezoidal.

The Correct Camera Distortion dialog box enables you to stretch and squeeze your image in various ways to eliminate distortion and straighten large objects. It also includes a vignette adjustment that removes shadowing around the edges of an image. Vignetting can be caused by camera or lens limitations.

Fix Keystone Distortion

① In the Editor, open a photo that has keystone distortion.

Note: For more on opening the Editor, see Chapter 1.

② Click **Filter**.

③ Click **Correct Camera Distortion**.

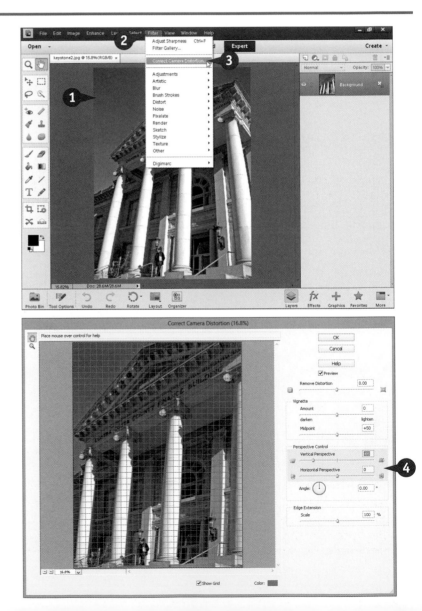

The Correct Camera Distortion window opens.

④ Click and drag the sliders (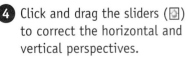) to correct the horizontal and vertical perspectives.

⑤ Click and drag the slider (◉) to correct distortion that fisheye lenses can cause.

Ⓐ You can click and drag the slider (◉) to scale the photo.

You can also type values for the horizontal and vertical perspectives, the distortion, and the scale.

⑥ Click **OK**.

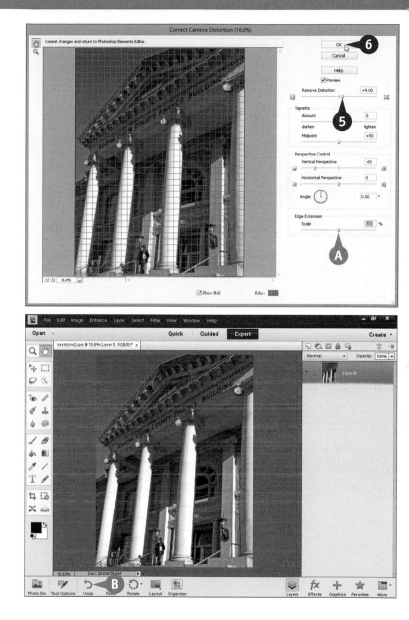

Photoshop Elements corrects the photo.

Ⓑ You can click **Undo** to undo the correction.

TIP

How can I use the Perspective command to correct buildings with keystone distortion?

In some cases, you may want to have more control over how a keystoned image is corrected. Using the Perspective command is another way to repair keystoning. Click **Image**, **Transform**, and then **Perspective**. Handles appear on the edges and corners of the image. Drag the top corner handles outward and the lower corner handles inward to fix the distortion. Click ☑ or press Enter to commit the changes.

CHAPTER 10

Enhancing Lighting and Color

Does your photo suffer from shadows that are too dark? Are the colors in your photo faded? You can correct lighting and color problems by using a variety of tools in Photoshop Elements.

Adjust Levels 204

Adjust Shadows and Highlights 206

Change Brightness and Contrast. 208

Using the Dodge and Burn Tools 210

Fix Exposure 212

Using the Blur and Sharpen Tools 214

Adjust Skin Color. 216

Adjust Color with the Sponge Tool 218

Replace a Color 220

Turn a Color Photo into Black and White. 222

Add Color to a Black-and-White Photo. 224

Adjust Colors by Using Color Curves. 226

Apply the Auto Smart Tone Tool. 228

Adjust Levels

You can use the Levels dialog box to fine-tune shadows, highlights, and midtones in your image. Input sliders enable you to manipulate the tonal qualities of an image, and the output sliders let you adjust contrast.

The Levels dialog box displays a *histogram*, which is a graph that shows the distribution of lighter and darker colors in the image. The amount of darker colors is represented on the left and the amount of lighter colors on the right. Adjusting the Levels settings changes how the colors are distributed.

Adjust Levels

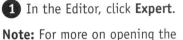

1 In the Editor, click **Expert**.

Note: For more on opening the Editor, see Chapter 1.

2 Click **Enhance**.

3 Click **Adjust Lighting**.

4 Click **Levels**.

Note: Alternatively, you can press Ctrl+L (⌘+L on a Mac).

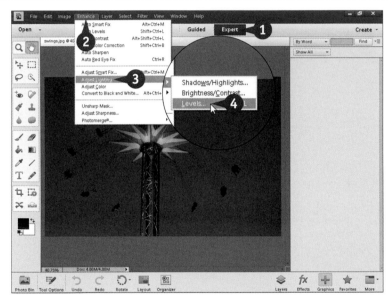

The Levels dialog box opens.

5 Make sure to click **Preview** (☐ changes to ☑).

The Preview option enables you to see your adjustments as you make them.

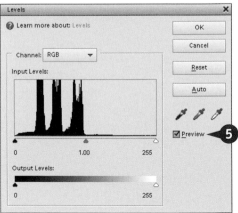

6 Click and drag the slider (⬛) to darken shadows and increase contrast.

7 Click and drag the slider (⬛) to adjust the midtones of the image.

8 Click and drag the slider (⬜) to lighten the bright areas of the image and increase contrast.

You can also type values to control the contrast and midtones.

Photoshop Elements displays a preview of the adjustments.

9 Click and drag the slider (⬛) to the right to lighten the image.

10 Click and drag the slider (⬜) to the left to darken the image.

11 Click **OK**.

Photoshop Elements applies the adjustments.

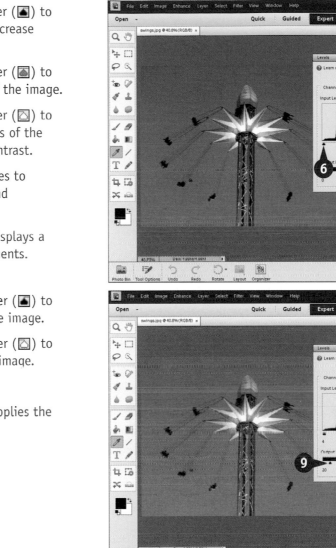

TIPS

How do I adjust the brightness levels of an image automatically?
Click **Enhance** and then **Auto Levels**. Photoshop Elements sets the lightest pixels to white and the darkest pixels to black and then redistributes the intermediate values proportionally throughout the rest of the image. Use Auto Levels to make immediate corrections to shadows, midtones, and highlights.

Can I tell Photoshop Elements what pixels to use as the darkest, midtone, and brightest levels in my image?
Yes. The Levels dialog box includes three Eyedropper tools, one for the darkest (🖊), midtone (🖊), and lightest tones (🖊). Click the Eyedropper tool for the tone you want to set and then click the appropriate pixel(s) in your image.

Adjust Shadows and Highlights

You can use the Shadows and Highlights feature to make quick adjustments to the dark and light areas of your image. The feature is less complicated than the Levels tool but also less flexible. The tool can be useful for fixing photos with poor exposure. The Lighten Shadows setting enables you to improve overly dark photos, whereas Darken Highlights can help correct photos that are too light.

You can adjust shadows and highlights in just a part of your image by making a selection or selecting a layer before executing the command. For more on making selections, see Chapter 6. For more on working with layers, see Chapter 8.

Adjust Shadows and Highlights

1 In the Editor, click **Expert**.

Note: For more on opening the Editor, see Chapter 1.

2 Click **Enhance**.

3 Click **Adjust Lighting**.

4 Click **Shadows/Highlights**.

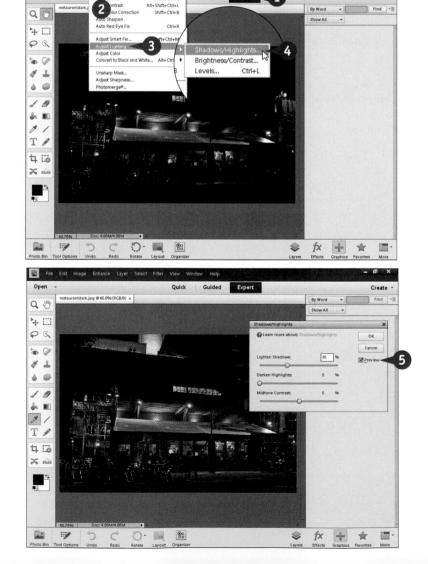

The Shadows/Highlights dialog box opens.

5 Make sure to click **Preview** (☐ changes to ☑).

The Preview option enables you to view your adjustments as you make them.

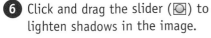

6 Click and drag the slider () to lighten shadows in the image.

7 Click and drag the slider () to darken highlights in the image.

8 Click and drag the slider () to adjust midtone contrast in the image.

You can also type values for the shadows, highlights, and contrast.

9 Click **OK**.

Photoshop Elements applies the adjustments.

TIPS

How do I cancel my adjustments without exiting the Shadows/Highlights dialog box?

If you press and hold Alt (Option on a Mac), Cancel changes to Reset. Click **Reset** to return the settings to their default values.

When I open the Shadows/Highlights dialog box, Photoshop Elements immediately adjusts my image. What is happening?

The Shadows/Highlights filter is set to automatically lighten shadows in your image by 35%. When you open the dialog box, you see this applied. You can reduce the effect by dragging the **Lighten Shadows** slider () to the left.

Change Brightness and Contrast

You can use the Brightness/Contrast dialog box to adjust the brightness and contrast levels in a photo or a selected portion of a photo. *Brightness* refers to the intensity of the lighter pixels in an image, and *contrast* refers to the relative difference between dark and light areas in an image.

The Brightness/Contrast tool is the easiest way to make simple adjustments to the lightness in your image in Photoshop Elements. To make more complex adjustments to the tonal qualities in an image, use the Levels dialog box. See the section "Adjust Levels" for more information.

Change Brightness and Contrast

1 In the Editor, click **Expert**.

Note: For more on opening the Editor, see Chapter 1.

2 Click **Enhance**.

3 Click **Adjust Lighting**.

4 Click **Brightness/Contrast**.

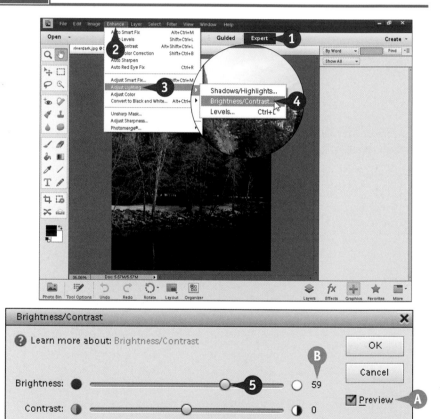

The Brightness/Contrast dialog box opens.

If you want to restrict changes to a selection or layer, select the layer or make the selection before executing the command.

Ⓐ The Preview check box is selected by default.

5 Click and drag the **Brightness** slider (◻) to adjust brightness.

Drag the slider to the right to lighten the image.

Drag the slider to the left to darken the image.

Ⓑ You can also type a number from 1 to 150 to lighten the image or from −1 to −150 to darken the image.

6 Click and drag the **Contrast** slider (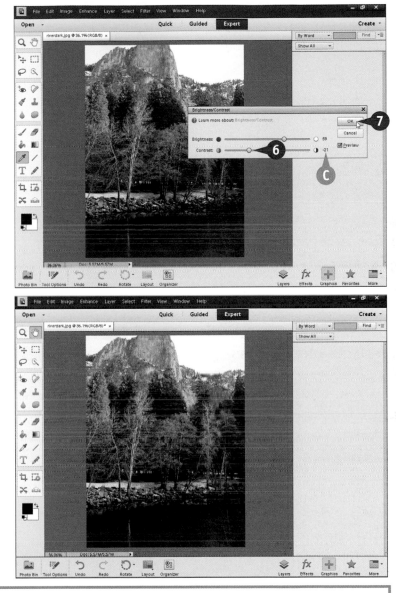) to adjust contrast.

Drag the slider to the right to increase contrast.

Drag the slider to the left to decrease contrast.

C You can also type a number from 1 to 100 to increase contrast or from −1 to −50 to decrease contrast.

7 Click **OK**.

Photoshop Elements applies the adjustments to the image, selection, or layer.

TIPS

How can I automatically adjust the contrast of an image?

Click **Enhance** and then **Auto Contrast** to automatically convert light and dark pixels. The Auto Contrast feature converts the very lightest pixels in the image to white and the very darkest pixels to black. Unlike with the Brightness/Contrast dialog box, you cannot fine-tune the contrast settings with Auto Contrast.

Does Photoshop Elements offer a tool for evaluating tones in an image?

Yes. Click **Window** and then **Histogram** to open the Histogram panel, which is a graphical representation of the light and dark pixels in an image plotted by intensity. The density of each color intensity is plotted, with the darker pixels on the left and the lighter pixels on the right.

Using the Dodge and Burn Tools

You can use the Dodge and Burn tools to quickly brighten or darken specific areas of an image, respectively. *Dodge* is a photographic term that describes the blocking of light when printing from a film negative. *Burn* is a photographic term that describes the addition of light when printing from a film negative.

These tools are an alternative to the Brightness/Contrast command, which affects the entire image. To brighten or darken the entire image, see the previous section, "Change Brightness and Contrast."

Using the Dodge and Burn Tools

Using the Dodge Tool

1 In the Editor, click **Expert**.

Note: For more on opening the Editor, see Chapter 1.

2 Click the **Sponge** tool (![sponge]).

A If the Tool Options panel is not open, click here to open it.

The Dodge tool shares space with the Sponge and Burn tools in the Tool Options panel.

3 Click the **Dodge** tool (![dodge]).

4 Click the ![arrow] and choose the brush you want to use.

B You can also choose the tool's size and exposure.

5 Click and drag over the area that you want to lighten.

Photoshop Elements lightens the area.

Using the Burn Tool

1 Click the **Sponge** tool ().

C If the Tool Options panel is not open, click here to open it.

The Burn tool shares space with the Sponge and Dodge tools in the Tool Options panel.

2 Click the **Burn** tool (🔘).

D You can select the brush, the range of colors you want to affect, and the tool's size and exposure.

3 Click and drag over the area that you want to darken.

Photoshop Elements darkens the area.

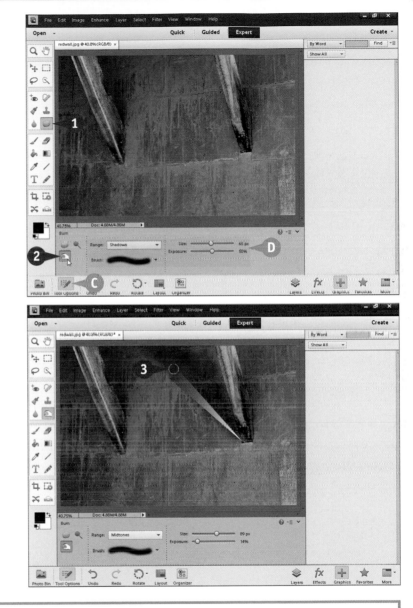

TIPS

Is there a way to gradually brighten an area?
If you set the Exposure level to a low value, you can drag repeatedly over the area you want to correct to gradually brighten the area, or you can click multiple times to gradually brighten just the area under the cursor.

How do I invert the bright and dark colors in an image?
Click **Filter**, **Adjustments**, and then **Invert**. You can also press Ctrl+I (⌘+I on a Mac) to apply the Invert command. Photoshop Elements inverts the bright and dark colors in the image. For more on filters in Photoshop Elements, see Chapter 13.

Fix Exposure

You can use the Photomerge Exposure tool to combine photos of the same scene taken with different exposure settings, which you can do if your camera has a manual mode or can take a series of exposure-bracketed photos. Photoshop Elements intelligently merges the photos to create an image that has optimal lighting throughout. It is best if you take the photos using a tripod and without zooming between shots to keep the photos perfectly aligned.

The Photomerge Exposure tool also enables you to manually choose areas with good lighting and contrast from one photo and then copy them to another photo where the areas are poorly lit.

Fix Exposure

1 In the Editor, click **Expert**.

Note: For more on opening the Editor, see Chapter 1.

2 **Ctrl**+click (**⌘**+click on a Mac) to select the photos in the Photo Bin.

3 Click **Enhance**.

4 Click **Photomerge**.

5 Click **Photomerge Exposure**.

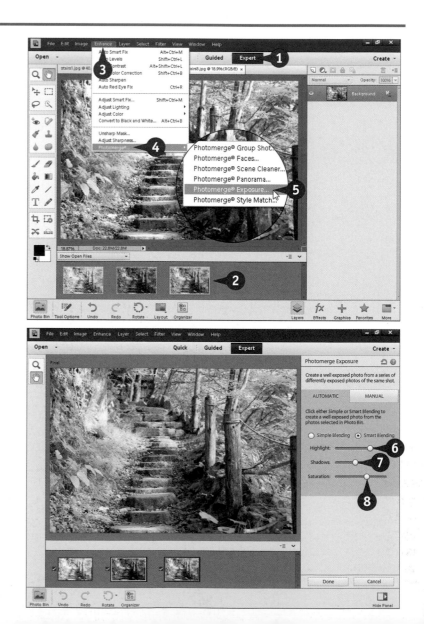

The Photomerge Exposure panel opens and automatically combines the photos to blend their exposures.

6 Click and drag the slider (○) to adjust the details in the lighter areas of the composite.

7 Click and drag the slider (○) to adjust the details in the darker areas of the composite.

8 Click and drag the slider (○) to adjust the overall color intensity.

Photoshop Elements applies the adjustments.

Ⓐ You can click here to remove a photo from the composite.

⑨ Click **Done** to save the changes and to close the Photomerge Exposure panel.

Ⓑ The merged image appears in the Photo Bin.

TIP

How can I manually combine the elements in my photos?

Repeat steps **1** to **5** to open the Photomerge Exposure panel. Click **Manual.** Click and drag a photo to the Final window. Click to select a photo with objects to combine with the Final photo. This photo appears in the Source window. Click the **Pencil** tool. Click and drag over an area to select it. Use the Eraser tool to remove areas. You can adjust the opacity of your selection to refine the Photomerge effect. Photoshop Elements merges the selected objects with the background photo.

Using the Blur and Sharpen Tools

You can sharpen or blur specific areas of your image with the Blur and Sharpen tools. This enables you to emphasize or de-emphasize objects in a photo. You can use the Blur tool to make tiny specks and other small flaws less noticeable in your photos. You can use the Sharpen tool to increase the contrast of edges. However, excessive sharpening can produce noise that can be especially apparent in areas of light, solid colors.

You can blur or sharpen the entire image by using one of the Blur or Sharpen filters located in the Photoshop Elements Filter menu. See Chapter 13 for more.

Using the Blur and Sharpen Tools

Using the Blur Tool

1 In the Editor, click **Expert**.

Note: For more on opening the Editor, see Chapter 1.

2 Click the **Blur** tool (📷).

Ⓐ If the Tool Options panel is not open, click here to open it.

The Blur tool shares space in the Tool Options panel with the Sharpen and Smudge tools.

3 Click the 🔽 and choose the brush you want to use.

Ⓑ To change the size and strength of the tool, click and drag the slider (🔲).

4 Click and drag the mouse pointer (⭕) to blur an area of the image.

Photoshop Elements blurs the area.

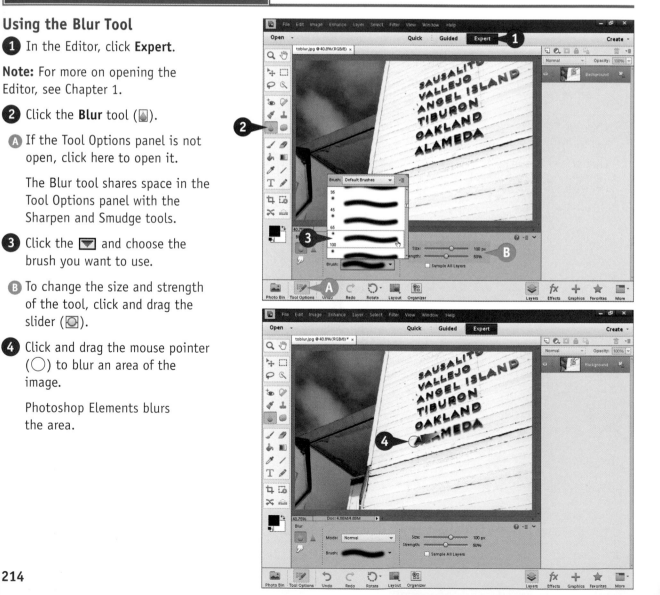

Using the Sharpen Tool

1 Click the **Blur** tool ().

C If the Tool Options panel is not open, click here to open it.

The Sharpen tool shares space in the Tool Options panel with the Blur and Smudge tools.

2 Click the **Sharpen** tool (▨).

3 Click the ▼ and choose the brush you want to use.

D To change the size and strength of the tool, click and drag the slider (◎).

4 Click and drag the mouse pointer (○) to sharpen an area of the image.

Photoshop Elements sharpens the area.

TIPS

What is the Smudge tool?

The Smudge tool (▨) is another tool you can use to create interesting blur effects in your photos. It simulates dragging a finger through wet paint, shifting and smearing colors in your image. The Smudge tool shares space in the Tool Options panel with the Blur and Sharpen tools.

Is there a filter I can use to sharpen or blur an entire image?

Yes. Photoshop Elements includes the Adjust Sharpness feature that you can use to sharpen the appearance of pixels in a photo. For more on sharpening an image, see Chapter 9. You can also select from several blurring filters, including Gaussian Blur, to make your image appear blurry. For more on blurring an image, see Chapter 13.

Adjust Skin Color

You can improve skin colors that may appear tinted or washed out in your images. After you sample an area of skin with the eyedropper, Photoshop Elements adjusts the skin color to make it look more natural. Photoshop Elements also adjusts other colors in the image based on the sampled skin.

You can fine-tune the adjustment to increase or decrease the tan or blush in the skin tones as well as the overall temperature of the image. To adjust all the colors in your image, not just the skin tones, see the other sections in this chapter.

Adjust Skin Color

1 In the Editor, click **Expert**.

Note: For more on opening the Editor, see Chapter 1.

2 Click **Enhance**.

3 Click **Adjust Color**.

4 Click **Adjust Color for Skin Tone**.

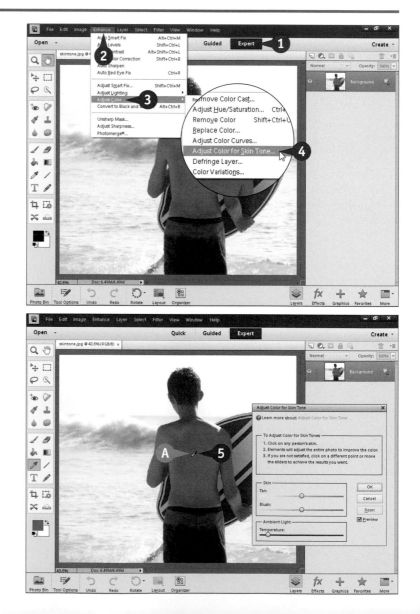

The Adjust Color for Skin Tone dialog box opens.

Ⓐ The mouse pointer (⬚) changes to an eyedropper (✐).

5 Click an area of skin in your image.

6 Click and drag the **Tan** slider () to adjust the level of brown in the skin tones.

7 Click and drag the **Blush** slider (◎) to adjust the level of red in the skin tones.

8 Click and drag the **Temperature** slider (◎) to adjust the overall coloring of the image.

Dragging to the left casts a cooler, bluish tint; dragging to the right casts a warmer, reddish tint.

9 Click **OK**.

Photoshop Elements makes adjustments to the skin in the image.

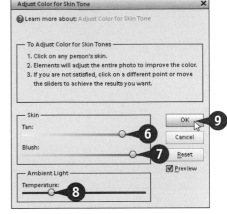

TIP

Can I have Photoshop Elements correct all the colors in my image automatically?

Yes. Follow these steps to apply the command.

1 Click the layer you want to adjust.

2 Click **Enhance**.

3 Click **Auto Color Correction**.

Photoshop Elements adjusts the image colors. You can press Ctrl + Z (⌘ + Z on a Mac) to undo the effect.

Adjust Color with the Sponge Tool

You can use the Sponge tool to make simple adjustments to the color saturation or color intensity of a specific area of an image. For example, you may want to make a person's clothing appear more colorful or tone down an element that is too colorful.

You apply the Sponge as you do the Brush tool, by clicking and dragging across a part of the image. You can adjust the size and softness of the brush to match the area you want to affect. You can click and drag multiple times to increase the effect of the tool.

Adjust Color with the Sponge Tool

Decrease Saturation

1 In the Editor, click **Expert**.

Note: For more on opening the Editor, see Chapter 1.

2 Click the **Sponge** tool ().

Ⓐ If the Tool Options panel is not open, click here to open it.

The Sponge tool shares space with the Dodge and Burn tools.

3 Click the ▼ and select a brush style.

Ⓑ To set a brush size, you can also click and drag the slider ().

4 Click the ▼ and select **Desaturate**.

5 Click and drag the mouse pointer (○) to decrease the saturation of an area of the image.

In this example, the cacti are desaturated.

To confine the effect to a particular area, you can make a selection prior to applying the tool. See Chapter 6 for more on making selections.

Increase Saturation

1 Perform steps **1** to **3** in the subsection "Decrease Saturation."

2 Click the ▼ and select **Saturate**.

3 Click and drag the mouse pointer (○) to increase the saturation of an area of the image.

In this example, the cacti's colors are intensified.

To confine the effect to a particular area, you can make a selection prior to applying the tool. See Chapter 6 for more on making selections.

TIPS

What does the Flow setting do?
The Flow slider (◉) in the Tool Options panel controls the intensity of the saturation. You can set the Flow anywhere from 1% to 100% to determine how quickly the sponge saturates or desaturates the pixels in your image. Start with a 50% Flow setting and then increase or decrease the percentage to get the amount of control you want.

How do I find the right brush style and size?
The Brush menu displays a variety of brush styles with soft, hard, and shaped edges. To blend your sponging effect into the surrounding pixels, select a soft-edged brush style. To make your sponging effect appear more distinct, use a hard-edged brush style. To change your brush size, click the **Size** ▼ in the Tool Options panel, or press [or] while sponging.

Replace a Color

The Replace Color command enables you to change one or more colors in your image by using the Hue, Saturation, and Lightness controls. By shifting the controls, you can change the color of objects or backgrounds just slightly or to wildly different tints.

If you make a selection before executing the Replace Color command, only the selected pixels are affected. Similarly, if you have a multilayered image, your adjustments affect only the selected layer. See Chapter 6 for more on making a selection, and see Chapter 8 for more on layers. Another option for replacing colors is the Smart Brush. See Chapter 12 for details.

Replace a Color

1 In the Editor, click **Expert**.

Note: For more on opening the Editor, see Chapter 1.

2 Click **Enhance**.

3 Click **Adjust Color**.

4 Click **Replace Color**.

To apply color corrections to a particular layer, select the layer before opening the Replace Color dialog box.

Note: See Chapter 8 for more on layers.

The Replace Color dialog box opens. The mouse pointer (⌖) changes to an eyedropper (✐).

5 Click in the image to select a color to replace.

Ⓐ Photoshop Elements turns the selected color to white in the preview window.

6 Click and drag the **Fuzziness** slider (▣) to control how many pixels with similar colors are affected within the image or selection.

Dragging to the right selects more color and dragging to the left selects less color.

You can also type a value for the fuzziness.

7 Click and drag the sliders () to change the colors inside the selected area.

You can also type values for the hue, saturation, and lightness.

8 Click **OK**.

Photoshop Elements replaces the selected color.

How can I replace more than one area of color?
You can press Shift and then click inside your image to add other colors to your selection. If you are viewing the Selection preview, the white area inside the preview box increases as you click. To deselect colors from your selection, press Alt (Option on a Mac) and then click a color inside your image.

How can I replace a color using the painting tools?
You can click the **Paint Bucket** tool (), select a foreground color, and then replace a color in your image with the selected color. You can retain details while applying the color by setting the mode to **Color** in the Tool Options panel. For more on using the painting tools in Photoshop Elements, see Chapter 12.

Turn a Color Photo into Black and White

You can change a color photo into a black-and-white photo to create a dramatic effect or before publishing the photo in a noncolor newsletter or brochure. The conversion tool in Photoshop Elements enables you to adjust the contributions of the different colors to the effect and to control the lighting and contrast.

You may want to copy the color image file before making the change and saving so the full-color original file remains intact. See Chapters 2 and 16 to learn how to save files.

Turn a Color Photo into Black and White

1 In the Editor, click **Expert**.

Note: For more on opening the Editor, see Chapter 1.

2 Click **Enhance**.

3 Click **Convert to Black and White**.

To confine the conversion to a particular area, you can make a selection prior to applying the command. See Chapter 6 for more on making selections.

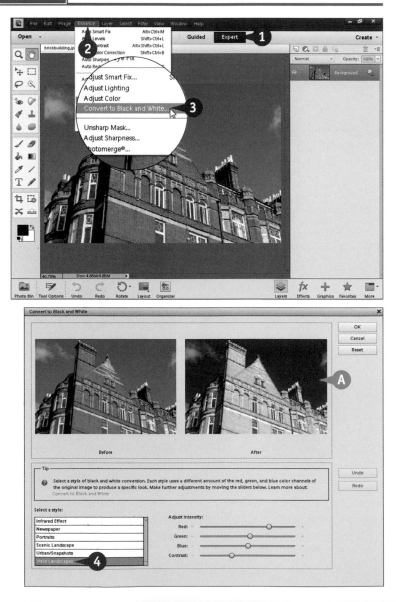

The Convert to Black and White dialog box opens.

4 Click a style.

A Photoshop Elements displays a preview of the black-and-white version.

5 You can click and drag the sliders (◙) to adjust the contributions of the original colors to the final black-and-white version.

6 You can also click this slider (◙) to increase or decrease the contrast.

7 Click **OK**.

Photoshop Elements converts the image to black and white.

How do I remove color from just one color channel?

1 Click **Enhance**, click **Adjust Color**, and then click **Adjust Hue/ Saturation**.

2 In the Hue/Saturation dialog box, click the ▼ and then choose a color channel.

3 Drag the **Saturation** slider (◙) to the left.

You can also type a value for the saturation.

4 Click **OK** to desaturate the color channel.

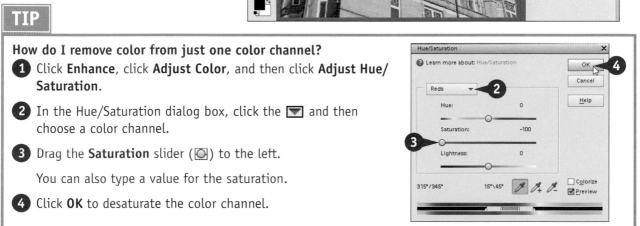

Add Color to a Black-and-White Photo

You can enhance a black-and-white photo by adding color with the painting tools in Photoshop Elements. For example, you can add color to a baby's cheeks or to articles of clothing. To add color, you must first make sure your image's mode is RGB Color. Setting the blending mode to Color for the layer you paint on enables you to add tints while keeping the details in the photo intact.

You can retain the original black-and-white version of your photo by making color changes on duplicate or adjustment layers. See Chapter 8 for more on layers.

Add Color to a Black-and-White Photo

1 In the Editor, click **Expert**.

Note: For more on opening the Editor, see Chapter 1.

2 Click **Image**.

3 Click **Mode**.

4 Click **RGB Color**.

If your image has multiple layers, you may need to flatten the layers before proceeding. In the prompt box that opens, click **Flatten** to continue.

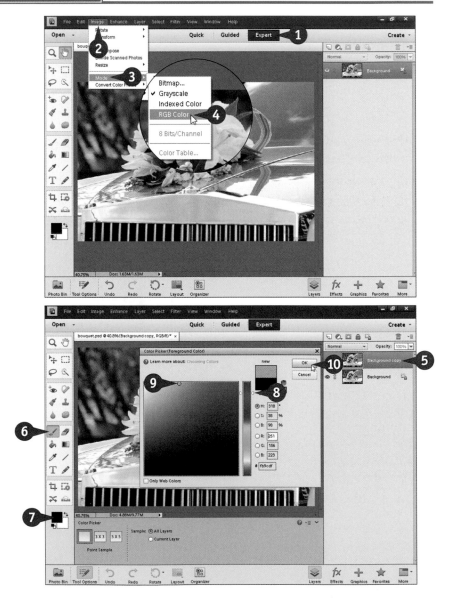

5 Duplicate the Background layer by selecting it and pressing **Ctrl**+**J** (**⌘**+**J** on a Mac).

6 Click the **Brush** tool (⬚).

7 Click the foreground color box.

The Color Picker dialog box opens.

8 To change the range of colors that appears in the window, click and drag the slider (◻).

9 Click a color.

You can also type values for a color.

10 Click **OK**.

11 Click the to set the blending mode to **Color**. This enables you to retain the lighting details of the objects that you paint over.

To confine the effect to a particular area, you can make a selection prior to applying the tool. See Chapter 6 for more on making selections.

12 Click and drag to paint the color on the photo.

Photoshop Elements applies the color to the black-and-white image.

This example shows pink color added to a bouquet of roses.

A You can click the visibility icon () to hide the layer with the color and revert the image to black and white.

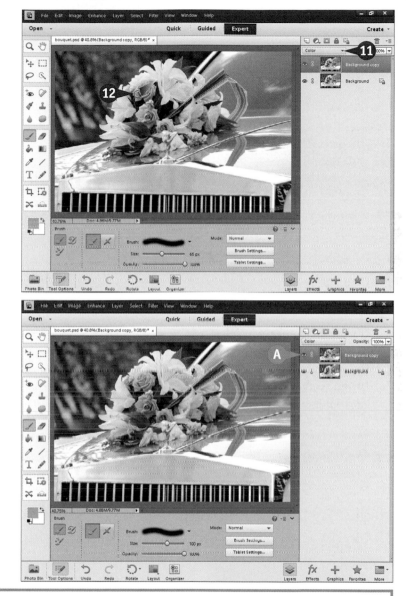

TIP

How do I tone down a layer color?
You can change the layer opacity in the Layers panel to make the color more transparent. Click the layer containing the color you want to edit. Click the **Opacity** and then click and drag the slider () that appears. Photoshop Elements adjusts the color as you drag. In this example the opacity has been reduced to 58%.

Adjust Colors by Using Color Curves

You can manipulate the tones and contrast of your image with the Color Curves dialog box. In the dialog box, a sloping line graph represents the colors in the image. The top right part of the line represents the highlights, the middle part the midtones, and the bottom left part the shadows. You can adjust colors in your photo by changing the curve in different ways.

You can adjust curves in just a part of your image by making a selection or selecting a layer before executing the command. For more on making selections, see Chapter 6. For more on working with layers, see Chapter 8.

Adjust Colors by Using Color Curves

1 In the Editor, click **Expert**.

Note: For more on opening the Editor, see Chapter 1.

2 Click **Enhance**.

3 Click **Adjust Color**.

4 Click **Adjust Color Curves**.

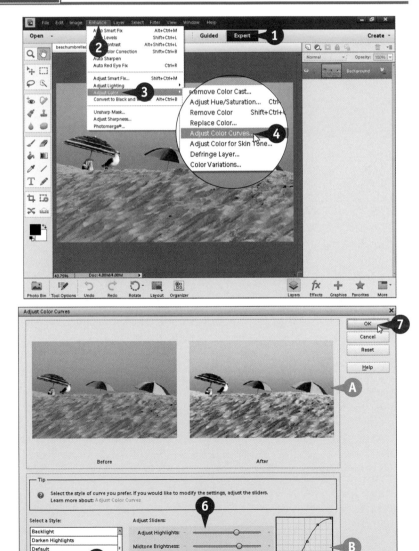

The Adjust Color Curves dialog box opens.

5 Click a style.

Ⓐ Photoshop Elements displays a preview of the adjusted version.

Ⓑ The curves graph changes depending on the style.

In this example, choosing the Increase Contrast style gives the graph a slight S shape.

6 You can click and drag the sliders (◎) to make more adjustments to the tones and contrast in the image; the curves graph changes accordingly.

7 Click **OK**.

226

Photoshop Elements applies
the adjustment to the image.

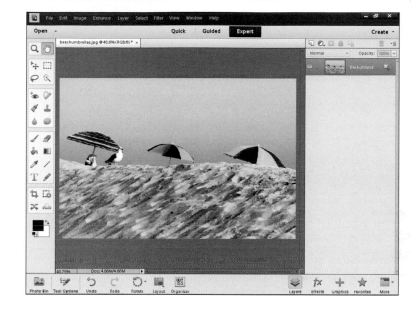

**How can I give the colors in my
image an out-of-this-world
appearance?**

You can choose the Solarize style
in the Color Curves dialog box.

1 Follow steps **1** to **4** in this section
to open the Adjust Color Curves
dialog box.

2 Click **Solarize** in the Select a
Style menu.

3 Click **OK** to apply the effect.

Apply the Auto Smart Tone Tool

You can use the new Auto Smart Tone tool to dynamically change the lighting and contrast by clicking and dragging across an image. The tool gives you a handy way to change different tonal aspects simultaneously and experiment with different lighting possibilities.

Auto Smart Tone combines aspects of the Levels, Shadows/Highlights, Brightness/Contrast, and Curves features discussed elsewhere in this chapter.

Apply the Auto Smart Tone Tool

1 In the Editor, click **Expert**.

Note: For more on opening the Editor, see Chapter 1.

2 Click **Enhance**.

3 Click **Auto Smart Tone**.

The Auto Smart Tone interface appears.

You enhance the tones in your image by clicking and dragging the center controller.

Ⓐ Thumbnails in each corner show how your photo will change as you drag in different directions.

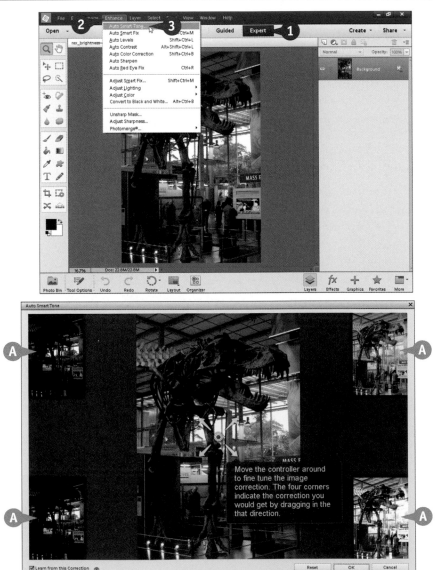

Move the controller around to fine tune the image correction. The four corners indicate the correction you would get by dragging in the that direction.

④ Click and drag the controller.

Ⓑ A grid appears to help you gauge dragging distances.

Dragging from the upper left to the lower right affects the lightness of the image.

Dragging from the upper right to the lower left affects the contrast of the image.

Ⓒ You can click **Learn from this Correction** to have Photoshop Elements initially set the controller based on past uses of the tool (☐ changes to ☑).

⑤ Click **OK**.

Photoshop Elements applies the tonal correction.

Ⓓ You can click **Undo** to undo the change.

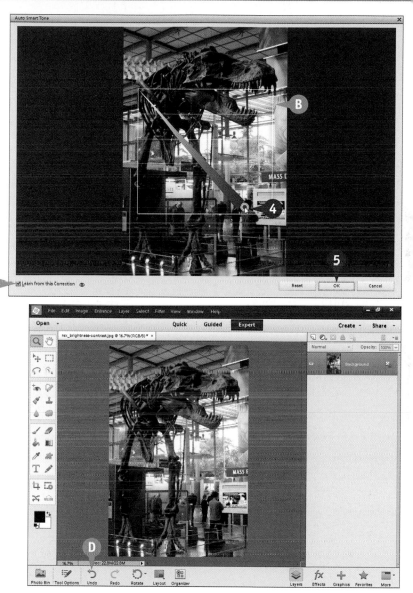

How do I reset the learning feature in Auto Smart Tone?

You can reset the learning feature in the Preferences. Click **Preferences** and then **General**. In the dialog box that appears, click **Reset Auto Smart Tone Learning**. Photoshop deletes whatever learning information it has saved.

How can I temporarily turn off the Auto Smart Tone effect?

While in the tool, you can click 👁 to temporarily turn off the enhancement (👁 changes to 👁). You can click 👁 to turn it back on. This allows you to view before and after versions of your image before closing the tool.

CHAPTER 11

Apply Guided Edits

Photoshop Elements' Guided mode features step-by-step instructions paired with tools for fixing photos and adding special effects. Items in the Guided panel let you retouch old photos, apply interesting color and blur effects, or even turn a photo into a jigsaw puzzle. They use the same tools and commands found in the other modes but present them in an ordered way that guides you to a specific end result.

Restore an Old Photo. 232

Improve a Portrait 234

Shift Colors 238

Apply a Lomo Camera Effect 240

Add Motion with Zoom Burst 242

Miniaturize Objects with Tilt Shift 244

Turn a Photo into a Puzzle 246

Apply a Reflection 248

Put an Object Out of Bounds 250

Apply a Low Key Effect. 252

Restore an Old Photo

You can use the Restore Old Photo steps in Guided mode to fix common problems found in aging snapshots. These problems may include creases, tears, fading, dust specks, and colorcasts.

The Restore Old Photo steps give you access to retouching tools that are useful in correcting these problems. For information about using these tools in Expert mode, see Chapter 9.

Restore an Old Photo

1 In the Editor, click **Guided**.

Note: For more on opening the Editor, see Chapter 1.

Guided mode opens.

A Make sure the Touchups list is open. You can click the arrow (⌄) to open it (⌄ changes to ⌃).

2 Click **Restore Old Photo**.

3 Click **Crop Tool**.

4 Click and drag the crop handles (☐) to define the area you want to keep.

By cropping, you can remove damaged or faded edges. For more about cropping, see Chapter 5.

5 Click ☑ or press Enter to accept the crop.

B To exit the tool without cropping, click ⊘ or press Esc.

Photoshop Elements crops the image.

6 Click here to scroll down in the panel.

7 Click **Spot Healing Tool**.

8 Click and drag across creases and tears to replace them with surrounding content.

Ⓒ You can also use the Healing Brush Tool and Clone Stamp Tool to fix imperfections. For details, see Chapter 9.

Photoshop Elements fixes the image.

9 Click here to scroll down in the panel.

10 Click **Blur Tool**.

11 Click and drag across areas of the image to remove dust specks.

Ⓓ The Dust Remover step works similarly but affects the entire image.

12 Click these buttons to make automatic adjustments. See the tip for details.

13 Click **Done**.

What are the color and contrast buttons in Restore Old Photo?
Auto Levels and Auto Contrast boost the contrast of a faded photo and bring out details. Auto Color analyzes the lighting distribution in your photo to automatically attempt to improve color balance.

How can I sharpen my photo?
You can optionally click **Sharpen** at the end of Restore Old Photo. However, this sharpening may counteract any blurring you have purposely added in previous steps.

Improve a Portrait

The Perfect Portrait tools enable you to fix common flaws on skin, add a subtle glow, and even slim a subject's figure. The Guided panel puts these tools in one place, and you can apply them one at a time to improve the appearance of a face or full-body shot.

Professional digital artists use such techniques to create the flawless portraits seen on magazine covers. You can use the techniques to take years off of friends and family in your photos.

Improve a Portrait

1 In the Editor, click **Guided**.

Note: For more on opening the Editor, see Chapter 1.

Guided mode opens.

Ⓐ Make sure the Touchups list is open. You can click the arrow (▾) to open it (▾ changes to ▴).

2 Click **Perfect Portrait**.

The Create a Perfect Portrait panel opens.

3 Click the **Zoom** tool (🔍).

4 Click to enlarge features you want to improve.

5 Click **Apply Smart Blur**.

The Smart Blur dialog box opens.

6 Click and drag the sliders (⬚) to apply an overall blur to the image.

7 Click **OK**.

8 Click **Reveal Original** to remove the blur.

9 Click the **Blur Brush** tool.

10 Click and drag to reapply the blurring to select areas of the photo to soften skin and deemphasize wrinkles.

11 Click here to scroll down in the panel.

12 Click the **Spot Healing** tool.

13 Click **Tool Options** to open the setting for the tool.

14 Click the ▼ to select a brush size.

15 Click to remove freckles or blemishes.

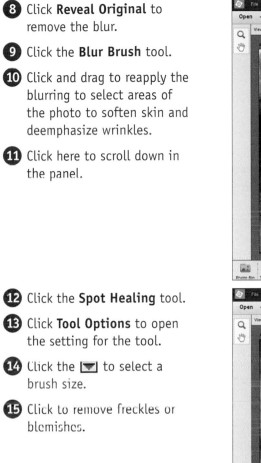

TIP

How can I whiten the teeth of a subject?
In the Create a Perfect Portrait panel, click **Whiten Teeth**. Click and drag the cursor across teeth to remove any mild colorcast (Ⓐ).

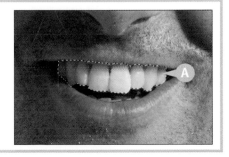

In the Perfect Portrait interface, you can erase wrinkles and blemishes using the Smart Blur and Spot Healing tools. The Dodge and Burn tools help you brighten eyes and darken eyebrows, respectively. Adding the Diffuse Glow filter subtly can give your image a glamorous feel.

When applying the different effects, Photoshop Elements applies them to different layers so you can easily remove them or decrease their intensity later. See Chapter 8 for more about layers.

Improve a Portrait (continued)

16 Click the **Brighten Eyes** tool.

17 Click and drag the slider () to select a brush about the size of the subject's iris.

18 Click the eyes to lighten their colors.

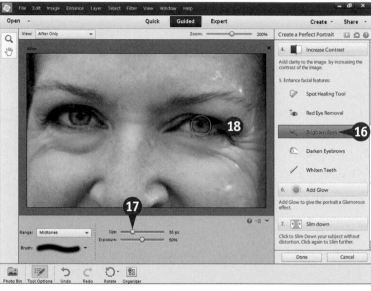

19 Click the **Darken Eyebrows** tool.

20 Click and drag the slider (⬚) to select a brush about the width of the subject's eyebrow.

21 Click and drag across the eyebrows to darken them.

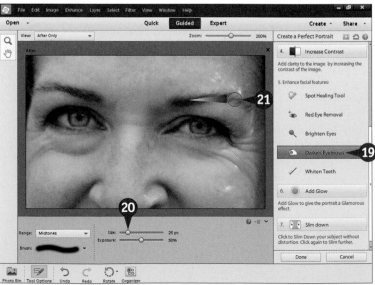

22 Click **Slim down**.

Ⓐ Photoshop Elements zooms out and narrows the image, and your subject, slightly.

You can click **Slim down** multiple times to narrow your subject further.

23 Click **Done**.

Photoshop Elements modifies your image.

24 Click **Expert** to switch to Expert mode.

25 Click **Layers** to view the Layers panel.

Ⓑ The different effects are applied via separate layers.

Note: For more about layers, see Chapter 8.

Ⓒ You can click **Undo** to undo the changes.

TIP

How do I add a glow to my portrait?
In the Perfect Portrait panel, click **Add Glow**. In the dialog box that appears, click and drag the sliders (▣) to adjust the glow. Click **OK** to apply the filter. For more about filters, see Chapter 13.

Shift Colors

You can shift the colors in your images by using the step-by-step instructions and adjustments in Guided mode. The mode enables you to compare before and after versions of an image as you adjust the colors.

By changing the saturation, you can increase or decrease the strength of the colors in an image. By changing the hue, you can convert colors in an image to completely new ones.

Shift Colors

1 In the Editor, click **Guided**.

Note: For more on opening the Editor, see Chapter 1.

Guided mode opens.

Ⓐ Make sure the Touchups list is open. You can click the arrow (🔽) to open it (🔽 changes to 🔼).

2 Click **Enhance Colors**.

Ⓑ You can click **Auto Fix** to have Photoshop Elements automatically balance the colors and contrast by using its built-in optimization routines. You can press Ctrl + Z (⌘+Z on a Mac) to undo the effect.

3 Click the **View** 🔽 and then select a **Before & After** setting to open before and after views of the image.

4 Click and drag the **Saturation** slider (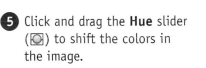) to change the intensity of the colors in the image.

Increasing the saturation in a washed-out image can make objects appear more vivid.

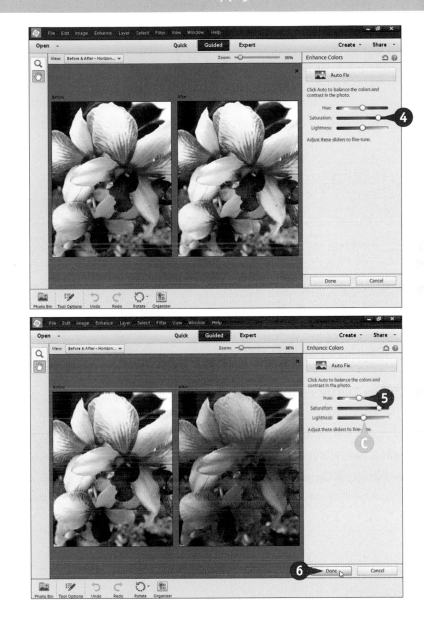

5 Click and drag the **Hue** slider (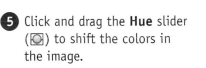) to shift the colors in the image.

Colors are shifted in the same order as they appear in a rainbow or on an artist's color wheel.

 You can also click and drag the **Lightness** slider (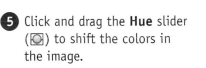) to change the lightness of the colors in the image.

6 Click **Done**.

TIP

How do I fix a colorcast in Guided mode?
In the Touchups list in Guided mode, you can click **Remove a Color Cast** to get rid of shading caused by different types of lighting. Improper film development or scanning can also cause colorcasts. To correct the colorcast, use the eyedropper tool in the steps to select a color in the image that should be pure white, gray, or black. Photoshop Elements uses that as a basis for correcting the entire image.

Apply a Lomo Camera Effect

You can make your image look as if it was shot with a Lomo film camera, a device known for creating vivid, high-contrast images. The Guided mode steps let you increase the saturation of your image as well as add shadowing around the image's edges, effects associated with Lomo cameras.

You can learn more about Lomo cameras and the pictures they take at www.lomography.com.

Apply a Lomo Camera Effect

1 In the Editor, click **Guided**.

Note: For more on opening the Editor, see Chapter 1.

Guided mode opens.

A Make sure the Photo Effects list is open. You can click the arrow (⬇) to open it (⬇ changes to ⬆).

2 Click **Lomo Camera Effect**.

3 Click **Lomo Camera Effect** to saturate the colors in your image and increase the contrast.

You can click the button multiple times to increase the effect.

4 Click **Apply Vignette** to add shadowing around the edges of the image.

You can click the button multiple times to increase the effect.

5 Click **Done**.

Photoshop Elements applies the effect.

B You can click **Undo** to undo the changes.

TIPS

How do I quickly add saturation to an image?
The Saturated Slide Film Effect feature in Guided mode enriches the colors in your image, giving them the appearance of those in traditional slide film. It is a one-button effect; click the button multiple times to increase the intensity.

How do I just add vignetting to an image?
The Vignette Effect in Guided mode enables you to add shadowing to the periphery of your image. The settings let you control the opacity, shape, and color of your vignette. You can apply a black or white vignette.

Add Motion with Zoom Burst

Y ou can add a striking sense of motion to your images with Zoom Burst, a new feature in Photoshop Elements 12. The feature adds radial motion blur to your image to reproduce the effect you can achieve by zooming your camera lens while the camera shutter is open.

Zoom Burst also allows you to specify an area of focus to remove the motion blur from the subject you are highlighting. You can also add a vignette to draw further attention to your subject.

Add Motion with Zoom Burst

1 In the Editor, click **Guided**.

Note: For more on opening the Editor, see Chapter 1.

Guided mode opens.

Ⓐ Make sure the Photo Effects list is open. You can click the arrow (☑) to open it (☑ changes to ☒).

2 Click **Zoom Burst Effect**.

Ⓑ You can optionally crop your photo to remove extraneous content. For more on cropping, see Chapter 5.

3 Click **Add Zoom Burst**.

Photoshop Elements adds radial blur to the image. You can click the button multiple times to intensify the effect.

④ Click **Add Focus Area**.

⑤ Click and drag from the center of the area on which you want to focus. The further you drag, the larger the area of focus.

Photoshop Elements removes the blur from the area.

⑥ Click **Apply Vignette** to add shadowing to the edges of the image.

You can click the button multiple times to darken the shadowing.

⑦ Click **Done**.

TIP

How else can I add the appearance of motion to my image?

Different blur filters are available that make objects in your image look like they are moving. Click **Expert** to switch to Expert mode. Click **Filter** and then **Blur** to access the Blur filter menu. Click **Radial Blur** to apply the effects seen in the Zoom Burst feature, or click **Motion Blur** to add blurring along a straight line.

You can make normal-size objects in a scene look smaller by applying tilt shift. In Photoshop Elements, this involves the blurring of a photo while keeping a horizontal band of content in focus.

In traditional photography, tilt-shift techniques are used to compensate for distortion that can occur when photographing tall structures. The fact that it can also make objects look miniature is a novel by-product. The Tilt Shift feature in Guided mode simulates this effect using the blur filter. For more about filters, see Chapter 13.

Miniaturize Objects with Tilt Shift

1 In the Editor, click **Guided**.

Note: For more on opening the Editor, see Chapter 1.

Guided mode opens.

A Make sure the Photo Effects list is open. You can click the arrow (⌄) to open it (⌄ changes to ⌃).

2 Click **Tilt-Shift**.

3 Click **Add Tilt-Shift**.

Photoshop Elements adds blurring across the image but leaves a center, horizontal band of focus.

4 Click **Modify Focus Area**.

5 Click and drag to adjust a band of focus. The further you drag, the larger the area of focus.

Photoshop Elements modifies the focus area.

6 Click **Refine Effect**.

7 Click and drag the sliders () to adjust the blur, contrast, and saturation.

Ⓑ The objects in the area of focus appear miniaturized.

8 Click **Done**.

TIP

What is an Orton effect?
In traditional photography, the Orton effect involves combining two photos of different exposures, one sharply focused and one out of focus. This often results in soft lighting and a dreamlike scene. You can simulate this with the Create Orton Effect, located under Photo Effects. You can control the blur, noise, and brightness associated with the effect.

Turn a Photo into a Puzzle

You can apply the Puzzle Effect in Guided mode to turn your photo into a jigsaw puzzle. The effect adds an overlay of interlocking jigsaw pieces to your image.

You can choose the size of the pieces that overlay the photo. You can also extract different jigsaw pieces from the result and move them on top of one another. The extracted pieces are placed in separate layers, which can be further edited in Expert mode.

Turn a Photo into a Puzzle

1 In the Editor, click **Guided**.

Note: For more on opening the Editor, see Chapter 1.

Guided mode opens.

Ⓐ Make sure the Photo Play list is open. You can click the arrow (⌄) to open it (⌄ changes to ⌃).

2 Click **Puzzle Effect**.

3 Click a size button to determine the size of the pieces.

Photoshop Elements adds a puzzle overlay to your image.

4 Click **Select Puzzle Piece**.

5 Click inside one of the pieces.

Ⓑ The piece is selected.

6 Click **Extract Piece**.

The piece is extracted and placed in the center of the puzzle.

7 Click **Move Tool**.

8 Click and drag to move the piece.

You can repeat steps **5** to **8** to rearrange the same piece or other pieces.

9 Click **Done**.

Photoshop Elements applies the effect.

10 Click **Expert**.

11 Click **Layers** to view the image layers.

C The extracted pieces are placed in separate layers

For more about layers, see Chapter 8.

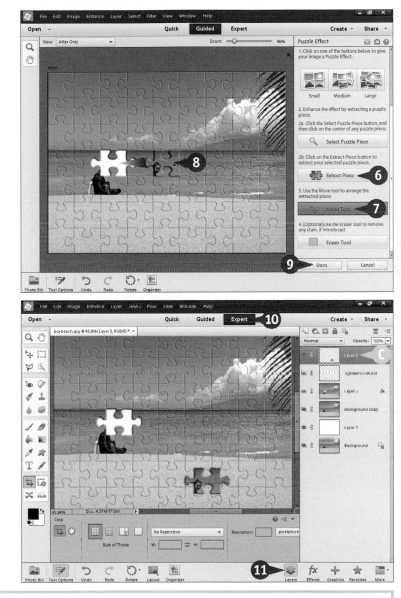

How can I turn an image into a photo collage?

The Picture Stack feature in Guided mode applies this effect to your image. It divides your image into smaller overlapping snapshots. You can choose how many snapshots — four, eight, or twelve. You can also select a border width for the photos. You can make further adjustments to the overlays by opening the Layers panel in Expert mode.

Apply a Reflection

In Guided mode, you can complete steps to create a realistic reflection of the content in your image. The result makes it appear that your content is next to a pond or shiny floor.

To produce the effect, Photoshop Elements duplicates your content and places it below the original image. Then you add color fill, blur, and a gradient to make the reflection more convincing.

Apply a Reflection

1 In the Editor, click **Guided**.

Note: For more on opening the Editor, see Chapter 1.

Guided mode opens.

A Make sure the Photo Play list is open. You can click the arrow () to open it (☑ changes to ⌃).

2 Click **Reflection**.

3 Click **Add Reflection**.

B Photoshop Elements duplicates the content to create a reflection.

4 Click **Eyedropper tool**.

5 Click inside the image to select a background color.

6 Click **Fill Background** to fill the reflection with the selected color.

7 Click an effect button to add texture to the reflection.

The Floor button adds blur, and the Glass and Water buttons add blur as well as distortion.

8 In the dialog box that appears, adjust the effect settings.

9 Click **OK** to apply the effect.

10 Click **Add Distortion** to shrink the reflection vertically.

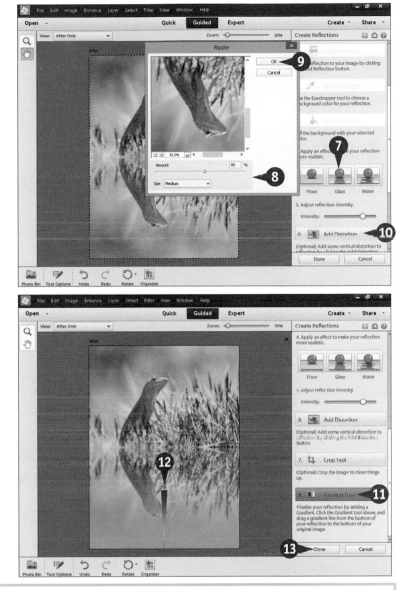

11 Click **Gradient Tool**.

12 Click and drag from the bottom of the reflection up to fade the reflection.

13 Click **Done**.

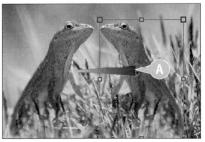

TIP

What is another way to make a mirror image of an object in my image?

In Expert mode, select the object using a selection tool. See Chapter 6 for information about selection tools. Then copy and paste the selection into its own layer. See Chapter 8 for more about layers. With the layer selected, click **Image**, **Rotate**, and then **Flip Layer Horizontal** to create a mirror image. Use the Move tool to adjust the position of the mirror image (A).

Put an Object Out of Bounds

In Guided mode, you can edit your image so that part of an object in it extends outside the bounds of the main image frame. For example, you can make a treetop stick out of the top of a picture of a park or a swinging bat extend out of the side of a baseball scene.

You create the effect by cropping to define the main content frame and then selecting the part of the object that should extend outside the cropped area. You can enhance the 3-D effect by adding a background gradient and drop shadow.

Put an Object Out of Bounds

1 In the Editor, click **Guided**.

Note: For more on opening the Editor, see Chapter 1.

Guided mode opens.

A Make sure the Photo Play list is open. You can click the arrow (∨) to open it (∨ changes to ∧).

2 Click **Out Of Bounds**.

3 Click **Add Frame**.

4 Click and drag the crop handles (☐) to define the main frame of your image. The part of the image that will be placed out of bounds should extend outside the frame.

You can click `Ctrl`+`Alt`+`Shift` (`⌘`+`Option`+`Shift` on a Mac) and drag the corner handles to skew the frame to give it depth.

5 Click ✓ or press `Enter` to accept the crop.

6 Click ✓ or press `Enter` a second time to complete the frame.

Photoshop Elements crops the content.

7 Click **Selection Tool**.

8 Click and drag the selection tool to define the out-of-bounds part of the image.

9 Click **Out of Bounds Effect**.

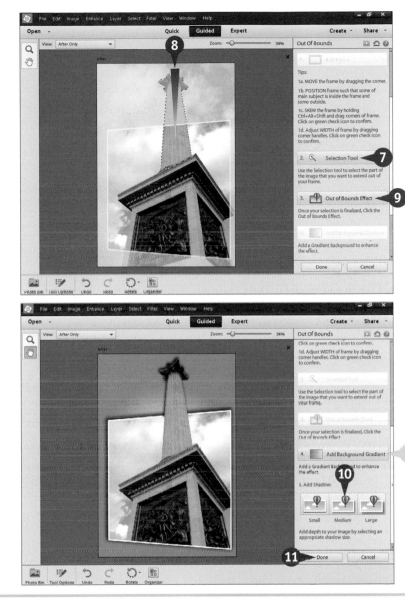

Photoshop Elements extends the selected content outside the main frame.

Ⓑ You can optionally click **Add Background Gradient** to enhance the background.

10 Click a Shadow button to apply a drop shadow and emphasize the out-of-bounds content.

11 Click **Done**.

TIP

How do I turn my photos into 1960s art?
You can convert your photos to vibrant, bitmapped masterpieces reminiscent of the Pop Art movement with the Pop Art feature in Guided mode. Located under Photo Play, the feature creates four versions of your photo, each a different color.

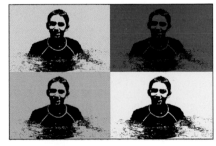

Apply a Low Key Effect

The Low Key feature in Guided mode enables you to add an artistic flavor to an image by throwing darker areas into complete shadow to highlight the image subject. When applying the effect, you also have the option of keeping the color in your image or converting it to black and white.

After you apply the Low Key effect, you can further darken the shadowed areas with a background brush. You can apply a reduce-effect brush to bring details back.

Apply a Low Key Effect

1 In the Editor, click **Guided**.

Note: For more on opening the Editor, see Chapter 1.

Guided mode opens.

A Make sure the Photo Effects list is open. You can click the arrow (⌄) to open it (⌄ changes to ⌃).

2 Click **Low Key**.

3 Click an **Add Low Key** button.

You can click **Color** to keep an image in color or **B&W** to convert colors to black and white.

Photoshop Elements converts the image.

④ Click **Background Brush**.

⑤ Click and drag the sliders (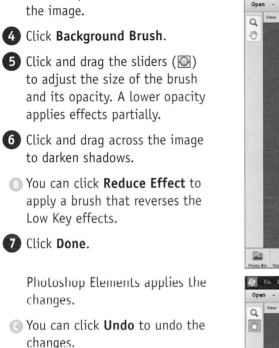) to adjust the size of the brush and its opacity. A lower opacity applies effects partially.

⑥ Click and drag across the image to darken shadows.

Ⓑ You can click **Reduce Effect** to apply a brush that reverses the Low Key effects.

⑦ Click **Done**.

Photoshop Elements applies the changes.

Ⓒ You can click **Undo** to undo the changes.

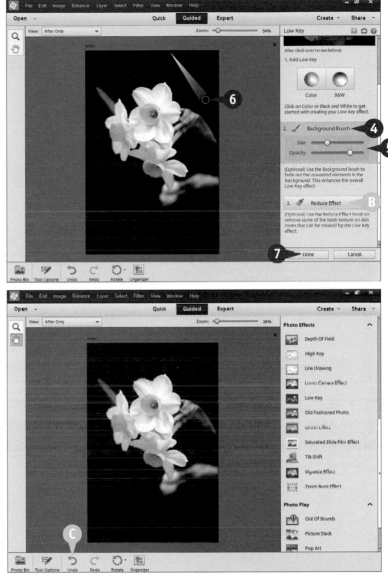

TIP

What is the High Key effect?
The High Key feature in Guided mode produces an effect opposite of Low Key. Light areas of an image are further lightened, which can result in a whitewashed background around your subject. You can intensify the effect in High Key by adding a diffuse glow.

CHAPTER 12

Painting and Drawing on Photos

Photoshop Elements offers a variety of tools you can use to paint and draw on your images as well as add shapes, colors, and gradients.

Set the Foreground and Background Colors 256

Add Color with the Brush Tool 258

Change Brush Styles 260

Using a Brush to Replace a Color 262

Adjust Colors with the Smart Brush 264

Draw a Shape 268

Draw a Line 270

Apply the Eraser 272

Apply a Gradient 274

Add Content from the Graphics Panel 276

Set the Foreground and Background Colors

You can select colors to use with many of the painting and drawing tools in Photoshop Elements by setting the foreground and background colors. The Brush and Pencil tools apply the foreground color, and the Eraser tool applies the background color when used on the Background layer.

See the next section, "Add Color with the Brush Tool," for more on how to paint on a photo. See the section "Apply the Eraser" for more on using the Eraser. Some filters in Photoshop Elements apply their effects to your image based on the current foreground and background colors. See Chapter 13 for more about filters.

Set the Foreground and Background Colors

Set the Foreground Color

1 In the Editor, click **Expert**.

Note: For more on opening the Editor, see Chapter 1.

2 Click the foreground color box.

The Color Picker dialog box opens.

3 Click and drag the slider (▣) to select a color range.

4 Click a color.

You can click outside the dialog box in the image window to select a color from your photo.

5 Click **OK**.

Ⓐ The selected color appears in the foreground color box.

Ⓑ Many tools, including the Type, Brush, and Shape tools, use the current foreground color when applied.

This example uses the Brush tool.

Note: For more on painting tools, see the next section, "Add Color with the Brush Tool."

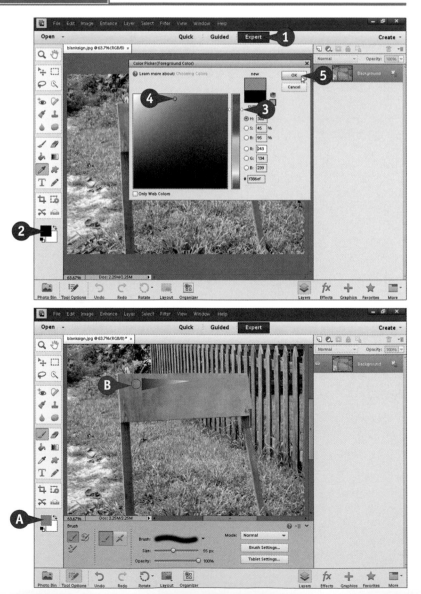

Set the Background Color

1 Click the background color box.

The Color Picker dialog box opens.

2 Click and drag the slider ([▨]) to select a color range.

3 Click a color.

You can click outside the dialog box in the image window to select a color from your photo.

You can also type values for a color.

4 Click **OK**.

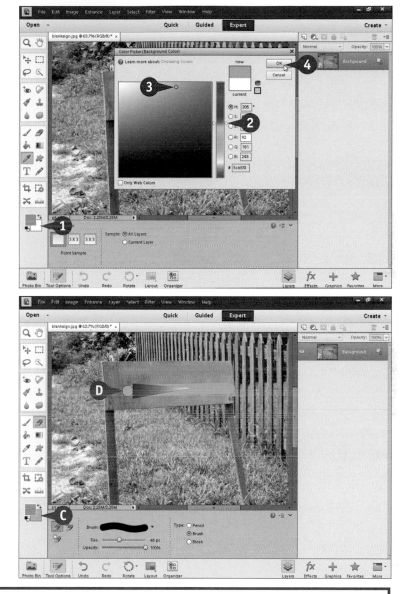

Ⓒ The selected color appears in the background color box.

Ⓓ Tools such as the Eraser apply the background color to a photo.

The Eraser tool applies color only in the Background layer; in other layers, the Eraser turns pixels transparent.

Note: See Chapter 8 for more on layers.

TIPS

How do I reset the foreground and background colors?

Click the **Default** button ([■]) or press [D] to reset the colors to black and white. You can also click the **Switch** icon ([⤢]) or press [X] to swap the foreground and background colors. This can be useful when you want to alternate between a pair of colors as you work.

Does Photoshop Elements offer a set of common colors?

Yes. Select a color to paint or draw on your photo from the Color Swatches panel, which includes sets of commonly used colors. To view the panel, click **Window** and then **Color Swatches**. Click the color you want to use; the foreground color box reflects your choice. To set the background color, [Ctrl]+click ([⌘]+click on a Mac) a color in the panel.

Add Color with the Brush Tool

You can use the Brush tool to add patches of solid color to your image. You can use the tool to cover unwanted elements or change the appearance of clothing or a backdrop. When applying the Brush tool, you can control the size of the brushstrokes by choosing a brush size. For realistic results, turn on the Airbrush feature to apply a softer line of color.

To limit where the brush applies color, create a selection before using the tool. For more about selections, see Chapter 6. The Brush tool can also be used to edit a layer mask in your image. See Chapter 8 for more about layer masks.

Add Color with the Brush Tool

1 In the Editor, click **Expert**.

Note: For more on opening the Editor, see Chapter 1.

2 Click the foreground color box to select a color with which to paint.

You can also press and hold Alt (Option on a Mac) and then click inside your image to select a color.

3 Click **OK**.

4 Click the **Brush** tool (📷).

5 Click the **Brush** ▼ and select a brush size and type.

A To set a brush size, you can also click and drag the slider (◯).

6 Press Enter to close the Brushes menu.

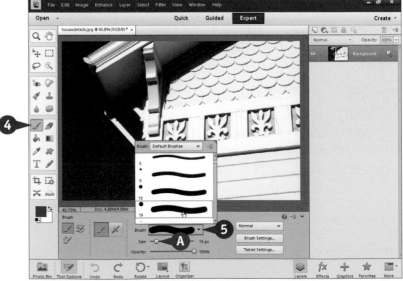

7 Click and drag the mouse pointer (○) on the image.

Photoshop Elements applies color to the image.

8 Click and drag the slider (○) to reduce the opacity of the paint effect.

9 Click and drag the mouse pointer (○) on the image.

Photoshop Elements applies transparent color to the image.

To undo the most recent brushstroke, you can click **Edit** and then **Undo Brush Tool** or click **Undo** in the Tool Options panel.

Note: To keep content in your image intact, you can duplicate a layer before painting. See Chapter 8 for more on layers.

TIPS

How do I paint hard-edged lines?
Use the Pencil tool (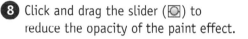), which is similar to the Brush tool (✏) except that it paints hard-edged lines. Like the Brush, the Pencil applies the foreground color. See the section "Draw a Line" for another way to draw lines.

What can I do with the Impressionist Brush tool?
The Impressionist Brush (✏) creates artistic effects by blending existing colors in an image together. The Impressionist Brush does not add any foreground or background color to your image. You can select the tool from the menu that appears when you right-click the Brush tool (✏).

Change Brush Styles

You can select from a variety of predefined brush styles in Photoshop Elements to apply color to your image in different ways. Brush styles can have hard or soft edges. Brush styles with specialized tips can apply speckled patterns of color to your image. Photoshop Elements offers a variety of predefined brush sets that you can access in the Tool Options panel.

You can also create a custom brush style by specifying spacing, fade, and other characteristics for your brush. This can be useful when you want to apply subtle or irregular patterns of colors.

Change Brush Styles

Select from a Predefined Set

1 In the Editor, click **Expert**.

Note: For more on opening the Editor, see Chapter 1.

2 Click the **Brush** tool ( ).

3 Click the **Brush** in the Tool Options panel.

4 Click the in the Brush menu and select a set of brushes.

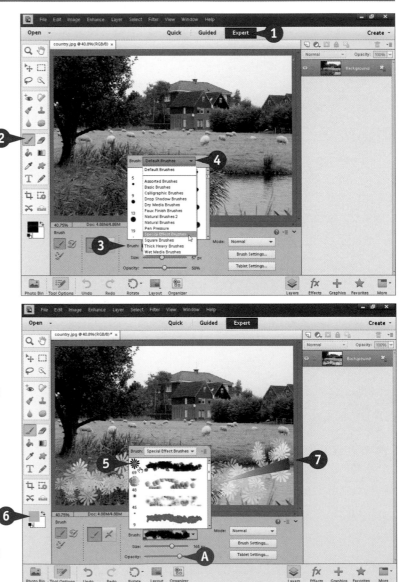

The set appears in the Brush menu.

5 Click a brush style to select it.

The mouse pointer changes to the new brush shape.

A You can click the slider ( ) to adjust the brush size.

6 Click the foreground color box to choose a color to apply with the brush. The actual color applied may vary depending on the brush type.

7 Click and drag the brush on the photo.

Photoshop Elements applies the brush to the area.

Customize a Brush

1 Click **Brush Settings**.

The Brush Settings dialog box opens.

2 Click and drag the sliders () to define the new brush attributes.

B You can limit the length of your brushstrokes with the Fade slider.

C You can randomize the painted color with the Hue Jitter slider.

D You can change the shape of the brush tip by clicking and dragging here.

3 Click and drag the brush on the photo.

Photoshop Elements applies the customized brush to the area.

Note: For more on applying the brush, see the previous section, "Add Color with the Brush Tool."

TIP

How can I make a brush apply dots instead of a line?

1 In the Tool Options panel, click **Brush Settings** to open the Brush Settings dialog box.

2 Click and drag the slider () to increase the Spacing value to greater than 100%.

A When you click and drag a brush shape, you get dots or patches instead of a contiguous line.

Using a Brush to Replace a Color

You can replace colors in your image with the current foreground color by using the Color Replacement tool. This gives you a free-form way of recoloring objects in your image while keeping the shading on the objects intact.

You can control the areas in your image that the tool affects by adjusting the Tolerance setting. A low tolerance value affects a narrow range of colors in the image, whereas a high tolerance value affects a wide range. You can also constrain how the tool is applied by selecting a brush size.

Using a Brush to Replace a Color

1 In the Editor, click **Expert**.

Note: For more on opening the Editor, see Chapter 1.

2 Click the **Brush** tool (▨).

3 In the Tool Options panel, click the **Color Replacement** tool (▨).

4 Click the foreground color box to select a color for painting.

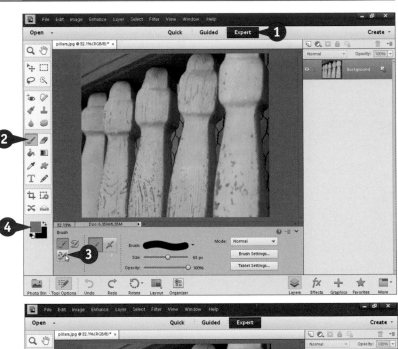

5 Click and drag the slider (◯) to select a brush size.

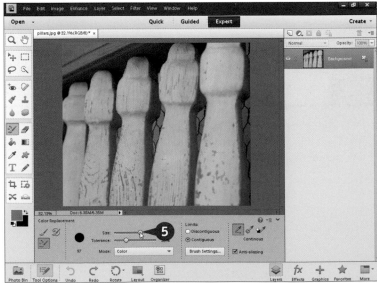

6 Click and drag the slider (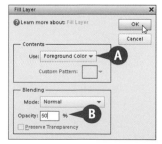) to set a tolerance from 1% to 100%.

The greater the tolerance, the greater the range of colors the tool replaces.

7 Click and drag in your image.

Photoshop Elements replaces the color.

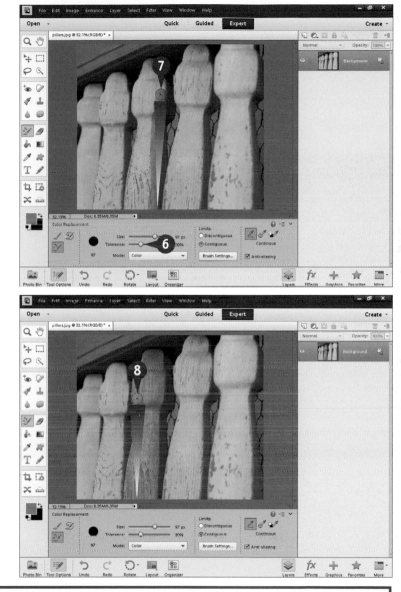

8 Continue to click and drag in your image.

Photoshop Elements replaces more color.

TIP

How do I fill a selection with a color?

Make a selection with a selection tool and then click **Edit** and **Fill Selection**. In the Fill Layer dialog box that appears, select the color you want to fill with (**A**) and then set an opacity for the fill color (**B**). Click **OK** to fill the selection.

Adjust Colors with the Smart Brush

You can simultaneously select objects in your photo and apply color adjustments to them with the Smart Brush tool. Different tool options enable you to increase, decrease, remove, or transform color in the objects. You can also darken overexposed areas or brighten areas that are in shadow.

The Smart Brush options in the Portrait category enable you to adjust facial colors to give photo subjects a tan, whiten teeth, or apply a lipstick tint to lips. Options in the Special Effects category apply striking, out-of-this world colors to objects.

Adjust Colors with the Smart Brush

Apply the Smart Brush Effect

1 In the Editor, click **Expert**.

Note: For more on opening the Editor, see Chapter 1.

2 Click the **Smart Brush** tool (📷).

3 Click the 🔽 to open a menu for choosing effects.

4 Click the 🔽 and select a preset category.

Photoshop Elements lists the painting effects in that category.

Ⓐ A thumbnail image shows an example of each painting effect.

5 Click an effect.

6 Press Enter to close the menu.

7 Click the slider (◯) and select a brush size.

⑧ Click and drag over objects in your image to apply the tool.

Photoshop Elements selects the objects and applies the painting effect.

Ⓑ The effect is stored as a new adjustment layer.

For more about adjustment layers, see Chapter 8.

Ⓒ You can click **Inverse** (☐ changes to ☑) to invert your selection and apply the effect to the other pixels in your layer.

Change Smart Brush Effects

While your painted area is still selected, you can switch effects.

① Click the 🔽 to open the effects menu.

② Click a different effect.

Ⓓ Photoshop Elements changes the Smart Brush effect.

continued ▶ 265

TIP

How do I decrease the effect of the Smart Brush so that it is only partially applied?
In the Layers panel, click the icon for the adjustment layer that the Smart Brush created. Click the **Opacity** 🔽 and then click and drag the slider (🔘) to the left. Photoshop Elements decreases the Smart Brush effect. You can click the visibility icon (👁) to turn off the adjustment layer and hide the effect.

Adjust Colors with the Smart Brush (continued)

You can change the behavior of new Smart Brush strokes by clicking selection icons in the Tool Options panel. The icons enable you to start a new Smart Brush selection, add to an existing selection, or subtract from a selection.

You can also switch to the Detail Smart Brush tool. The tool has a similar effect as the regular Smart Brush except you have more control over what areas the brush affects. The Detail Smart Brush does not automatically select similarly colored nearby pixels as you click and drag; it changes only the colors you drag over.

Adjust Colors with the Smart Brush (continued)

Apply to a New Selection

After applying a Smart Brush effect to one part of the image, you can apply a different effect to another part.

1 Click the **Smart Brush** tool (⬚).

2 In the Tool Options panel, click the **New Selection** button (⬚).

3 Click the ⬛ to change the Smart Brush effect.

4 Click and drag over a new area in your image.

Photoshop Elements applies the painting effect.

Ⓐ To add to a selected layer with the Smart Brush, you can click ⬚ before painting.

Ⓑ To subtract from a selected layer, you can click ⬚.

Paint Details

1 In the Tool Options panel, click the **Detail Smart Brush** tool (▨).

2 Click and drag the slider (◉) to adjust the brush size.

3 Click the **New Selection** button (▨).

C To add to an existing selection, you can click ▨.

D To subtract from an existing selection, you can click ▨.

4 Click the ▼ to change the Detail Smart Brush effect.

E To examine details in your image, you can use the Zoom tool (🔍). For details, see Chapter 5.

5 Click and drag over a detail in your image.

Photoshop Elements applies the painting effect.

TIPS

How can I apply Smart Brush textures?
Click **Textures** in the Smart Brush presets menu. Effects include Behind Net, which covers your selection with thin black lines, and Lizard Skin, which applies a scaly look. You can also apply texture effects using one of the Photoshop Elements texture filters (see Chapter 13).

What is a Smart Brush mask?
Photoshop Elements constrains the effects of the Smart Brush by adding a mask to an adjustment layer. The mask is a special black-and-white overlay that appears as a thumbnail in the Layers panel. Adjustments are applied to the white area of the mask but not the black area. For more about masks and how to edit them, see Chapter 8.

Draw a Shape

You can create solid shapes in your image by using the many shape tools in Photoshop Elements. Shapes offer an easy way to add whimsical objects, labels, or buttons to an image.

When you add a shape to an image, Photoshop Elements places the shape on its own layer. This makes it easy to move and transform the shape later on. Because shape objects are vector graphics in Photoshop Elements, they can be resized without a loss in quality. For more on layers, see Chapter 8. You can overlay text on a shape to create signs or labeled buttons. See Chapter 14 for more about adding text.

Draw a Shape

① In the Editor, click **Expert**.

Note: For more on opening the Editor, see Chapter 1.

② Click the **Custom Shape** tool (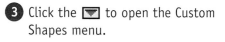).

The Custom Shape tool shares space in the Tool Options panel with the other shape tools.

③ Click the ▼ to open the Custom Shapes menu.

④ Click a shape.

⑤ Press **Enter** to close the menu.

Ⓐ You can click the panel menu (▼≣) to access hundreds of additional shapes in 24 categories.

Ⓑ You can click the ▼ to select a style, such as a 3-D style, for your shape.

6 Click the  and select a color for your shape.

7 Press **Enter** to close the menu.

8 Click and drag your mouse pointer (+) to draw the shape. You can adjust the ratio of the shape's height and width as you drag.

C Photoshop Elements places the shape on its own layer.

D To add to an existing shape layer when you draw your shape, you can select that layer in the Layers panel and click **Add to shape area** (□).

Note: For more on layers, see Chapter 8.

You can click and drag multiple times to create more than one shape.

TIP

How do I resize a shape after I draw it?
Click the shape's layer. Click **Image**, **Transform Shape**, and then a transform command such as **Scale**, **Skew**, or **Distort**. You can also press **Ctrl**+**T** (**⌘**+**T** on a Mac). Resize the shape by clicking and dragging a corner handle (□) (**A**).

Draw a Line

Y ou can use the Line tool in Photoshop Elements to draw straight lines in your image. You can customize the line with arrowheads, giving you an easy way to point out elements in your image.

When you add a line to an image with the Line tool, Photoshop Elements places the line on its own layer. This makes it easy to move and transform the line later on. Because line objects are vector graphics in Photoshop Elements, you can resize and otherwise transform them without a loss in quality. For more on layers, see Chapter 8.

Draw a Line

1 In the Editor, click **Expert**.

Note: For more on opening the Editor, see Chapter 1.

2 Click the **Custom Shape** tool ().

3 Click the **Line** tool ().

The Line tool shares space in the Tool Options panel with the other shape tools.

4 Click the and then click **At the start** or **At the end** to include an arrowhead on your line. You can click **At Both Ends** to put arrowheads on both ends.

A You can also specify the shape of the arrowheads by typing values here. You can specify the width, length, and concavity.

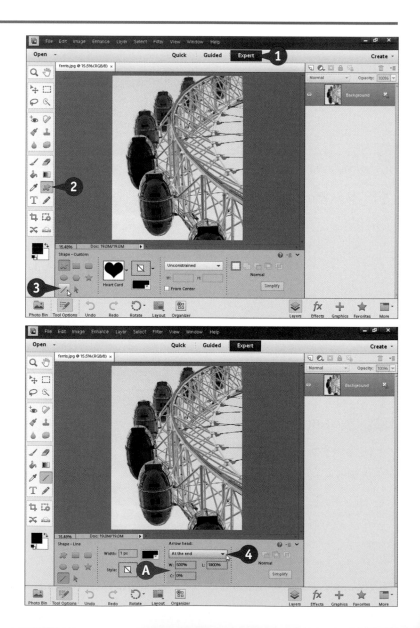

5 Type a line width.

6 Click the 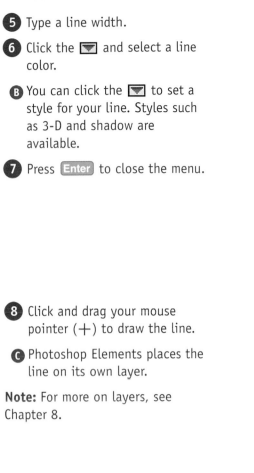 and select a line color.

B You can click the 🔽 to set a style for your line. Styles such as 3-D and shadow are available.

7 Press **Enter** to close the menu.

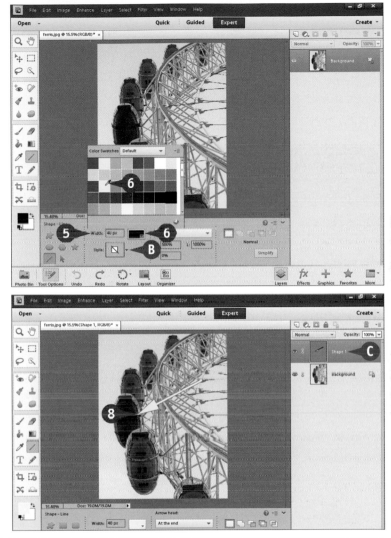

8 Click and drag your mouse pointer (**+**) to draw the line.

C Photoshop Elements places the line on its own layer.

Note: For more on layers, see Chapter 8.

TIP

How can I add an outline along a selection in my image?

1 Click **Edit**.

2 Click **Stroke (Outline) Selection**.

3 In the Stroke dialog box, type a width for the line.

4 Click a location (**○** changes to **⊙**).

5 Click **OK**.

A Photoshop Elements applies the stroke.

Apply the Eraser

You can use the Eraser tool to erase unwanted areas of your photo. When you apply the Eraser tool in the Background layer, the erased pixels are replaced with the current background color. When you erase in other layers, the Eraser tool turns the pixels transparent, revealing any underlying layers.

In the Tool Options panel, you can control the size of the eraser and the softness of its edges. Using a soft-edged eraser can be useful for removing content around objects that have fuzzy edges, whereas a hard-edged eraser can be better for high-contrast objects. You can also change the opacity of the tool to only partially erase content in your image.

Apply the Eraser

Adjust the Eraser Settings

1 In the Editor, click **Expert**.

Note: For more on opening the Editor, see Chapter 1.

2 Click the **Eraser** tool ().

3 Click the background color box to choose a color to appear in place of the erased pixels.

Note: For more, see the section "Set the Foreground and Background Colors."

4 Click the **Brush** to choose an eraser size and type.

Ⓐ You can also click and drag the slider (◯) to set an eraser size.

Erase the Background Layer

① Click the Background layer.

② Click and drag the mouse pointer (○) to erase.

Portions of the Background layer are erased and filled with the background color.

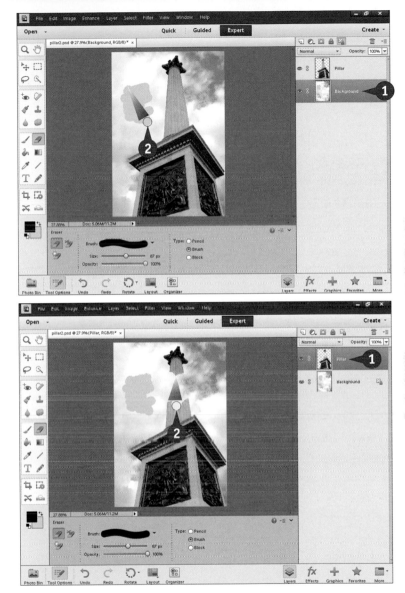

Erase a Normal Layer

① Click a normal layer.

② Click and drag the mouse pointer (○) to erase.

Portions of a layer are erased to reveal the underlying layer.

TIPS

What other eraser tools are available in the Tool Options panel?

You can use the Background Eraser tool () to sample a color in your image and erase only that color as you drag the tool over your image. The Magic Eraser tool () erases all the adjacent, similarly colored pixels when you click it.

Which eraser shape should I use?

In the Tool Options panel, you can choose from three eraser shapes, or *modes*: Brush, Pencil, and Block. Brush mode, which is the default, enables you to apply the eraser to your image similar to the Brush tool. The Pencil mode acts like the Pencil tool while erasing, with the strokes having a harder edge. The Block mode turns the eraser mouse pointer into a hard-edged square shape for erasing.

Apply a Gradient

You can apply a *gradient*, which is a blend from one color to another, to give objects in your image a radiant or 3-D look. You can apply a gradient to a selected portion of an image or the entire image.

Setting the geometry of a gradient controls the direction of the color blend. A linear gradient changes as it moves across your image. A radial gradient changes color from a center point moving outward.

The Gradient Editor enables you to choose from predefined color combinations for your gradient or choose your own custom colors. You can also edit the sharpness of the color transitions.

Apply a Gradient

1 In the Editor, click **Expert**.

2 Make a selection.

Note: For more on opening the Editor, see Chapter 1. See Chapter 6 for more on making selections.

> If you do not make a selection, the gradient is applied to the entire image.

3 Click the **Gradient** tool (▦).

A A linear gradient (▭) is the default. You can select different geometries in the Tool Options panel.

4 Click the gradient swatch.

> The Gradient Editor dialog box opens.

5 Click a preset gradient type from the top box.

B You can define a custom gradient by changing these settings.

6 Click **OK**.

7 Click and drag the mouse pointer (+) inside the selection.

This defines the direction and transition of the gradient.

Dragging a long line with the tool produces a gradual transition.

Dragging a short line with the tool produces an abrupt transition.

Photoshop Elements generates a gradient inside the selection.

TIP

How can I highlight an object in my image by using a gradient?
Place the object on its own layer. Create a new layer below the object and then select the new layer. Click the **Gradient** tool (■) and then click the **Radial Gradient** button (□) in the Tool Options panel. Click and drag the mouse pointer (+) from the center of the object outward to create the gradient (**A**).

Add Content from the Graphics Panel

You can add backgrounds, frames, graphics, and other elements to your image from the Graphics panel. The panel enables you to quickly add free clip art to decorate your imaging projects. Graphics added from the panel appear in separate layers in your image. You can move, resize, and transform those layers to achieve a pleasing final product.

The panel comes with hundreds of different decorative elements in dozens of categories. Some of the Graphics content is stored online and requires an Internet connection to retrieve. Photoshop Elements downloads the content after you install the program and initially access the panel.

Add Content from the Graphics Panel

Add a Background

1 In the Editor, click **Expert**.

Note: For more on opening the Editor, see Chapter 1.

2 Click **Graphics**.

A The Graphics panel opens.

3 Click the  and select **By Type**.

4 Click the  and select **Backgrounds**.

Photoshop Elements displays backgrounds.

5 Click and drag a background to the image window.

B Photoshop Elements replaces the current background layer with the selected background.

C Any other layers in your image appear above the new background layer.

Note: For more on layers, see Chapter 8.

276

Add a Graphic

① Click the ▼ and select
Graphics.

Photoshop Elements displays
a collection of graphics.

② Click and drag a graphic to
the image window.

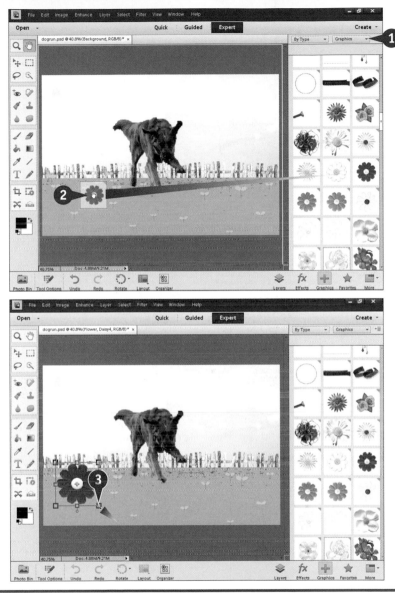

Photoshop Elements adds the
graphic as a new layer.

③ Click and drag a handle to
resize the graphic.

The graphic is resized.

TIP

How do I search for content by keyword?

① In the Content panel, click the ▼ and select **By Word**.

② Type a keyword.

③ Click **Find**.

Ⓐ Photoshop Elements displays related content.

CHAPTER 13

Applying Filters

You can use the filters in Photoshop Elements to quickly and easily apply enhancements to your image, including artistic effects, texture effects, and distortions. Filters can help you correct defects in your images or enable you to turn a photograph into something resembling an impressionist painting. This chapter highlights a few of the more than 100 filters available in Photoshop Elements. For more on all the filters, see the help documentation.

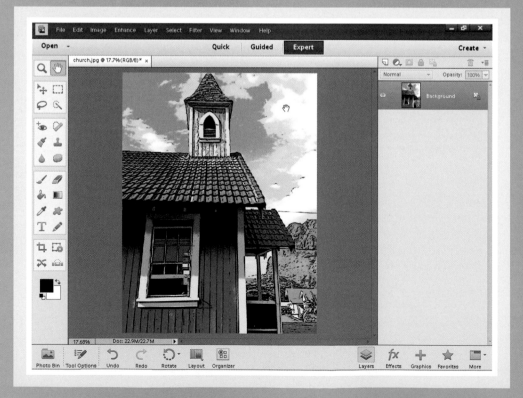

Blur an Image 280

Distort an Image 282

Turn an Image into a Painting 284

Turn an Image into a Sketch 286

Add Noise to an Image 288

Pixelate an Image 290

Emboss an Image 292

Apply Multiple Filters 294

Blur an Image

You can use the Blur filters to apply a variety of blurring effects to your photos. For example, you can use the Gaussian Blur filter to obscure background objects while keeping foreground objects in focus. The Motion Blur filter applies directional blurring, making objects appear to move fast.

To blur a background behind an object, select the object using one or more selection tools and then invert the selection. For more about making and inverting a selection, see Chapter 6. After inverting, you can apply the Blur filter.

Blur an Image

1 In the Editor, select the layer to which you want to apply the filter.

Note: For more on opening the Editor, see Chapter 1. For more about layers, see Chapter 8.

In this example, the scenery around the lock has been selected, and the image has a single Background layer.

Note: For more about making selections, see Chapter 6.

2 Click **Filter**.

3 Click **Blur**.

4 Click **Gaussian Blur**.

The Gaussian Blur dialog box opens, displaying a preview of the filter's effect.

5 Click the minus sign (⊟) or plus sign (⊞) to zoom out or in.

6 Click and drag the **Radius** slider (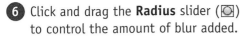) to control the amount of blur added.

In this example, boosting the radius value increases the amount of blur.

7 Click **OK**.

Photoshop Elements applies the filter.

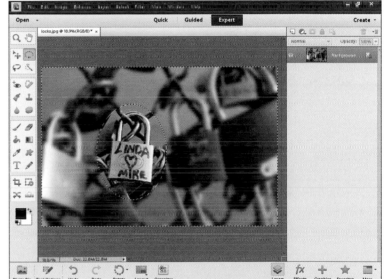

How do I simulate a short depth of field in an image?
Short depth of field is a photographic effect where one object in the scene is focused (**A**) and the rest of the scene is blurred. You can achieve this with a Guided mode feature. Click **Guided** at the top of the Photoshop Elements workspace. On the right, under Photo Effects, click **Depth of Field**. Follow the steps to define an area of focus and to blur the rest of the image. Click **Done** to apply the effect.

Distort an Image

You can use any of the Distort filters to stretch and squeeze your image, creating the appearance of waves, glass, swirls, and more. For example, the Twirl filter turns the image into a swirl of colors, and the Ripple filter adds wavelike effects. Settings in the filter dialog boxes enable you to increase or decrease the distortion. The Distort filters such as Glass and Ocean Ripple make your image appear as though viewed through a distorted, transparent surface, and the Shear filter lets you tilt your image at an angle.

To apply the filter to just part of your image, select that portion by using a selection tool. For more on selection tools, see Chapter 6.

Distort an Image

1 In the Editor, select the layer to which you want to apply the filter.

Note: For more on opening the Editor, see Chapter 1. For more about layers, see Chapter 8.

In this example, the image has a single Background layer.

2 Click **Filter**.

3 Click **Distort**.

4 Click a filter.

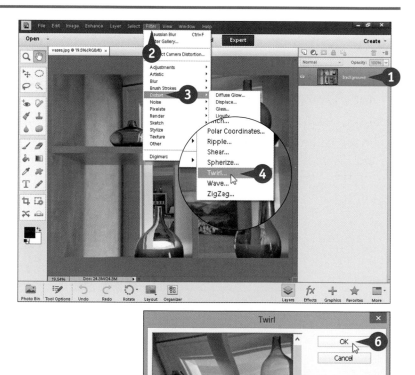

The filter's dialog box opens.

5 Make adjustments to the filter's settings to fine-tune the effect.

With some filters, you can preview the effect before applying it to the image.

6 Click **OK**.

Photoshop Elements applies the filter.

In this example, the Twirl distortion filter is applied.

In this example, the Ripple distortion filter is applied.

Ⓐ You can also apply distortion effects with the Reflection tool. To access it, click **Guided**. The tool is located under Photo Play.

TIPS

How many filters does Photoshop Elements offer?
Photoshop Elements has more than 100 filters grouped into 13 categories. You can experiment with each one to find out what effect it has on your image. You can also download additional filters from third-party companies. Some of these filters are free, but others must be purchased.

Is there another way to distort a selection?
Yes. You can use the Distort command to reshape a selected element in your photo. After selecting the element, click **Image**, **Transform**, and then **Distort**. You can also press Ctrl+T (⌘+T on a Mac). Photoshop Elements surrounds the selection with handles, which you can drag to distort the element. See Chapter 7 for more on distorting selections.

Turn an Image into a Painting

Y ou can use many of the Artistic filters in Photoshop Elements to make your image look as if you created it with a paintbrush or other art media. The Watercolor filter, for example, applies a painted effect by converting similarly colored areas in your image to solid colors. The Palette Knife creates a similar but softer effect. The Colored Pencil filter applies a layer of crosshatched color to your image using the current background color.

To apply a filter to just part of your image, select that portion by using one or more selection tools. For more on selection tools, see Chapter 6.

Turn an Image into a Painting

① In the Editor, select the layer to which you want to apply the filter.

Note: For more on opening the Editor, see Chapter 1. For more about layers, see Chapter 8.

In this example, the image has a single Background layer.

② Click **Filter**.

③ Click **Artistic**.

④ Click a filter.

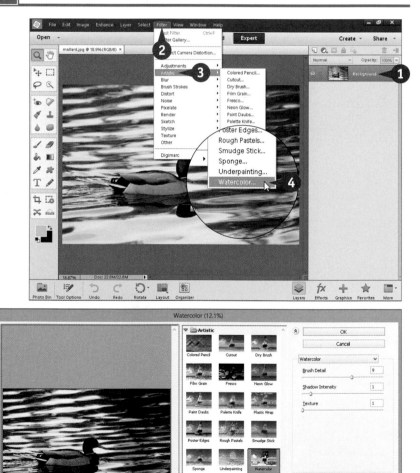

The Filter Gallery dialog box opens, displaying a preview of the filter's effect.

Ⓐ You can click the minus sign (⊟) or the plus sign (⊞) to zoom out or in.

5 Adjust the filter's settings to fine-tune the effect.

6 Click **OK**.

Photoshop Elements applies the filter. In this example, the Dry Brush filter is applied.

Turn an Image into a Sketch

The Sketch filters add outlining effects to your image. The Comic filter, for example, makes an image look as if it was drawn for a comic book, using black lines and colors from your image. You can adjust filter settings to change the contrast and richness of the colors in the final result. Other Sketch filters, such as the Charcoal filter, use the current foreground color as the line color and the background color as the paper color. Changing these colors alters the filter's effect. For more on adjusting colors, see Chapter 10.

Turn an Image into a Sketch

1 In the Editor, select the layer to which you want to apply the filter.

Note: For more on opening the Editor, see Chapter 1. For more about layers, see Chapter 8.

In this example, the image has a single Background layer.

2 Click **Filter**.

3 Click **Sketch**.

4 Click **Comic**.

The Filter Gallery dialog box opens, displaying a preview of the filter's effect.

5 Click the minus magnifying glass (🔍) or plus magnifying glass (🔍) to zoom out or in.

6 Click and drag the **Color** sliders (🔘) to control the way the filter changes the image's color.

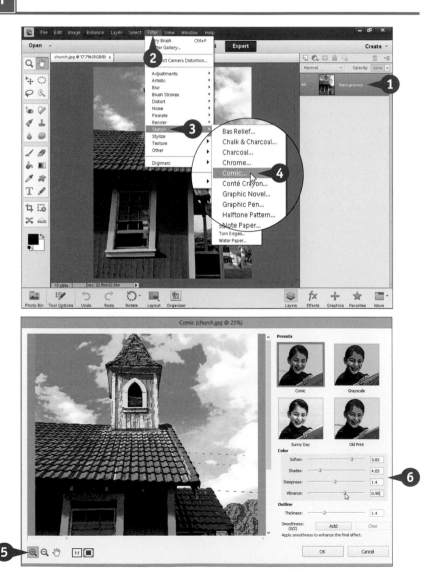

Click and drag the **Outline** slider () to control the filter's outline effect.

8 Click **OK**.

Photoshop Elements applies the filter.

In this example, the thickness of the lines increases and the colors change.

TIP

What does the Graphic Novel filter do?
The Graphic Novel filter makes an image look like a drawing from a black-and-white illustrated book. Follow steps **1** to **4** in this section, selecting **Graphic Novel** in step **4**. In the Filter Gallery dialog box, click and drag the sliders () to control the detail and darkness of the colors. Click **OK** to apply the filter.

Add Noise to an Image

Filters in the Noise menu add graininess to or remove it from your image. You can add graininess with the Add Noise filter to reduce detail or add a static effect. You can adjust the effect to control how much of your image continues to show through.

Other filters under the Noise menu remove extraneous elements from your image. For example, the Dust & Scratches filter applies blurring to get rid of dust and scratches in old scanned photos.

To apply the filter to just part of your image, select that portion by using a selection tool. For more on selection tools, see Chapter 6.

Add Noise to an Image

① In the Editor, select the layer to which you want to apply the filter.

Note: For more on opening the Editor, see Chapter 1. For more about layers, see Chapter 8.

In this example, the image has a single Background layer.

② Click **Filter**.

③ Click **Noise**.

④ Click **Add Noise**.

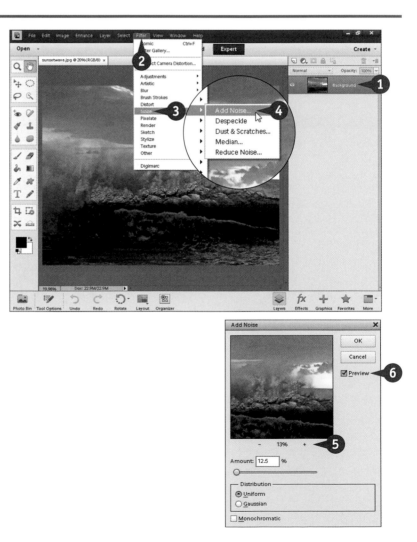

The Add Noise dialog box opens, displaying a preview of the filter's effect.

⑤ Click the minus sign (⊟) or plus sign (⊞) to zoom out or in.

⑥ Click **Preview** to preview the effect in the main window (☐ changes to ☑).

288

⑦ Click and drag the **Amount** slider () to change the noise or type the amount of noise you want to apply to an image.

In this example, the Amount value is increased.

⑧ Click an option to determine how you want the noise distributed (○ changes to ⊙).

The Uniform option spreads the noise more evenly than Gaussian.

⑨ Click **OK**.

Photoshop Elements applies the filter.

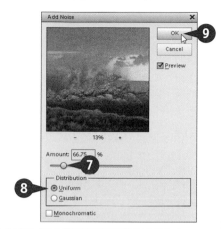

TIPS

What does the Monochromatic setting in the Add Noise dialog box do?

If you click **Monochromatic** (☐ changes to ☑), Photoshop Elements adds noise by lightening or darkening pixels in your image. Pixel hues stay the same. At high settings with the Monochromatic option on, the filter produces a television-static effect.

Can I apply filters from a Photoshop Elements Effects panel?

Yes. If you click **Effects** to open the Effects panel and click **Filters**, you can access most of the filters also found under the Filter menu. You can choose different filter categories from the panel menu.

Pixelate an Image

The Pixelate filters divide areas of your image into solid-colored dots or shapes, generating an abstract effect. The Crystallize filter, one example of a Pixelate filter, re-creates your image by using colored polygons. You control the size of the polygons with a setting in the Pixelate dialog box.

You can apply the Pointillize filter to turn your image into a pointillist painting, with colors throughout the image turned into dots. The background color determines the color of the canvas on which the dots are placed. To apply a filter to just part of your image, select a portion by using a selection tool. For more on selection tools, see Chapter 6.

Pixelate an Image

① In the Editor, select the layer to which you want to apply the filter.

Note: For more on opening the Editor, see Chapter 1. For more about layers, see Chapter 8.

In this example, the image has a single Background layer.

② Click **Filter**.

③ Click **Pixelate**.

④ Click **Crystallize**.

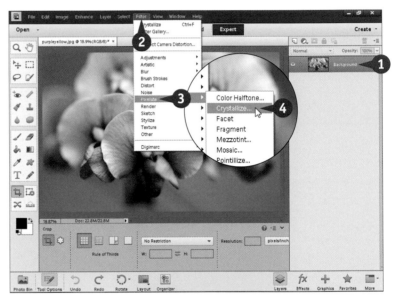

The Crystallize dialog box opens, displaying a preview of the filter's effect.

⑤ Click the minus sign (🔲) or plus sign (🔲) to zoom out or in.

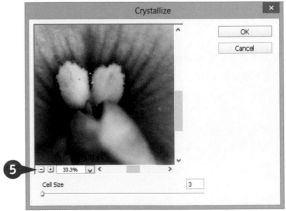

6 Click and drag the **Cell Size** slider () to adjust the size of the shapes.

The size can range from 3 to 300. In this example, the Cell Size has been increased.

7 Click **OK**.

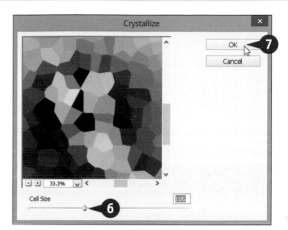

Photoshop Elements applies the filter.

TIP

What does the Mosaic filter do?
The Mosaic filter converts your image to a set of solid-color squares. Click **Filter**, **Pixelate**, and then **Mosaic** to open the Mosaic dialog box. You can click and drag the slider (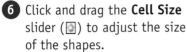) to specify the mosaic square size (**A**). Click **OK** to apply the filter. By making a selection before applying, the Mosaic filter can be used to obscure an object in a scene.

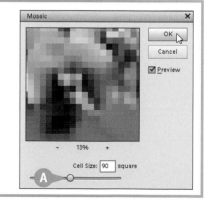

Emboss an Image

You can achieve the effect of a three-dimensional shape pressed into paper with the Emboss filter. You may find this filter useful for generating textured backgrounds. With settings for the filter, you can control the strength of the embossing by determining the height of the embossing and the types of edges it recognizes.

The Emboss filter is located under the Stylize submenu, which holds a grab bag of filters that can affect your image in a variety of ways, some quite dramatically.

To apply the filter to just part of your image, select that portion by using a selection tool. For more on selection tools, see Chapter 6.

Emboss an Image

1 In the Editor, select the layer to which you want to apply the filter.

Note: For more on opening the Editor, see Chapter 1. For more about layers, see Chapter 8.

In this example, the image has a single Background layer.

2 Click **Filter**.

3 Click **Stylize**.

4 Click **Emboss**.

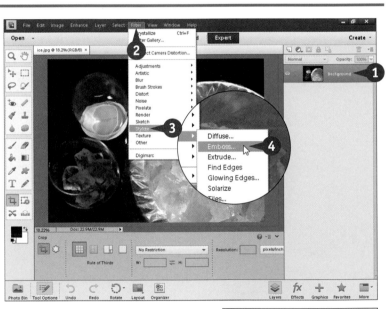

The Emboss dialog box displays a preview of the filter's effect.

5 Click the minus sign (▭) or the plus sign (⊞) to zoom out or in.

6 Type an angle value to specify the direction of the shadow.

7 Click and drag the **Height** slider (◉) to set the strength of the embossing or type a number for the height.

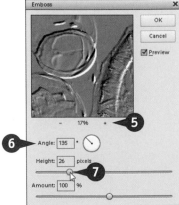

8 Click and drag the **Amount** slider (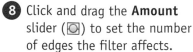) to set the number of edges the filter affects.

9 Click **OK**.

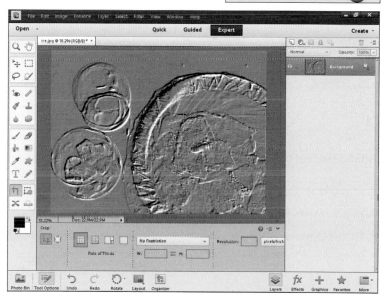

Photoshop Elements applies the filter.

Do I have another way to create an embossed effect in an image?
Yes. You can use the Bas Relief filter to get a similar effect. Follow steps **1** to **4** in this section, clicking **Sketch** in step **3** and **Bas Relief** in step **4**. In the Filter Gallery dialog box that appears, you can click and drag sliders (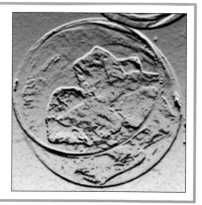) to control the detail and smoothness of the effect. Click **OK** to apply the filter.

Apply Multiple Filters

You can apply more than one filter to an image by using the Filter Gallery interface. The interface enables you to preview a variety of filter effects and apply them in combination. For example, you can apply the Diffuse Glow filter to add bright lighting across an image and also the Find Edges filter to apply contrast to edges of objects.

Many filters open the Filter Gallery interface when you apply them, including the Dry Brush filter, which is covered earlier in this chapter. Not all the effects listed under the Filter menu appear in the Filter Gallery. Ones not shown can be accessed in the Filter menu.

Apply Multiple Filters

① In the Editor, select the layer to which you want to apply the filters.

Note: For more on opening the Editor, see Chapter 1. For more about layers, see Chapter 8.

In this example, the image has a single Background layer.

② Click **Filter**.

③ Click **Filter Gallery**.

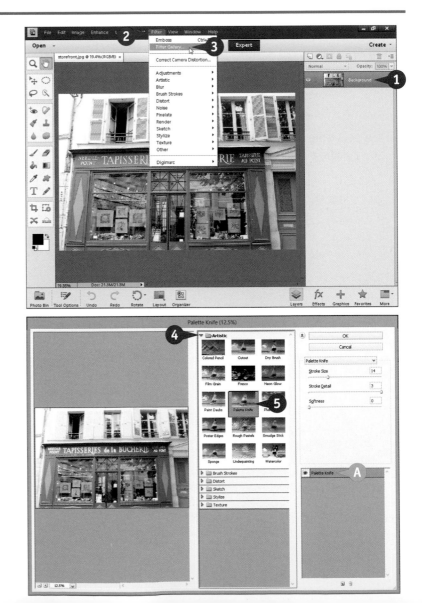

The Filter Gallery dialog box opens.

The left pane displays a preview of the filtered image.

④ Click an arrow (▷) to display filters from a category (▷ changes to ▽).

⑤ Click a thumbnail to apply a filter.

Ⓐ The filter appears in the filter list.

6 Click the **New Effect Layer** button ().

B The new effect appears in the filter list.

You can click and drag effects in the list to change their order and change the look of your image.

Note: For more on rearranging layers, see Chapter 8.

7 Click a different arrow (▶) to display filters from another category (▶ changes to ▼).

8 Click a thumbnail to apply another filter.

You can repeat steps **6** to **8** to apply additional filters.

9 Click **OK**.

Photoshop Elements applies the filters.

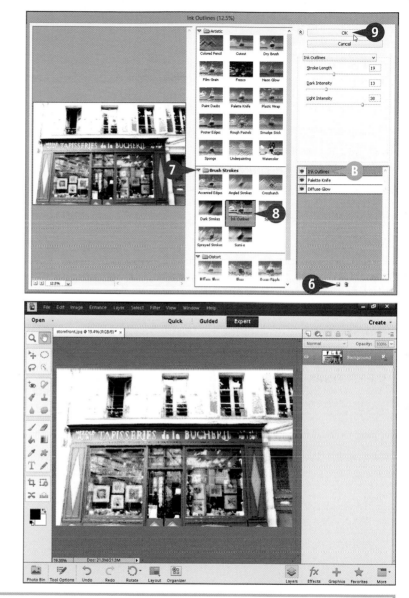

TIP

How can I apply filters to text?

Select a type layer, and select a filter under the Filter menu. A dialog box opens, asking if you want to simplify the type layer. Click **OK**. Photoshop Elements converts the type layer to a regular layer. Apply the filter as you would to any other layer. Keep in mind that after a type layer is converted to a regular layer, the type cannot be edited. Here, the Sponge and Graphic Pen filters are applied to orange text.

CHAPTER 14

Adding Text Elements

Do you want to add letters and words to your photos and illustrations? Photoshop Elements enables you to add text to your images and precisely control the appearance and layout of text. You can also stylize your text by using effects and other tools in Photoshop Elements.

Add Text. 298

Change the Formatting of Text 300

Change the Color of Text 302

Create Warped Text. 304

Add an Effect to Text. 306

Add Text along a Selection 308

Add Text in a Shape 310

Add Text

Adding text enables you to label elements in your image or use letters and words in artistic ways. You insert text in Photoshop Elements using the Type tool. In the Tool Options panel, you can select horizontal and vertical versions of the tool as well as a version that enables you to place text along a selection.

Text that you add appears in its own layer. You can manipulate text layers in your image to move or stylize text. Text in Photoshop Elements is vector-based, so you can resize and transform it without a loss in quality.

Add Text

1 In the Editor, click **Expert**.

Note: For more on opening the Editor, see Chapter 1.

2 Click the **Horizontal Type** tool (⊤).

3 Click in the image where you want the text to begin.

You can also click and drag to define a bounding box to contain your text.

4 Select a font, style, and size for your text from these menus.

5 Click the ⏷ and select a color for your text.

By default, the foreground color is selected.

6 Type your text.

To create a line break, press Enter.

7 When you finish typing your text, click ☑ or press Ctrl+ Enter (⌘+Enter on a Mac).

Ⓐ You can click ⊘ or press Esc to cancel.

Ⓑ Photoshop Elements places the text in its own layer.

Note: To reposition text, click the layer of text in the Layers panel, click the **Move** tool (⊕), and then click and drag the text. For more on moving a layer, see Chapter 8.

How do I add vertical text to my image?

With the **Horizontal Type** tool (T) selected, click the **Vertical Type** tool (I͟T) in the Tool Options panel. Your text appears with a vertical orientation, and lines are added from right to left.

You can change the orientation of existing text in your image by selecting a text layer and then clicking the **Change the Text Orientation** button (T͟I). This converts horizontal text to vertical text and vice versa. Using vertical text can be useful when applying some Asian language characters or when you want to add letters to a vertical sign.

Change the Formatting of Text

You can change the font, style, size, and other characteristics of your text. This can help emphasize or de-emphasize your text.

Photoshop Elements has access to all the fonts on your computer's operating system. A number of fonts are added when you install Photoshop Elements. Available styles for text include italic, bold, and other options that can vary depending on the font being used. The default size measurement is the point, which is 1/72 of an inch. You can enter other units of measurement in the size field in the Tool Options panel, such as **5 cm**, and Photoshop Elements converts the value to points.

Change the Formatting of Text

1 In the Editor, click **Expert**.

Note: For more on opening the Editor, see Chapter 1.

2 Click the **Horizontal Type** tool (![T]).

3 Click the text layer that you want to edit.

Note: For more on how to open the Layers panel, see Chapter 1.

4 Click and drag to select some text from the selected layer.

A You can double-click the layer thumbnail to select all the text.

5 Click the ▼ and choose a font.

6 Click the ▼ and choose the text's style.

7 Click the ▼ and choose the text's size.

8 Click **Anti-aliasing** (□ changes to ☑) to control the text's anti-aliasing.

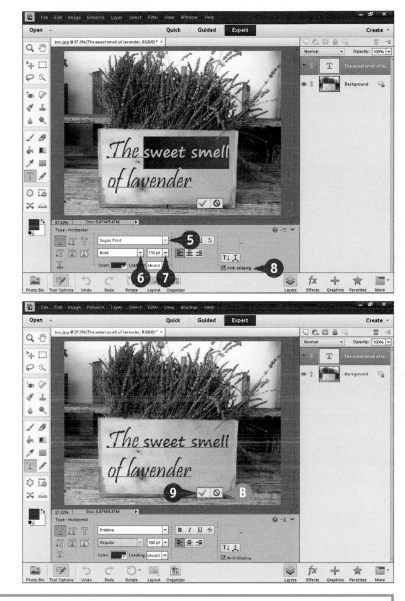

9 When you finish formatting your text, click ☑ or press **Ctrl**+**Enter** (**⌘**+**Enter** on a Mac).

Ⓑ You can click ◎ or press **Esc** to cancel.

Photoshop Elements applies the formatting to your text.

TIPS

What is anti-aliasing?
Anti-aliasing is the process of adding semitransparent pixels to curved edges in digital images to make the edges appear smoother. You can apply anti-aliasing to text to improve its appearance. Text that you do not anti-alias can sometimes look jagged. You can control the presence and style of your text's anti-aliasing in the Tool Options panel. At very small text sizes, anti-aliasing can be counterproductive and cause blurring.

How do I change the alignment of my text?
When creating your text, click one of the three alignment buttons in the Tool Options panel: Left Align Text (▤), Center Text (▤), or Right Align Text (▤). You may find these options useful when you create multiline passages of text.

Change the Color of Text

You can change the color of your text to make it blend or contrast with the rest of the image. You can change the color of all or just part of your text. By default, Photoshop Elements colors your text the current foreground color. For more about setting the foreground color, see Chapter 12.

You can also change the color of your text by changing the opacity setting of a text layer. Lowering the opacity of a layer makes it more transparent, and therefore makes text in that layer lighter in color and see-through. For more about changing opacity of layers, see Chapter 8.

Change the Color of Text

1 In the Editor, click **Expert**.

Note: For more on opening the Editor, see Chapter 1.

2 Click the **Horizontal Type** tool (T).

3 Click the text layer that you want to edit.

Note: For more on how to open the Layers panel, see Chapter 1.

4 Click and drag to highlight some text.

A You can double-click the layer thumbnail to highlight all the text.

5 Click the ⮟ and choose a color.

When you position your mouse pointer (⮜) over a color, it changes to an eyedropper (✐).

Ⓑ You can click the **Color Picker** button (◼) for more color options.

Ⓒ You can click the ⮟ to change the colors available in the menu.

6 Press Enter to close the Color Swatches menu.

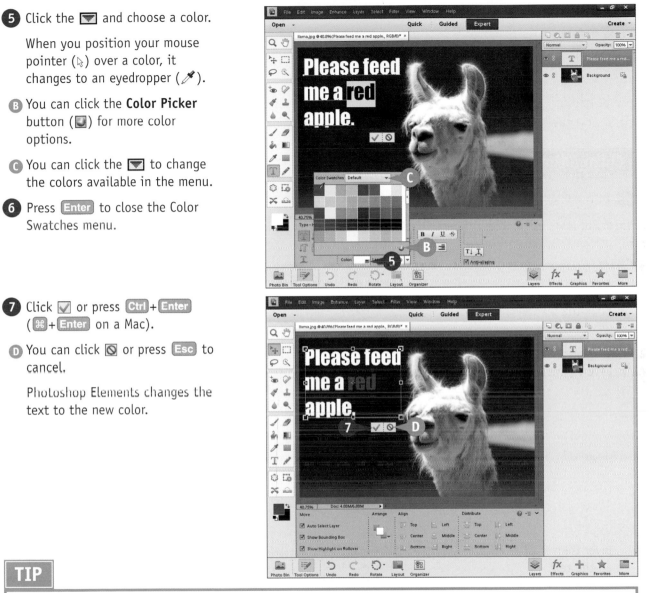

7 Click ✓ or press Ctrl+Enter (⌘+Enter on a Mac).

Ⓓ You can click ◯ or press Esc to cancel.

Photoshop Elements changes the text to the new color.

TIP

How do I change type color by using the Color Swatches panel?
Click **Window** and then **Color Swatches** to open the panel. Click the text layer in the Layers panel. Click and drag in the image window to highlight the text you want to recolor (Ⓐ). Click a color in the Color Swatches panel (Ⓑ). The text changes color.

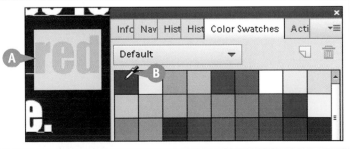

Create Warped Text

Yᵒou can easily bend and distort layers of text by using the Warped Text feature in Photoshop Elements. This can help you stylize your text to match the theme of your image. For example, text in a sky can be distorted to appear windblown.

Style options include Arc and Arch, which curve text in one direction across the image, and Flag and Wave, which curve the text back and forth across the image. Which direction the warping occurs depends on whether the warp is set to horizontal or vertical.

Create Warped Text

1 In the Editor, click **Expert**.

Note: For more on opening the Editor, see Chapter 1.

2 Click the **Horizontal Type** tool (T).

3 Click the text layer that you want to warp.

Note: For more on how to open the Layers panel, see Chapter 1.

4 Click the **Create Warped Text** button (T).

The Warp Text dialog box opens.

5 Click the **Style** ▼ and choose a warp style.

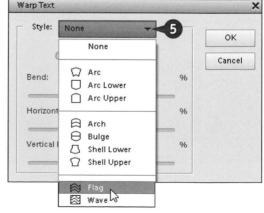

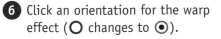

6 Click an orientation for the warp effect (○ changes to ◉).

7 Adjust the Bend and Distortion values by clicking and dragging the sliders (▢).

You can also type Bend and Distortion values.

The Bend and Distortion values determine how Photoshop Elements applies the warp.

For all settings, a value of 0% means Photoshop Elements does not apply that aspect of a warp.

8 Click **OK**.

Photoshop Elements warps the text.

You can still edit the format, color, and other characteristics of the type when you apply a warp. See the other sections in this chapter for more.

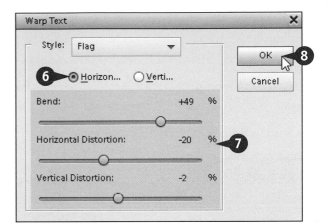

TIP

How do I unwarp text?

1 Follow steps **1** to **4** in this section.

2 In the Warp Text dialog box, click the **Style** ▼ and choose **None**.

3 Click **OK**.

Your text unwarps.

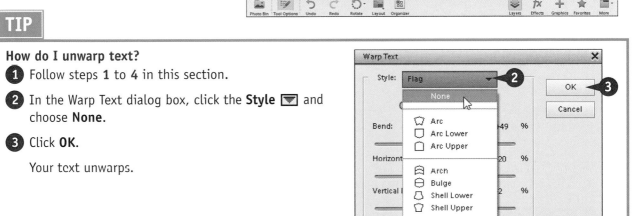

Add an Effect to Text

You can add a variety of special effects to text layers in your image. You can make the characters in the layer stand out by adding an outline that contrasts with the background. You can also give text a 3-D look with beveling effects or a drop shadow.

After applying an effect, you can open the Style Settings dialog box to fine-tune the effect's characteristics. For more ways to make layers look fancy, see Chapter 15.

Add an Effect to Text

1 In the Editor, click **Expert**.

2 In the Layers panel, click the text layer to which you want to apply the effect.

Note: For more on opening the Editor or panels, see Chapter 1.

3 Click **Effects**.

The Effects panel opens.

4 Click **Styles**.

5 Click the and then choose a category.

In this example, Strokes is chosen. You could also choose a different category such as Bevels or Drop Shadows.

Photoshop Elements displays the styles for that category.

6 Double-click a style.

Photoshop Elements applies the effect to the text.

7 Click **Layers**.

The Layers panel appears.

8 Double-click the **Style** icon () in the affected layer.

The Style Settings dialog box opens.

9 Click and drag the sliders () to adjust the effect characteristics.

10 For the stroke effects, click the color box to select a different stroke color.

11 Click **OK**.

Photoshop Elements applies the style settings.

TIP

How do I add a second effect, such as beveling, to the layer that I have outlined?

1 Double-click the **Style** icon () for the layer to open the Style Settings dialog box.

2 Click **Bevel** (☐ changes to ☑).

3 Click and drag the slider () to adjust the size of the beveling.

4 Click **OK**.

Photoshop Elements applies beveling to the layer.

307

Add Text along a Selection

With the Text on Selection tool, you can select an object in your image and then add text along the edge of the object. This enables you to place text along curved or bumpy edges, such as the circumference of a wheel or the ridge of a mountain. The angles of the letters follow the curves of the selection.

The text you add to a selection appears in its own text layer. You can format the text just as you can regular text in Photoshop Elements.

Add Text along a Selection

1 In the Editor, click **Expert**.

Note: For more on opening the Editor, see Chapter 1.

2 Click the **Horizontal Type** tool (T).

3 In the tool settings, click the **Text on Selection** tool (T).

4 Click and drag to select an object in your image.

Note: You select the object just as you do with the Quick Selection tool. See Chapter 6 for more about the Quick Selection tool.

5 Click ✓ or press Enter to commit the selection.

A You can click ⊘ or press Esc to deselect the selection and start over.

Photoshop Elements converts the selection to a path, which appears as a solid line.

6 Click on the path with the cursor.

A blinking text-entry cursor (⌁) appears on the path.

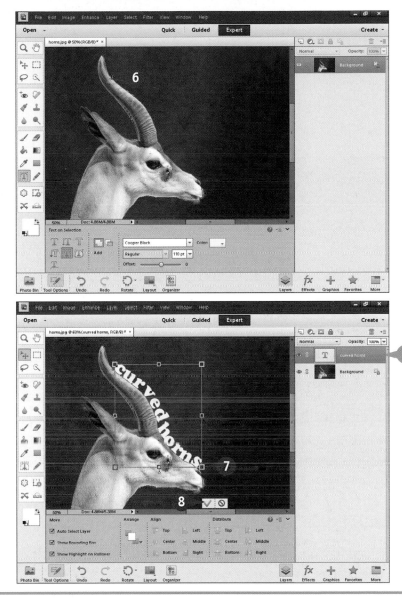

7 Type your text.

The text appears along the path.

8 Click ✓ or press **Ctrl**+**Enter** (**⌘**+**Enter** on a Mac).

Ⓑ The text appears as a layer in the Layers panel.

For details about formatting the text in a layer, see the other sections in this chapter.

TIP

How do I add text along a shape?
Click the **Horizontal Type** tool (🔤). In the tool settings, click the **Text on a Shape** tool (🔤). Click a shape. Click and drag to draw the shape (**Ⓐ**). Click on the edge of the shape and type your text (**Ⓑ**). Photoshop Elements offers several different shapes for drawing on, including rectangular, elliptical, and speech-balloon shapes.

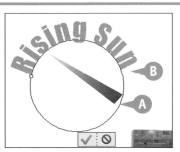

Add Text in a Shape

You can add text within the confines of a shape in Photoshop Elements. You can color, style, and align your shape text just as you can regular text. As you add the text, it wraps based on the geometry of the shape.

Adding text in a shape can make the text more interesting and readable than placing the text by itself. You can use the variety of shapes that come installed with Photoshop Elements, including speech bubbles and banners.

Add Text in a Shape

1 In the Editor, click **Expert**.

Note: For more on opening the Editor, see Chapter 1.

2 Click the **Custom Shape** tool (■).

3 Click the ▼ and select a custom shape to draw.

Ⓐ You can click the ▼ and select different categories to access more shapes.

4 Press Enter to close the Shapes menu.

5 Click the ▼ to select a shape color.

6 Click and drag to draw the shape.

Ⓑ A shape layer appears in the Layers panel.

Note: See Chapter 12 for more about drawing shapes.

7 Click the **Horizontal Type** tool ().

8 Move the tool over the shape (🔲 changes to ①).

9 Click inside the shape.

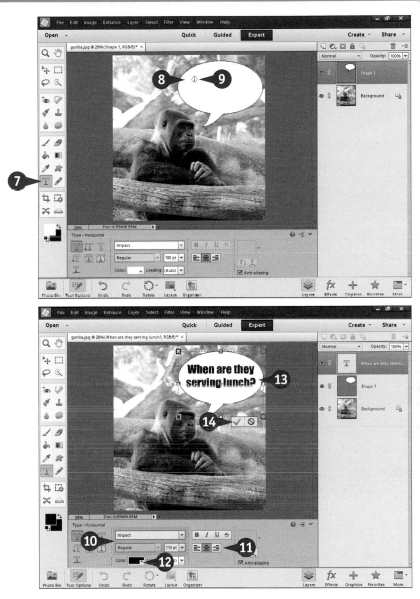

10 Click here to select the font, size, and style for the text.

11 Click a text alignment (▤, ▤, or ▤).

12 Click the ▼ to select a text color.

13 Type your text.

14 When you are done, click ✓ or press **Ctrl**+**Enter** (**⌘**+**Enter** on a Mac).

TIPS

How can I create a sign with vertical lettering?
Draw a rectangular shape in your image and then add text to it using the Vertical Type tool (🔲). You can access the tool in the Tool Options panel when a text tool is selected.

Can I confine my text using a shape but hide the shape?
Yes. Complete steps in this section to add your text inside a shape and then click 👁 in the Layers panel to hide the shape layer. Your text floats above your image, still restricted by the shape.

CHAPTER 15

Applying Styles and Effects

You can apply special effects to your images by using the built-in styles and effects in Photoshop Elements. The effects enable you to add shadows, glows, and a 3-D appearance to your art. You can also add special effects to your layers with layer styles.

Add a Drop Shadow to a Layer 314

Add a Fancy Background 316

Add an Outer Glow to a Layer 318

Add a Fancy Covering to a Layer 320

Add a Watermark 322

Apply a Photomerge Style 324

Apply an Effect with an Action 326

Add to Favorites 328

Add a Drop Shadow to a Layer

Y ou can add a drop shadow to a layer to give the layers in your photo a 3-D look. Style settings enable you to control the placement of the shadow. You can decrease the opacity to make the shadowing more subtle, increase the offset distance to make the photo appear farther off the canvas, or change the shadow color to something other than black.

Photoshop Elements offers a number of predefined drop-shadow styles in the Effects panel that apply shadowing with hard and soft edges and that are different distances from the layer.

Add a Drop Shadow to a Layer

1 In the Editor, click **Expert**.

2 Click **Layers** to open the Layers panel.

Note: For more on opening the Editor or panels, see Chapter 1.

3 Select the layer to which you want to add a drop shadow.

4 Click **Effects**.

5 Click **Styles**.

6 Click the ▼ and then choose **Drop Shadows** from the menu.

The Drop Shadow styles appear.

7 Double-click a drop shadow style.

Ⓐ Photoshop Elements applies the drop shadow to the layer.

8 Click 🌑 to open the Style Settings dialog box.

314

The Style Settings dialog box opens.

9 Click and drag the **Lighting Angle** dial to specify the direction of the shadowing.

10 Click and drag the **Distance** slider () to increase or decrease the distance of the shadow from your layer.

11 Make other adjustments to refine the effect.

12 Click **OK**.

Photoshop Elements applies the style settings.

Note: To add a 3-D look to text in your image, you can add a drop shadow to a type layer. For more about type, see Chapter 14.

TIP

How can I add color shading to a layer?
You can use the Photographic Effects layer styles.

1 Repeat steps **1** to **6** in this section, selecting **Photographic Effects** from the menu.

2 Double-click an effect to apply the shading.

Photoshop Elements offers several blue and green tones as well as an orange gradient.

Add a Fancy Background

You can add a fancy background to your image with one of several texture effects in Photoshop Elements. The backgrounds that Photoshop Elements provides include rainbow designs, molten textures, and a brick pattern. For a more subtle use of the effect, you can duplicate a layer, apply the background to the top copy, and then reduce the opacity of that layer. For more about duplicating layers and opacity, see Chapter 8.

You can scale the background effect applied to your image to make the pattern appear larger or smaller behind the rest of the image content. See the tip for details.

Add a Fancy Background

1. In the Editor, click **Expert**.

2. Click **Layers** to open the Layers panel.

Note: For more on opening the Editor or panels, see Chapter 1.

3. Select the layer to which you want to apply the fancy background.

4. Click **Effects**.

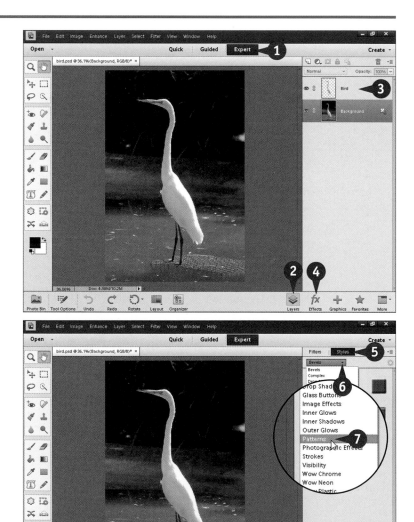

5. Click **Styles**.

6. Click the .

7. Click **Patterns**.

The Pattern styles appear.

8 Double-click a style.

If you selected the Background layer in step **3**, a dialog box opens, asking if you want to make your background a normal layer.

9 Click **OK.**

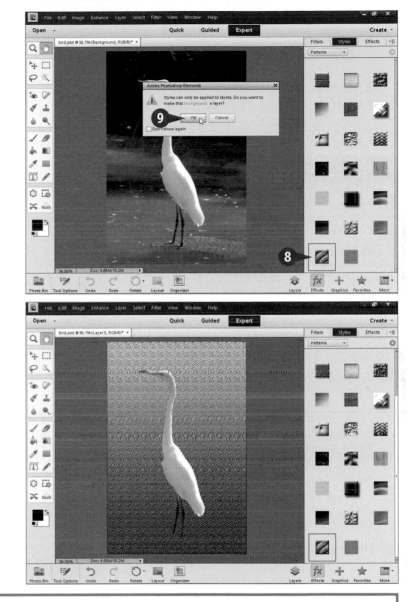

Photoshop Elements applies a pattern to the selected layer, creating a background behind the other layers.

TIPS

How can I reduce the strength of an effect that I just applied?

In cases where the effect is applied to a duplicate layer, you can reduce the opacity of the new layer to lessen the effect. Reducing the opacity to less than 100% allows the original content underneath to show through.

How can I change the size of a layer's background pattern?

To adjust the size of your pattern, click the pattern layer in the Layers panel. Then click **Layer**, click **Layer Style**, and then click **Scale Effects**. You can adjust the Scale setting in the Scale Layer Effects dialog box to resize the pattern. For example, you can increase the Scale setting to make the bricks in a brick pattern larger.

Add an Outer Glow to a Layer

The Outer Glows styles add fancy coloring to the outside edges of a layer's content, which can help highlight the layer. The effect can give an object in your image a ghostly or electric look and feel, depending on the color and size of the outer glow.

If you are not pleased initially with a style after applying it, you can open the Style Settings dialog box for the style and adjust the color, size, and opacity of the outer glow. Solid color added to the edge of a layer is called a *stroke*. See the section "Add an Effect to Text" in Chapter 14 for an example of this.

Add an Outer Glow to a Layer

1 In the Editor, click **Expert**.

2 Click **Layers** to open the Layers panel.

Note: For more on opening the Editor or panels, see Chapter 1.

3 Click the layer to which you want to apply the outer glow.

4 Click **Effects**.

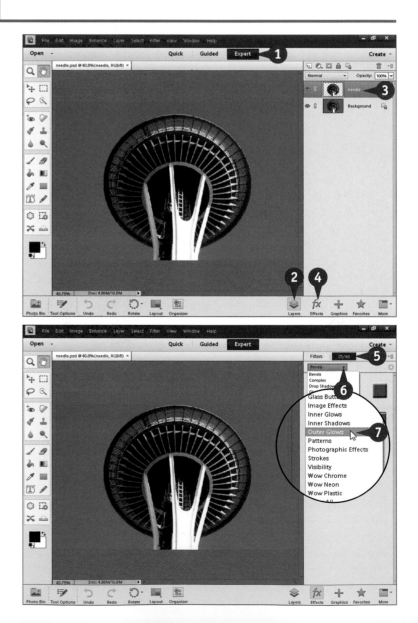

5 Click **Styles**.

6 Click the ▼.

7 Click **Outer Glows**.

Photoshop Elements displays the Outer Glows styles.

⑧ Double-click an outer glow style.

Photoshop Elements applies the outer glow to the layer.

⑨ Click 🔅 to open the Style Settings dialog box.

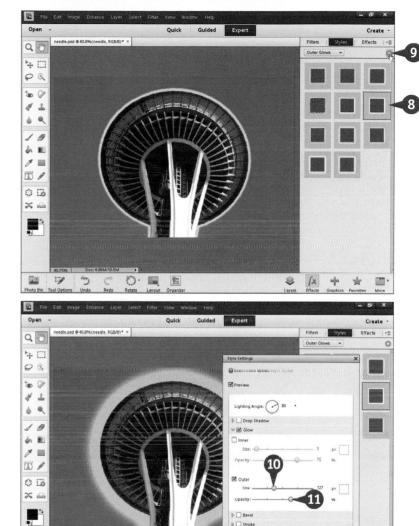

The Style Settings dialog box opens.

⑩ Click and drag the **Size** slider (🔲) to increase or decrease the outer glow size.

You can also type a size.

⑪ Make other adjustments to refine the effect.

⑫ Click **OK**.

Photoshop Elements applies the style settings.

TIP

How do I add a glow to the inside edge of layer objects?
Follow steps **1** to **6** in this section and then select **Inner Glows** from the Effects panel menu. Double-click an inner glow style to add it to your image. You can select glows of different sizes and colors, including a fiery orange-and-red glow.

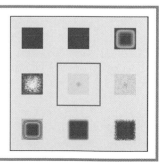

Add a Fancy Covering to a Layer

You can apply any of a variety of layer effects that can make a layer appear covered in colorful metal or glass. The glass effects are located in the Glass Buttons category in the layer styles. Photoshop Elements offers 14 different glass colors to choose from. A metal effect called Diamond Plate is located under the Complex category and gives your layer a look of textured chrome. You can find other metallic effects under the Patterns category.

In some cases, you can apply multiple effects to a layer simultaneously. For example, after adding a glass covering, you can further customize the layer with a drop shadow.

Add a Fancy Covering to a Layer

Cover with Glass

1. In the Editor, click **Expert**.

2. Click **Layers** to open the Layers panel.

Note: For more on opening the Editor or panels, see Chapter 1.

3. Click the layer that you want to cover.

4. Click **Effects**.

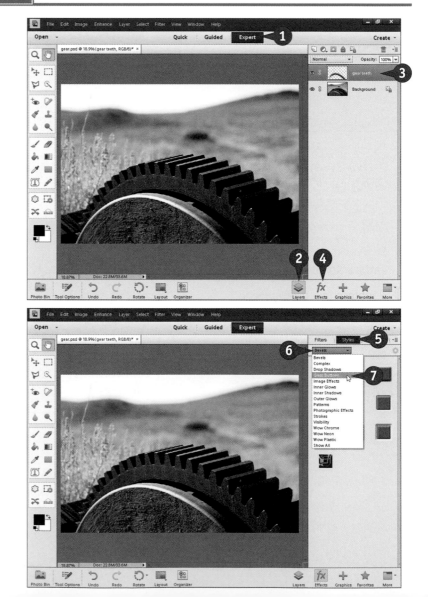

5. Click **Styles**.

6. Click the .

7. Click **Glass Buttons**.

Photoshop Elements displays a number of glass styles.

8 Double-click a style.

Photoshop Elements applies the style to the layer.

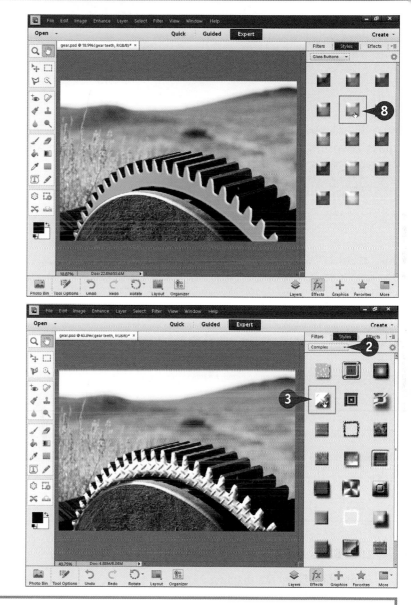

Cover with Metal

1 Repeat steps **1** to **5** in the previous subsection, "Cover with Glass."

2 Click the  and then choose **Complex** from the menu.

Photoshop Elements displays various styles.

3 Double-click the **Diamond Plate** style.

Photoshop Elements applies the style to the layer.

How do I remove a style from a layer?

1 In the Layers panel, click a layer that has a style applied, indicated by a Style icon ().

2 Click **Layer**.

3 Click **Layer Style**.

4 Click **Clear Layer Style**.

Note: You can also right-click the layer and then click **Clear Layer Style**.

Photoshop Elements removes the style from the layer.

Add a Watermark

Photoshop Elements can automatically add watermarks to a collection of photos. Watermarks are semiopaque words or designs overlaid on images to signify ownership and discourage illegal use. Before you can begin, you need to create a source folder and a destination folder for your images. To work with folders, see your operating system's documentation.

Photoshop Elements enables you to choose custom text — for example, your name or company name — to use as your watermark and also specify a font and color. You can decrease the opacity of the watermark text to let the image content below the text show through.

Add a Watermark

1. Place the images to which you want to add watermarks into a source folder.

2. Create an empty destination folder in which to save your watermarked files.

3. In the Editor, click **File**.

Note: For more on opening the Editor, see Chapter 1.

4. Click **Process Multiple Files**.

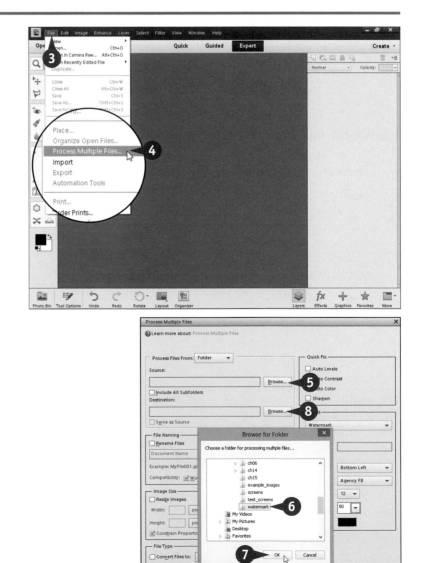

The Process Multiple Files dialog box opens.

5. Click **Browse** next to the Source box.

The Browse for Folder dialog box opens.

6. Click the source folder containing your images.

7. Click **OK**.

8. Click **Browse** next to the Destination box and then repeat steps **6** and **7** for the destination folder.

322

9 Click the ▼ and then choose **Watermark**.

10 Type your watermark text.

11 Select the position, font, and size for the text.

12 Click the ▼ and specify an opacity from 1 to 100. The lower the opacity, the more transparent the watermark will be.

You can also type an opacity value.

13 Click the color box and then choose a watermark color.

You may want to select a color that contrasts with the colors in your photo.

14 Click **OK**.

A Photoshop Elements adds watermarks to the photos in the source folder and saves them in the destination folder.

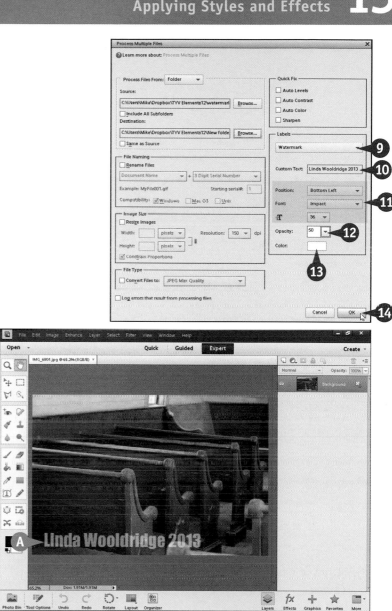

TIPS

How can I automatically add captions to my photos?
In the Process Multiple Files dialog box, you can select **Caption** under the top menu in the Labels panel. With Caption chosen, Photoshop Elements applies text associated with the photo to the top of the photo. Similar to applying a watermark, you can specify the positioning, font, size, opacity, and color of the caption.

What kinds of captions can I add to my photos?
You can add the filename, date modified, and description as a caption. You can add this information by itself — for example, just the filename — or in combination by clicking one or more check boxes (☐ changes to ☑).

Apply a Photomerge Style

Photoshop Elements can apply the color and tone styles from one image to another with the Photomerge Style Match tool. The tool is useful if you like the ambience of the scene in one photo and want to duplicate the look and feel in a very different photo.

After you apply the style match, you can selectively remove it from areas of your image with the Style Eraser tool or add it back with the Style Painter tool. These tools enable you to apply the matched colors and tones to specific objects in your image.

Apply a Photomerge Style

1 Open the image to which you want to apply the style.

2 Click **Enhance**.

3 Click **Photomerge**.

4 Click **Photomerge Style Match**.

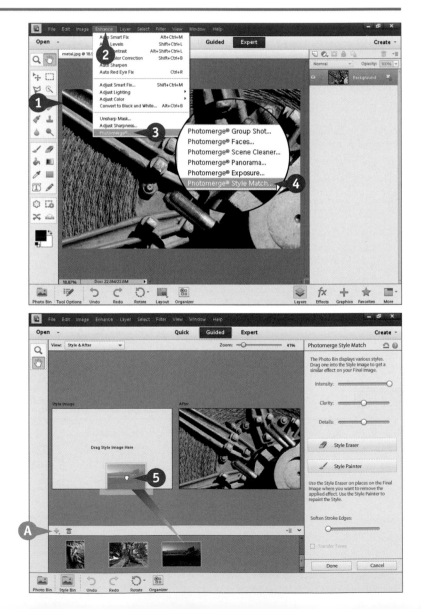

Photoshop Elements displays a set of images in the Style Bin.

Ⓐ You can click the **Add Styles Images** button (🖼) to add images to the Style Bin.

5 Click and drag an image to the Sample window.

B Photoshop Elements merges the color and tones from the sample image.

6 Click and drag the sliders (◻) to adjust how the style is merged.

C You can click **Reset** (◻) to undo the merge and select a different sample image.

7 Click **Done**.

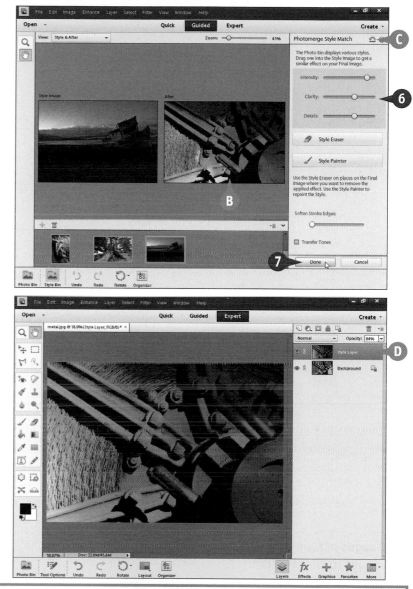

Photoshop Elements applies the final style settings to the image.

D The merged style is placed in its own layer in the Layers panel. You can adjust the opacity of the layer to lessen the effect of the merge.

Note: See Chapter 8 for more about changing layer opacity.

TIP

How can I remove a merged style from parts of an image?

1 Complete steps **1** to **5** to merge the styles.

2 Click the **Style Eraser** tool.

3 Click and drag to remove the style.

A You can use the **Style Painter** tool to reapply erased styles.

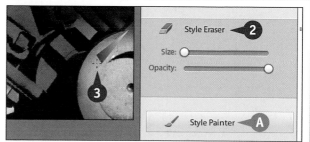

Apply an Effect with an Action

You can apply complex effects to an image by playing actions from the Actions panel. An *action* is an automated procedure made up of several Photoshop Elements commands. Using actions can save time because you can execute multiple commands with a single click.

Photoshop Elements comes with a variety of actions preloaded and grouped into sets. Default sets include those for adding borders, cropping, and applying special effects.

Apply an Effect with an Action

1 Open the image to which you want to apply the action.

2 In the Editor, click **Expert**.

Note: For more on opening the Editor, see Chapter 1.

3 Click **Window**.

4 Click **Actions**.

The Actions panel opens.

A You can click the ▶ (▶ changes to ▼) to open different action sets.

5 Click to select an action.

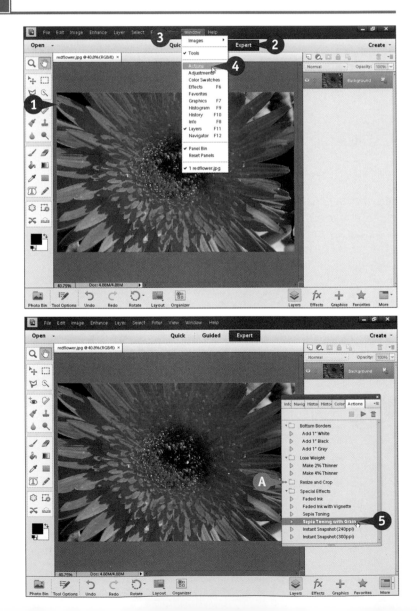

6 Click the **Play** button ().

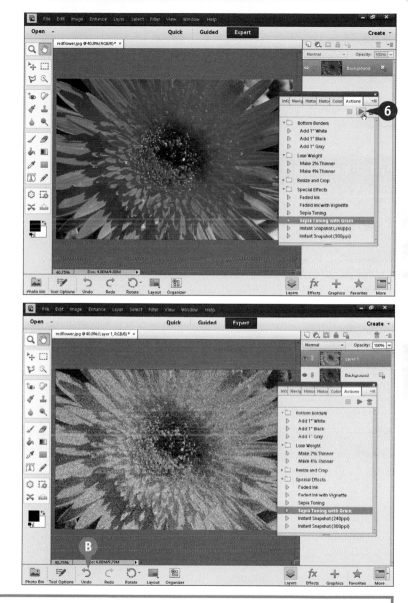

Photoshop Elements executes the steps for that action on the image.

B You can click **Undo** to revert the action steps one at a time.

TIP

How can I view the steps that comprise an action?
Follow these steps:

1 For the action, click the ▷ (▷ changes to ▽).

A Photoshop Elements lists the steps for that action.

If you select a specific step and click the **Play** button (▶), Photoshop Elements plays all the steps for that action from the selected step forward.

Add to Favorites

You can save your favorite, most-used effects and graphics in a separate Favorites panel. This can save you time because hundreds of effects and graphics are available in their respective panels, most of which you may never use.

Items in the Favorites panel are signified by the same thumbnail image that you see in the other panels. You access the panel via Favorites at the bottom of the workspace.

Add to Favorites

Add an Effect

1 In the Editor, click **Expert**.

2 Click **Effects** to open the Effects panel.

Note: For more on opening the Editor or panels, see Chapter 1.

3 Right-click an effect.

4 Click **Add to Favorites**.

The effect is added to the Favorites panel.

Add a Graphic

1 Click **Graphics** to open the Graphics panel.

2 Right-click a graphic.

3 Click **Add to Favorites**.

The graphic is added to the Favorites panel.

Apply a Favorite

 Click **Favorites** to open the Favorites panel.

The favorites appear.

2 Double-click an item.

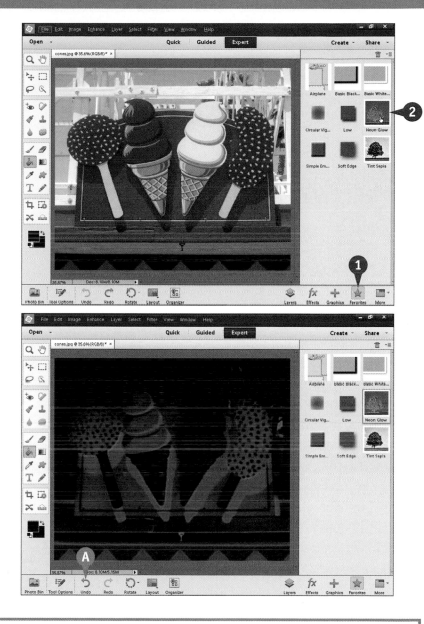

Photoshop Elements applies the favorite to your image.

Ⓐ You can click **Undo** to undo the change.

How can I remove an item from the Favorites panel?

To remove a favorite, right-click the item and then click **Remove from Favorites** from the menu that appears. The item is deleted from the Favorites panel but not from its original place in the Effects or Graphics panel.

How do I change the thumbnail sizes shown in the panels?

You can click the panel menu (▼≡) in the Effects, Graphics, and Favorites panels and then choose a thumbnail view. In the Layers panel, you can click the panel menu (▼≡) and then click **Panel Options**.

CHAPTER 16

Saving and Sharing Your Work

You can save your photos in different file formats, print them, store them on CD or DVD, or share them online via Facebook. You can also create slide shows and photo books.

Save a Photo for the Web. 332

Convert File Types 334

E-Mail Images with Photo Mail 336

Print Photos 340

Create a Slide Show 342

Create a Photo Book 346

Share Photos on Facebook 350

Share a Photo on Twitter 354

Export Photos 356

Export Photos to Adobe Revel. 358

Back Up Photos 360

Save a Photo for the Web

You can save an image for the web in one of a number of formats. These formats shrink the file size of images so that they can be efficiently transmitted online. When saving for the web in Photoshop Elements, you can also resize the dimensions of your image.

The JPEG — Joint Photographic Experts Group — format is the preferred web format for saving photographic images. Many digital cameras also use it for saving their photos. If you are saving a nonphotographic image, such as a line drawing or illustration with lots of solid color, consider saving your image in the GIF or PNG-8 format. See the tips for more details.

Save a Photo for the Web

1 In the Editor, click **File**.

Note: For more on opening the Editor, see Chapter 1.

2 Click **Save for Web**.

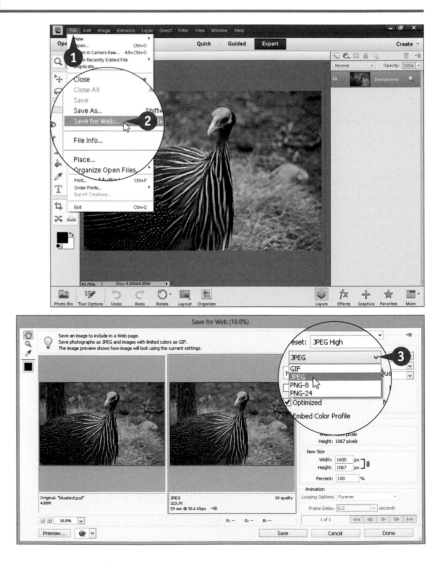

The Save For Web dialog box opens.

Your original image appears in the top or left pane and a preview of the version to be saved is in the bottom or right pane.

3 Click the ⊡ to choose a file type.

This example shows a photo saved in the JPEG format.

332

④ Select optimization settings to specify a quality and file size for your image. The higher the quality setting, the larger the resulting file size.

⑤ Check that the file quality and size are acceptable in the preview area.

Ⓐ You can resize the resulting image by typing dimensions or a percentage and then clicking the image preview.

⑥ Click **Save**.

The Save Optimized As dialog box opens.

⑦ Click the ☑ to choose a folder in which to save the file.

⑧ Type a filename. Photoshop Elements automatically assigns the correct extension if you do not specify an extension.

⑨ Click **Save**.

Photoshop Elements saves the image file, and the original image file remains open.

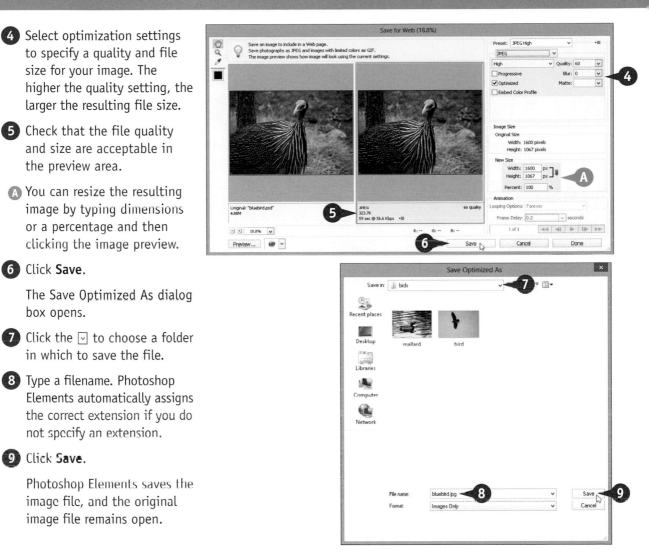

TIPS

What is GIF?

GIF, or Graphic Interchange Format, is good for saving illustrations that have a lot of solid color. The format supports a maximum of 256 colors (versus the millions of colors supported by JPEG). If the image is simple, you can save it with even fewer colors and decrease the file size. You can include transparency and animation in GIF images.

What is PNG?

PNG, or Portable Network Graphics, is a high-quality alternative to JPEG and GIF. You can save two types of PNG files in Photoshop Elements. PNG-24, similar to JPEG, supports millions of colors and is good for photographic images. PNG-8 is an alternative to GIF and supports up to 256 colors in a single image. PNG supports transparency.

Convert File Types

You can quickly and easily convert images from one file type to another in Photoshop Elements by using the Process Multiple Files feature. This easily converts a collection of PSD files to the JPEG format for sending by e-mail or posting on the web.

This feature can also resize the images as they are processed, enabling you to shrink the size of the resulting files. You can also rename the converted files using a serial number, the current date, and other options. During the process, Photoshop Elements opens each image, makes the conversions, and then saves the updated image.

Convert File Types

1 Place the images that you want to convert in a folder.

Note: To work with folders, see your operating system's documentation.

2 In the Editor, click **File**.

Note: For more on opening the Editor, see Chapter 1.

3 Click **Process Multiple Files**.

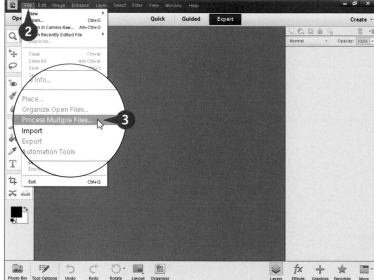

Note: If a dialog box appears warning about multipage documents and project files, click **OK**.

The Process Multiple Files dialog box opens.

4 Click **Browse**.

The Browse for Folder dialog box opens.

5 Click ▷ to open folders on your computer (▷ changes to ◢).

6 Click the folder containing your images.

7 Click **OK**.

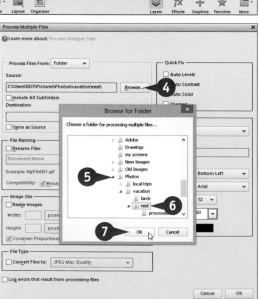

8 Click **Browse** and then repeat steps **5** to **7** to specify a destination folder where you want your processed images to be saved.

Ⓐ You can optionally click **Resize Images** (☐ changes to ☑) and type a new width and height. Photoshop Elements will resize the images before saving.

Ⓑ You can also click **Rename Files** (☐ changes to ☑) and choose a naming scheme for the converted images.

Note: For more on resizing images, see Chapter 5.

9 Click **Convert Files to** (☐ changes to ☑).

10 Click the ▼ and choose a file format to convert to.

11 Click **OK**.

Photoshop Elements processes the images.

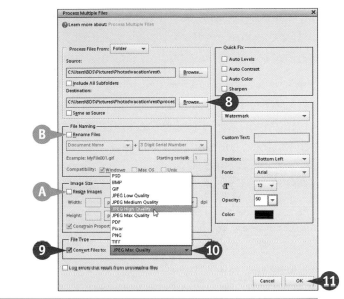

TIPS

How can I automatically fix color and lighting problems in my converted photos?
There are automatic optimization settings under the Quick Fix heading in the Process Multiple Files dialog box. You can select them to have Photoshop Elements improve the color, contrast, and sharpness of your photos before conversion. For more on these settings, see Chapter 9.

How can I quickly add labels to my converted photos?
Under the Labels heading in the Process Multiple Files dialog box are tools for adding captions and watermarks to your converted photos. You can automatically add filename, description, and date information as captions as well as specify the size and style of the caption font. For more on adding watermarks, see Chapter 15.

E-Mail Images with Photo Mail

You can embed your images in an e-mail message and then send them to others by using the Photo Mail feature in Photoshop Elements. With Photo Mail, you can select custom stationery that inserts colors, graphics, and captions next to your images. You can store recipient information in your Photo Mail Contact Book so you do not have to re-enter the same e-mail information.

This feature requires that you already have an e-mail program, such as Microsoft Outlook or Apple Mail, set up on your computer. Photoshop Elements does not come with e-mail capability.

E-Mail Images with Photo Mail

1 In the Organizer, click **Share**.

Note: For more on using the Organizer, see Chapter 3.

2 Click **Photo Mail**.

Note: Photoshop Elements may display a dialog box asking you to choose your e-mail client. If so, choose the software with which you prefer to send e-mail and then click **Continue**.

Note: The Photo Mail feature is not available in the Mac version of Photoshop Elements.

The Photo Mail pane opens.

3 Click and drag images you want to mail from the main Organizer window into the Photo Mail pane.

Ⓐ Photoshop Elements totals the file sizes.

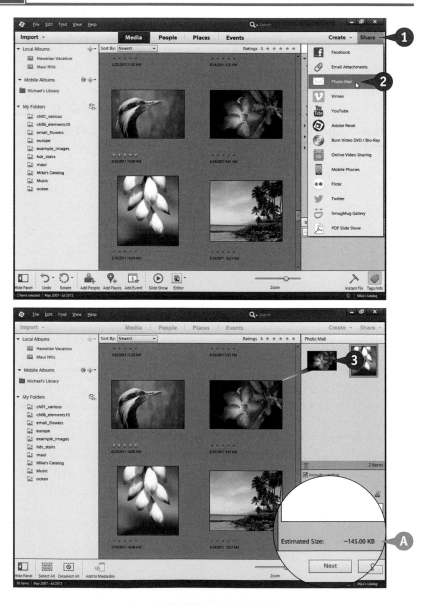

④ To add a new recipient, click the **Edit recipients in contact book** icon (🖾).

The Contact Book dialog box opens.

⑤ Click **New Contact**.

The New Contact dialog box opens.

⑥ Type the contact details for the recipient.

⑦ Click **OK** to save the details.

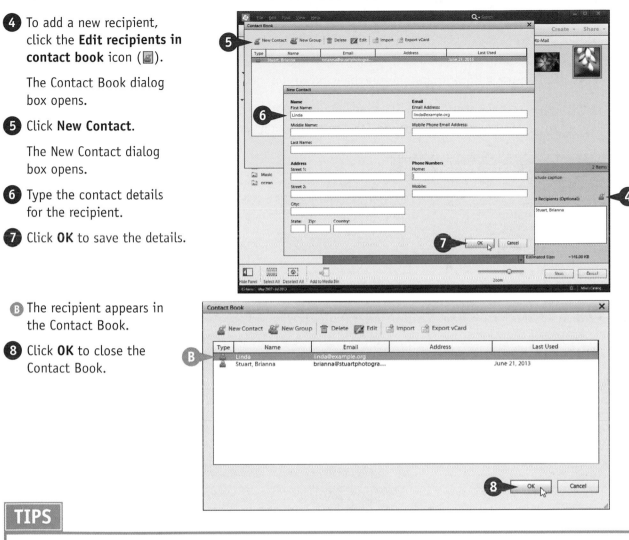

Ⓑ The recipient appears in the Contact Book.

⑧ Click **OK** to close the Contact Book.

continued ▶

TIPS

Can I send my images as e-mail attachments?
If you want to send your photos as plain e-mail attachments instead of as embedded items in an e-mail message, click the **E-mail Attachments** option in the Organizer's Share menu. Sending attachments is similar to sending Photo Mail but without the steps where you select stationery and a layout. It also allows users to more easily view your photos outside of their e-mail client.

How can I keep the file sizes of my images small when e-mailing them?
If you are worried about the file sizes of your images when e-mailing, choose the **E-mail Attachments** option instead of the Photo Mail option in the Organizer's Share menu. With the E-mail Attachments option, you can adjust both the dimensions of your photos and the JPEG compression applied prior to sending.

Photo Mail includes more than 50 stationery designs that you can apply to the photos that you e-mail. You can select stationery with animal, seasonal, or party themes. Photoshop Elements embeds your images and the stationery into the e-mail message by using HTML, which is the language used to create web pages.

Some e-mail programs do not display HTML embedded in e-mail. Recipients using such e-mail programs will not be able see the styles and graphics offered in the Photo Mail feature.

E-Mail Images with Photo Mail (continued)

The new contact appears in the Select Recipients list.

9 Click each intended recipient (☐ changes to ☑).

10 Click **Next**.

The Stationery & Layouts Wizard opens.

11 Click a category to open stationery options.

12 Click a stationery with which to style your e-mail.

A You can click inside the stationery design to add or edit captions for your images.

13 Click **Next Step**.

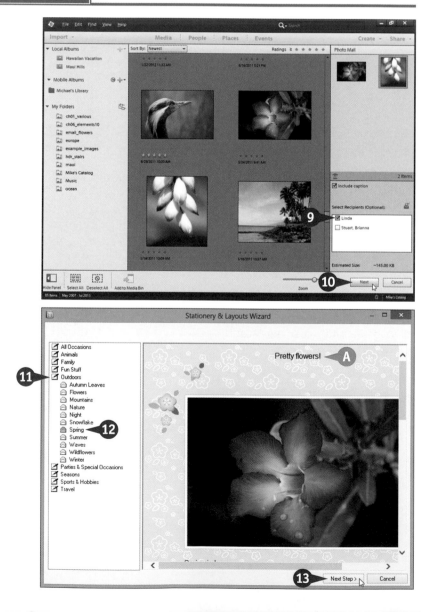

The layout options appear.

⓮ Click the layout options to organize and size your images.

Ⓑ You can optionally customize your text.

Ⓒ You can set other options. The available options vary depending on the stationery selected in step **12**.

⓯ Click **Next**.

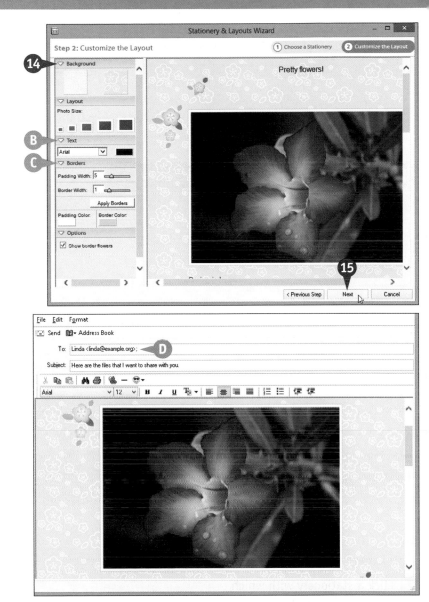

Photoshop Elements opens a new message in your e-mail client software.

Ⓓ The recipient is added to the To field.

Your message text, layout design, and images are included in the body of the message.

Note: For more on sending your message, see the documentation for your e-mail application.

TIP

How can I view a history of what I have e-mailed?
Click **Find**, **By History**, and then **E-mailed to**. A dialog box opens, showing a history of e-mail messages and number of items sent through Photoshop Elements. You can double-click an entry to view the photos that were sent (Ⓐ).

Print Photos

Y ou can print your Photoshop Elements images to create hard copies of your work. You can then add your photos to a physical photo album or frame them.

After you select your photos to print, you can choose the paper size and the printed size for your photos on the page. Photoshop Elements automatically arranges the images on the page for printing. You can zoom and pan your photos within the print dimensions to focus on just the content you want printed. Additional printing options enable you to include a filename, caption, or date with the photo.

Print Photos

① In the Organizer, select the photos to print.

Note: For more on using the Organizer, see Chapter 3.

② Click **File**.

③ Click **Print**.

You can also print by pressing **Ctrl**+**P** (**⌘**+**P** on a Mac).

This example shows printing from the Organizer. You can also open an image and follow from step **2** forward to print from the Editor.

Note: On a Mac, you are switched to the Editor workspace to print.

Note: See Chapter 1 for more on the Editor and Organizer.

The Prints dialog box opens.

④ Select your printer and paper settings. These vary depending on the make and model of your printer.

⑤ Click the ▼ and select a print type.

In the Print Type menu, you can select Contact Sheet to arrange your photos in rows and columns. You can select Picture Package to access more photo layouts.

⑥ Click the ▼ to select a print size.

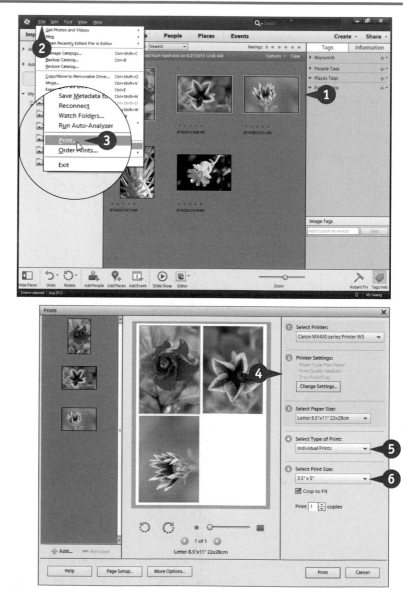

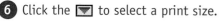

Click a photo to adjust.

 Click and drag the slider (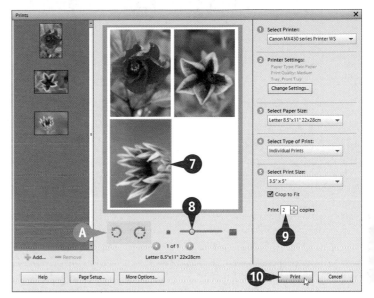) to zoom the photo.

Ⓐ You can click an icon to rotate the photo.

You can click and drag to pan your photo within the print size boundary.

⑨ Type the number of copies to print.

⑩ Click **Print**.

Photoshop Elements prints the photos.

TIP

How can I add captions and other text to my printed photo?

① In the Prints dialog box, click **More Options**.

② Click **Printing Choices**.

③ Click this option (☐ changes to ☑) to print a caption if your photo has one.

Ⓐ You can click these options (☐ changes to ☑) to print the date the photo was taken or the filename.

Ⓑ You can use these settings to print a solid border around the photo.

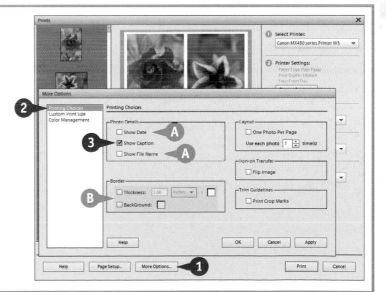

Create a Slide Show

You can use the Organizer to combine images from your collection into a custom slide show that includes music, text, graphics, and even narration. The resulting slide show can be shared with friends and family online, as a DVD, or as an Adobe PDF document. On a Mac, only PDF slide shows are available.

Once you choose the photos to create a slide show in the Organizer, you can select a default slide duration and transition to be applied to all the slides. You can rearrange the slide order by clicking and dragging thumbnails in the Slide Show Editor.

Create a Slide Show

1 In the Organizer, **Ctrl**+click (⌘+click on a Mac) the images you want to put in your slide show.

Note: For more on using the Organizer, see Chapter 3.

2 Click **Create**.

3 Click **Slide Show**.

The Slide Show Preferences dialog box opens.

4 Choose a duration, a transition, and other options.

5 Specify the quality of the preview photos. Choosing a lower quality results in a shorter load time.

6 Click **OK**.

The Slide Show Editor dialog box opens.

 To add more photos to your slide show, you can click **Add Media**.

 Photoshop Elements displays thumbnails for the slides and icons for the transitions along the bottom of the Slide Show Editor.

7 Click a slide to which you want to add text.

8 Click **Add Text**.

The Edit Text dialog box opens.

9 Type your text.

10 Click **OK**.

Photoshop Elements adds the text to the selected slide.

The text properties appear in the right-hand pane.

11 Click and drag inside the text to position it.

12 Choose formatting options for your text.

13 Repeat steps **7** to **12** for the other slides in your slide show.

continued ▶   **343**

TIPS

How do I rearrange the photos in my slide show?
In the Slide Show Editor, click and drag the thumbnails at the bottom to change their order in the slide show. To remove a slide, right-click it and choose **Delete Slide**. If you have a lot of slides, click **Quick Reorder** to view and rearrange them in a larger window.

How do I add music to my slide show?
To add music or narration to a slide show, click **Add Media** and then choose an audio option in the Slide Show Editor. You can add an audio file that plays in the background while the slide show runs. Organizer supports MP3, WAV, WMA, and AC3 audio file formats. Click **Fit Slides To Audio** to sync your slide show with the audio.

Create a Slide Show (continued)

When creating a slide show, you can edit the transition effect and slide duration for each slide as well as set the show to loop continuously. Transition effects control how one slide flows to the next. You can also caption your slides with text or add clip art to give them extra decoration.

Organizer saves your slide show as either a WMV file (Windows only) or a PDF file. The WMV format can be viewed with Windows Media Player. You can view PDFs with a variety of applications, including the free Adobe Reader. Slide shows are easy to share with others by copying the finished file onto a disc or e-mailing it.

Create a Slide Show (continued)

14 If the Extras panel is closed, click **Extras** to open it.

15 Click a slide to which you want to add clip art.

16 Click and drag the clip art to the slide.

You can click and drag the clip art to reposition it.

A You can choose options to resize or recolor the clip art.

17 Click a transition icon between the slides.

The transition properties appear.

18 Click the ⬇ to choose a transition duration.

19 Click the ⌄ to choose a transition style.

20 Click the **Play** button (▶) to preview your slide show.

Photoshop Elements cycles through the slides.

B You can click **Full Screen Preview** to preview the slide show at maximum size. To exit Full Screen Preview, you can press Esc.

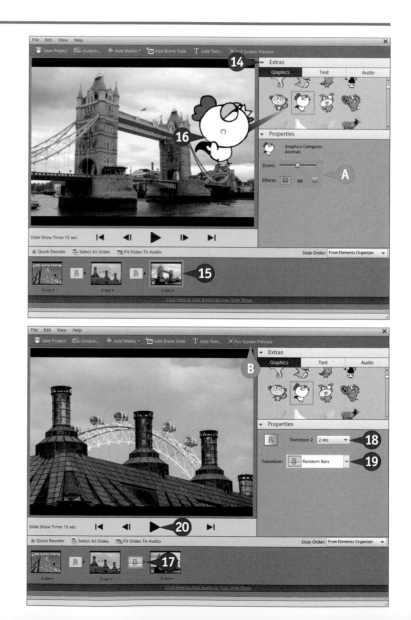

344

21 Click **Save Project**.

A dialog box opens, asking you to name your slide show.

22 Type a name.

23 Click **Save**.

24 Click the ☒ to close the Slide Show Editor and return to the Organizer. You can also press **Ctrl**+**Q** (**⌘**+**Q** on a Mac).

C You can click **Output** to save the slide show as a PDF file or movie or burn it to a CD or DVD.

Note: Only PDF slide shows are available in the Mac version of Photoshop Elements.

D Photoshop Elements saves your slide show in the Organizer and labels it with a ▣.

You can double-click the slide show to continue to edit it.

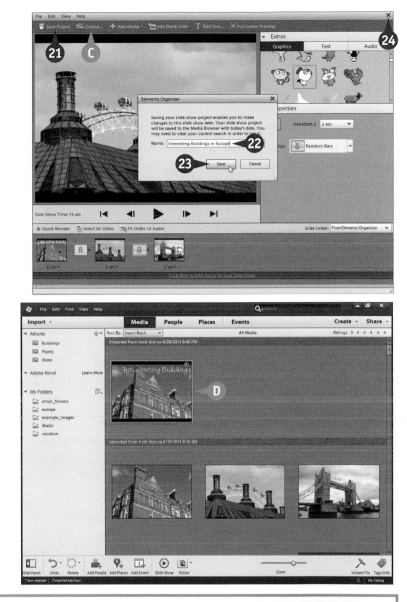

How do I add a title page to my slide show?
Click a slide thumbnail. Click **Add Blank Slide**. Photoshop Elements adds a blank slide to your slide show. Click **Add Text**. In the dialog box that opens, type a title for your page, and then click **OK**. You can click and drag the new title page to reposition it.

Interesting
Buildings
in
Europe

Create a Photo Book

Photoshop Elements lets you arrange the favorite photos from your collection into a professional-looking photo book. This enables you to have a hard copy of your photos that you can share with friends and family.

You can select from a variety of styles, colors, and layouts for your book pages. Photoshop Elements can automatically assemble photos selected in the Organizer into the pages of your book. You can then review the pages of the book and make custom changes to the positioning of the photos and add text to describe what is happening in each image.

Create a Photo Book

Set Up the Book

1 In the Organizer, **Ctrl**+click (⌘+click on a Mac) the images you want to include in your photo book.

Note: For more on using the Organizer, see Chapter 3.

2 Click **Create**.

3 Click **Photo Book**.

The Photo Book dialog box opens in the Editor.

4 Click a book size.

Ⓐ If you select a size under a printing partner, an order button appears after you create your book.

5 Click a book theme.

Ⓑ By default, Photoshop Elements automatically fills the pages with your images.

6 Type the number of pages in your photo book. Page limits vary with the type of book.

7 Click **OK**.

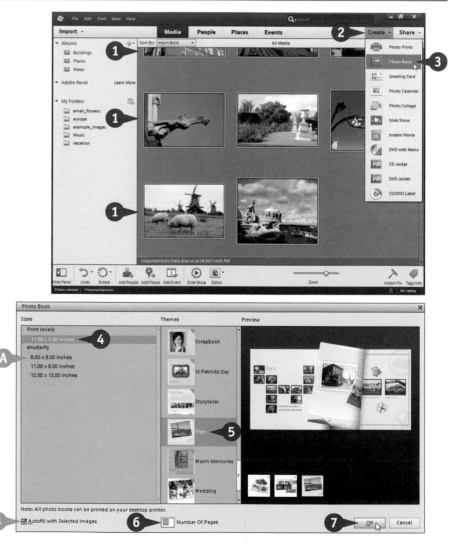

Photoshop Elements adds the photos to the book.

8 Click the **Zoom** tool (Q) to magnify the currently selected page.

9 Click the arrow to cycle through the pages sequentially.

10 Click a page to edit.

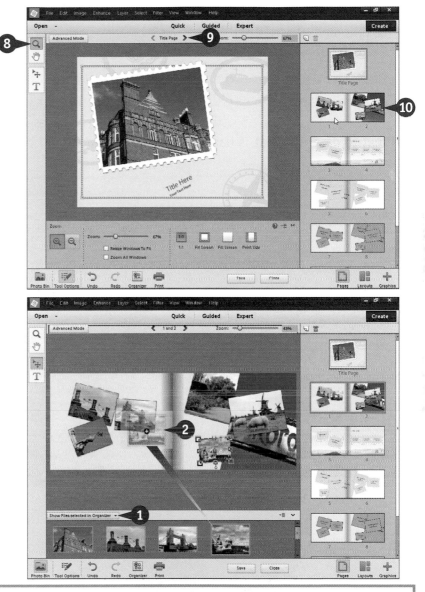

Edit a Photo

1 Click the ▼ and select **Show Files selected in Organizer**.

2 Click and drag a file to a photo on the page.

continued ▶ **347**

TIP

How do I change the title page text?

Complete steps **1** to **9** and click the first page in your book under the Pages tab to view it. Click the **Horizontal Type** tool (T). Double-click the title page text to select it, and type to change the text (**A**). Click ☑ or press Enter (⌘+Enter on a Mac) to finish editing the title page text.

After you complete your photo book, you can save it as a project in Photoshop Elements. The photo book appears in the Organizer along with your images and other creations. To get an idea of what the final photo book will look like, or to create a do-it-yourself book, you can print the pages on your local printer. To get a professionally printed version, you can order your book through one of the printing partners in the Photo Book interface.

Create a Photo Book (continued)

Ⓐ Photoshop Elements replaces the photo.

③ Click the **Move** tool (⬚).

④ Click and drag inside a photo.

Ⓑ You can click a selection handle to resize the photo.

Ⓒ You can click and drag the rotation handle to turn the photo.

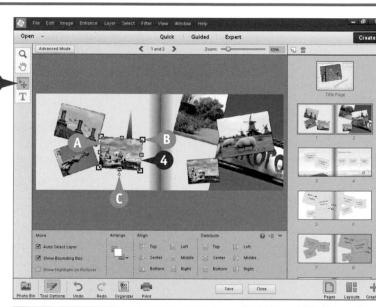

Ⓓ Photoshop Elements moves the photo.

Add Text

① Click the **Horizontal Type** tool (Ⓣ).

② Select the font, size, and other formatting.

③ Click where you want to add text on the page.

④ Type your text.

⑤ Click ☑ or press **Enter** (⌘+**Enter** on a Mac) to finish adding the text.

Finish the Book

1. Click **Pages**.

2. Click to select other book pages.

3. Repeat steps **1** to **4** in the subsection "Edit a Photo" to edit photos and steps **1** to **5** in the subsection "Add Text" to add text.

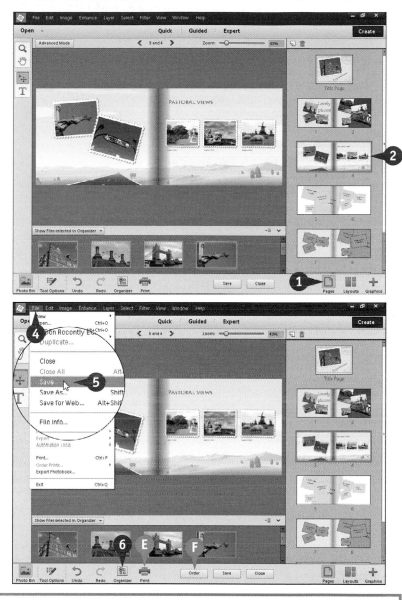

4. Click **File**.

5. Click **Save** to save your photo book.

6. Click **Organizer** to return to the Organizer.

E. You can click **Print** to print the photo book on your printer.

F. If you selected a printer partner size in the subsection "Set Up the Book," you can click **Order** to order a professionally printed copy.

TIP

How do I change the layout of a page?

1. Click **Pages** and click the page whose layout you want to change.

2. Click **Layouts**.

   Photoshop Elements displays a list of layouts.

3. Double-click a layout.

   Photoshop Elements applies the layout to the page.

Share Photos on Facebook

You can select photos in your Organizer catalog and post them to an album on the social network Facebook. You can upload the photos directly to Facebook by giving Photoshop Elements permission to communicate directly with your Facebook account. After the photos are posted, your Facebook friends can view the photos.

This sharing feature requires an Internet connection and a Facebook account. Anyone 13 years of age or older with an e-mail address can sign up for a Facebook account. You can visit Facebook at www.facebook.com.

Share Photos on Facebook

1 In the Organizer, Ctrl+click (⌘+click on a Mac) to select the photos you want to share.

2 Click **Share**.

Note: For more on using the Organizer, see Chapter 3.

3 Click **Facebook**.

An authorization dialog box appears.

4 Click **Authorize**.

Ⓐ By default, Photoshop Elements downloads your list of friends from Facebook and makes them available when you define people in the Organizer. For more about defining people in your photos, see Chapter 4.

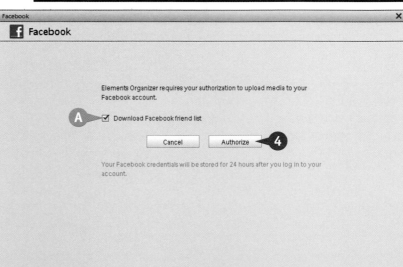

A Facebook login page opens in a web browser.

5 Type the e-mail address for your Facebook account.

6 Type your Facebook password.

Ⓑ If you do not have a Facebook account, you can click the link to sign up for one.

7 Click **Log In** to sign in to Facebook.

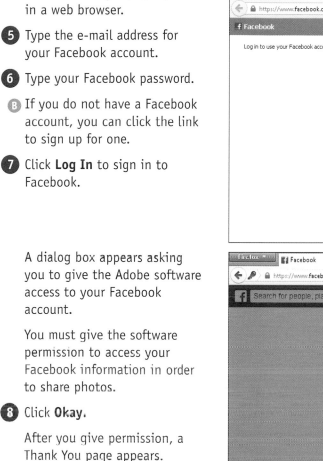

A dialog box appears asking you to give the Adobe software access to your Facebook account.

You must give the software permission to access your Facebook information in order to share photos.

8 Click **Okay.**

After you give permission, a Thank You page appears.

9 Close your web browser and return to Photoshop Elements.

TIP

How else can I share my photos online?
You can share your photos directly from Photoshop Elements to two other online photo-sharing sites, Flickr and SmugMug. In the Organizer, click the **Share** tab. Ctrl+click (⌘+click on a Mac) to select the photos you want to share. Click **Flickr** to upload to Flickr. Click **SmugMug Gallery** to upload to SmugMug. You can visit Flickr at www.flickr.com or SmugMug at www.smugmug.com.

continued ▶

Facebook organizes your photos into albums, which enables you to keep photos of specific events in one place. You can control who can view the albums that you post. In the Share to Facebook dialog box in Photoshop Elements, you can specify whether just your Facebook friends, friends of your friends, or everyone on Facebook can see the photos.

You can also upload the photos in one of two different resolutions. The higher resolution offers better viewing quality online but takes longer to upload.

Share Photos on Facebook (continued)

10 Click **Complete Authorization**.

The Facebook dialog box appears with thumbnail versions of your images.

Ⓐ You can click the plus sign (⊞) to add more photos from the Organizer to the album. To remove a photo from the album, click a thumbnail and then click the minus sign (⊟).

11 Type your Facebook album details.

Ⓑ You can click this option (○ changes to ⊙) to add your photos to an existing album on Facebook.

12 Click the ▾ to specify who can see your photos.

13 Click an option (○ changes to ⊙) to specify the upload resolution.

14 Click **Upload**.

Facebook — **f Facebook**

Thank you for authorizing Elements Organizer to upload to your Facebook Account. Select 'Complete Authorization' to continue uploading the media to your Facebook account.

Your Facebook friend list will be downloaded in the background.

Complete Authorization ◀ **10**

Your Facebook credentials will be stored for 24 hours after you log in to your account.

Facebook — **f Facebook** — Signed in as: **Brianna** Log Out?

Ⓑ ○ Upload Photos to an existing album
Select an album ...

⊙ Upload Photos to a new album
Name : Ocean Visit
Location :
Description : Scenes from our trip to the coast ◀ **11**

Who can see these photos?
Friends Only ◀ **12**

Choose your photo upload quality
13 ⊙ Standard (Recommended, fast upload)
○ High (slow upload)

☑ Upload people tags in these photos

Cancel   Upload ◀ **14**

Ⓐ + −

Photoshop Elements uploads the photos to Facebook.

15 You can click **Visit Facebook** to access Facebook to view the shared photos.

TIP

How can I automatically tag friends in my photos?

On Facebook, you can highlight friends that appear in your photos by tagging the photos with friends' names. If you applied People keyword tags in the Organizer, you can have Photoshop Elements apply those tags as Facebook tags.

1 In the Organizer, tag photos with People keyword tags.

Note: See Chapter 4 for more about keyword tags.

2 Follow the steps in this section to share the photos to Facebook.

3 In the Share to Facebook dialog box, make sure **Upload people tags in these photos** is checked ().

The uploaded Facebook photos are tagged with the friends' names.

Share a Photo on Twitter

You can select a photo in your Organizer catalog and add it to a post on Twitter. Twitter is a microblogging service that enables you to post short messages, or *tweets*, that other Twitter users can see. When you add an image to a tweet, a link is included in the message. Clicking the link displays the image.

This sharing feature requires an Internet connection and a Twitter account. Anyone with an e-mail address can sign up for a Twitter account. You can visit Twitter at www.twitter.com.

Share a Photo on Twitter

1 Click the photo you want to share.

You can share only one photo at a time.

2 In the Organizer, click **Share**.

3 Click **Twitter**.

An authorization dialog box appears.

4 Click **Authorize**.

The first time you share via Twitter, a Twitter login page opens in a web browser.

5 Type your Twitter login information.

Ⓐ If you do not have a Twitter account, you can sign up for one.

6 Click **Authorize app**.

After authorizing, a Thank You page appears.

7 Close your web browser and return to Photoshop Elements.

8 In the Twitter dialog box, click **Done**.

A dialog box appears enabling you to add a message to post with your image.

9 Type the text for your tweet.

B Numbers show you how many characters you have left and the total available.

10 Click **Tweet**.

Photoshop Elements sends the image and text to Twitter and displays a confirmation dialog box. You can click **Done** to close the dialog box or click **Visit Twitter** to view your tweet.

TIPS

How can I categorize my Twitter postings?
You can categorize your postings, and make them more searchable, with hashtags. To create a hashtag, you choose a word related to your tweet, precede that word with a hash symbol (#), and include the text in your tweet. You can include multiple words in a hashtag, but you need to remove the spaces between the words. You might add the hashtags #pet and #germanshepherd to a post that includes an image of your dog. You can search for tweets about German Shepherds by searching for #germanshepherd on Twitter.

How can I tell if I have shared a photo on Twitter?
In the Organizer, right-click the photo and click **Show File Info** in the menu that appears. The Information panel opens. Click **History** in the Information panel. Look for the word Twitter listed next to Shared With.

Export Photos

You can export the photos in the Organizer to a folder. This is helpful if you want to move the photos to another computer or give them to another person. Photoshop Elements enables you to export your photos in a variety of file formats. You can export JPEG or PNG versions for sharing electronically. TIFF or PSD versions are best for saving high-quality originals with layers. A size menu lets you export to a variety of common image dimensions. When exporting JPEG photos, you can control the quality of the exported files.

Export Photos

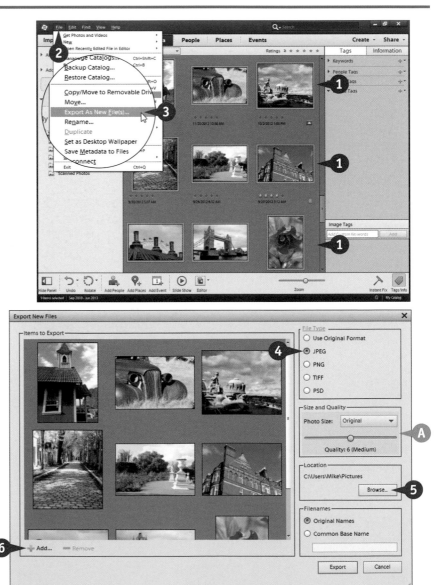

1 In the Organizer, **Ctrl**+click (**⌘**+click on a Mac) to select the photos you want to export.

Note: For more on using the Organizer, see Chapter 3.

If you do not select any photos, Photoshop Elements exports all the photos currently shown.

2 Click **File**.

3 Click **Export As New File(s)**.

The Export New Files dialog box opens, showing the selected photos listed.

4 Click a file type (○ changes to ◉).

A Some file types allow you to specify a size or quality.

5 Click **Browse** to choose a destination folder for the images.

6 To select more images to export, click **Add**.

The Add Media dialog box opens.

⑦ Ctrl +click (⌘+click on a Mac) to select the photos you want to add.

Ⓑ You can use these settings to limit the displayed photos.

⑧ Click **Done**.

Photoshop Elements adds the photos.

Ⓒ To remove a photo from the export list, click the photo and then click **Remove**.

⑨ Click **Export**.

Photoshop Elements exports your images.

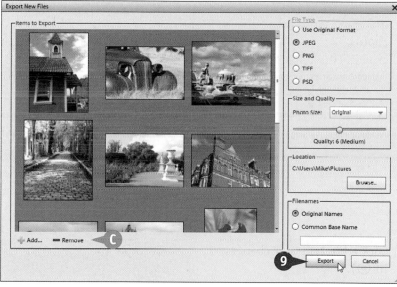

Export Photos to Adobe Revel

You can export photos from Photoshop Elements to Adobe Revel, Adobe's cloud-based photo management service. Revel enables you to store and access your photos from online servers managed by Adobe.

Using Revel gives you backup copies of your image files in the event your computer hard drive fails. Revel also gives you a central place from which to view your photos from different devices. See the tips for more about accessing Revel from different devices. Accessing Adobe Revel requires an Internet connection.

Export Photos to Adobe Revel

1 In the Organizer, click **File**.

2 Click **Sign In to Adobe Revel**.

A sign-in window appears.

Ⓐ If you do not have an Adobe ID to sign in with, click **Create an Adobe ID** to create one.

3 Type your Adobe ID. It is the e-mail address you signed up with.

4 Type your password.

5 Click **Sign In**.

A welcome screen appears.

6 Click here to share all your photos and videos in the Organizer with Revel (O changes to ●).

Ⓑ You can click here to share only specific content.

7 Click **Next**.

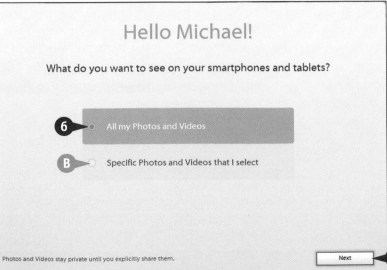

A confirmation screen appears.

⑧ Click the ▼ to select a default Revel library for your shared photos. You can create new libraries from within Revel.

⑨ Click **Done.**

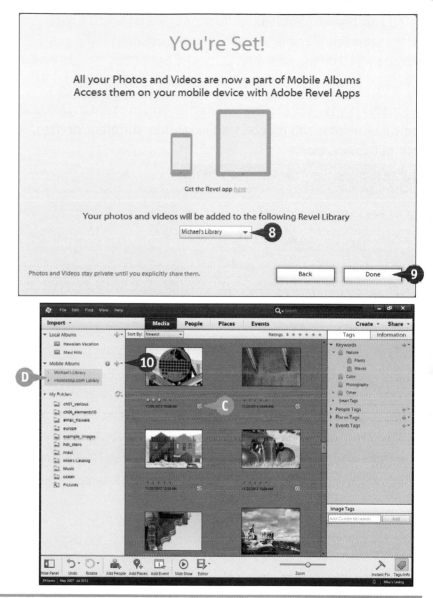

① Shared photos are marked with an icon (⊚).

① Revel libraries are listed here. If you have multiple Revel libraries, you can click a library name to display a library's photos.

⑩ To log out of Adobe Revel, click ▼ and then **Settings.**

⑪ Click **Sign Out** in the dialog box that appears.

How can I view my Revel photos in a web browser?
In your web browser, visit www.adoberevel.com and then sign into your Revel account using your Adobe ID and password. From the Revel website, you can access your libraries and see the photos you have exported from Photoshop Elements. You can also export photos directly from your computer to Revel via the website.

How can I view my Revel photos on my mobile device?
You can download the Revel app to your iPhone, iPad, or Android-based device. After you sign into your Revel account on your mobile device, you can view your Revel photos. You can also export photos you take with your mobile device into Revel and then access those photos in Photoshop Elements.

Back Up Photos

You can back up your digital photos by using the Organizer's backup tool. This feature walks you through the steps for backing up your files to a CD or DVD (Windows only) or hard drive (Windows or Mac). Regularly backing up your work to external media is a good idea in case the storage on your computer fails.

A standard CD can hold up to 700MB of data. A standard DVD can hold up to 4.38GB of data. Photoshop Elements can also burn to the Blu-ray disc format, which can hold up to 50GB. How many images a disc holds depends on the size of the images and the format in which they are saved.

Back Up Photos

1 In the Organizer, open the catalog you want to back up, or **Ctrl**+click (**⌘**+click on a Mac) to select specific photos to back up.

Note: For more on catalogs, see Chapter 3.

2 Click **File**.

3 Click **Backup Catalog**.

Note: Photoshop Elements may display a warning about missing files. If this happens, click **Reconnect** to perform a check. See the tip for more details.

The Backup Catalog to CD, DVD, or Hard Drive dialog box opens.

4 Click **Full Backup** (○ changes to ◉).

Ⓐ For subsequent backups, you can click **Incremental Backup** (○ changes to ◉). Incremental Backup backs up files that have changed or been added since the last backup, and is faster than a full backup when you have saved a catalog previously.

5 Click **Next**.

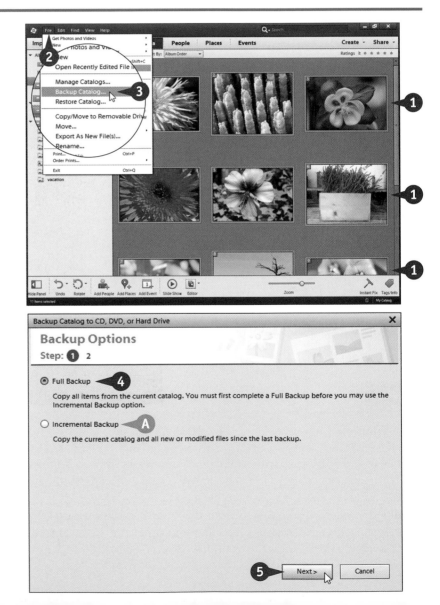

360

6 Click the drive to which you want to copy the backup files.

B You can type a name for the backup in this text box.

C Depending on your backup drive selection, the wizard displays an estimated file size and creation time.

7 Click **Save Backup**.

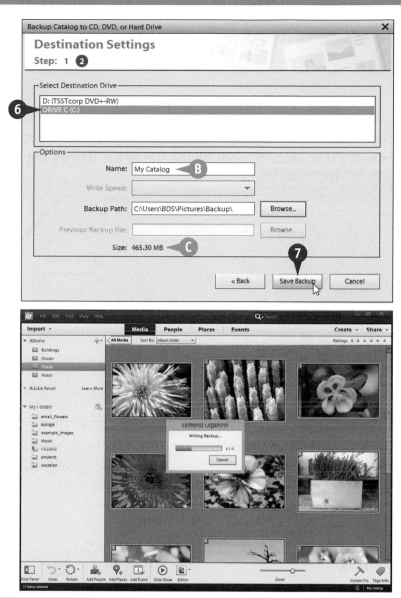

Photoshop Elements backs up your photos.

A prompt box alerts you when the procedure is complete.

Depending on the media you used, you may have the option of verifying your backup when the backup is finished.

The Organizer prompts me to find missing files before backing up my photos. What do I do?
If any of the catalog photos no longer contain valid links to original files, the backup tool displays a prompt asking you to reconnect any missing files. A file can appear to be missing if you move it after adding the photo to the Organizer or if you rename the file outside the Organizer. Click **Reconnect** to allow Photoshop Elements to look for the missing links and then continue with the backup.

How do I restore my backed-up files?
Click **File** and then **Restore Catalog** to restore backups of your photos to your computer. The Restore dialog box offers options for restoring backed-up photos and catalogs to their original location or to a new location.

Index

A

A (Quick Selection) tool, 12, 130–131
actions, applying effects to, 326–327
Add Noise dialog box, 288–289
Add Noise filter, 288
Adjust Sharpness dialog box, 192–193
Adjust Sharpness feature, 215
adjustment layers, 159, 174–175, 177
adjustments, canceling, 207
Adobe Revel, exporting photos to, 358–359
advanced dialog box (Photo Downloader), 29
advanced searches, performing, 70–71
advanced tools
    applying Instant Fix, 88–89
    defining
        events, 82–83
        people in photos, 76–77
        places, 78–79
    finding by visual similarity, 92–93
    keyword tags, 72–75
    performing advanced searches, 70–71
    Smart Events, 84–85
    stacking photos, 90–91
    viewing places, 80–81
    working with people, place, and event tags, 86–87
albums, 39, 48, 60–61
alignment, changing for text, 301
allocating memory, 22
anti-aliasing, 301
Arrange commands, reordering layers with, 167
Aspect option (marquee tools), 123
assigning keyword tags, 73
attachments, e-mail, 337
Auto Smart Tone tool, 228–229
automatic optimization settings, 335

B

B (Brush) tool, 13, 258–259
background color, 13, 256–257
Background Eraser tool, 273
Background layer, 161, 273
backgrounds
    adding, 276, 316–317
    deleting, 155
    moving selections in, 142
    resizing patterns, 317
    setting color, 256–257
backing up photos, 360–361

Bas Relief filter, 293
beveling, 307
bitmap images, 6
black-and-white photos, 222–225
blending layers, 176–177
blur filters, 243, 280–281
Blur (R) tool, 12, 214
BMP (Bitmap), 35
borders, feathering, 154–155
Brightness/Contrast dialog box, 208–209
Brush menu, 219
Brush Settings dialog box, 261
Brush Strokes filters, 285
Brush (B) tool, 13, 258–259
brushes, 260–263
Burn tool, 211, 236

C

C (Crop) tool, 13, 115
canceling adjustments, 207
canvas size, changing, 108–109, 114
captions
    adding, 58–59, 323, 341
    searching by, 63
card readers, importing photos from, 28–29
Catalog Manager, 48–49
catalogs
    about, 5, 44
    changing security settings for, 49
    creating, 48–49
    searching, 45
    switching, 49
categorizing Twitter postings, 355
Charcoal filter, 286
Clone Stamp (S) tool, 12, 188–189
closing
    photos, 41
    Tool Options panel, 17
collage, photo, 247
color. *See* lighting and color
color button (Restore Old Photo), 233
color channel, 223
Color Curves, adjusting color with, 226–227
Color Curves dialog box, 226–227
Color effect, 177
Color Picker dialog box, 172–173
color shading, adding to layers, 315
Color Swatches panel, 257, 303
colorcast, fixing in Guided mode, 239
Colored Pencil filter, 284

Comic filter, 286
commands, 99, 158. *See also specific commands*
content
    adding from Graphics panel, 276–277
    organizing photos with the same, 93
    searching for by keyword, 277
Content-Aware Move (Q) tool, 13, 144–145
contrast button (Restore Old Photo), 233
Cookie Cutter tool, 115
Copy command, 146
copying and pasting, into layers, 161
Correct Camera Distortion dialog box, 200–201
coverings, adding to layers, 320–321
Create button (Editor), 9
Crop (C) tool, 13, 115
Crystallize dialog box, 290–291
Custom Shape (U) tool, 13
customizing
    brushes, 261
    marquee tools, 123
    names of exported images, 357
    slide shows, 55

D

date
    changing on photos, 57
    filtering events by, 85
    finding photos by, 62
decorations, adding, 5
decreasing
    magnification, 101
    saturation, 218
default settings, for tools, 17
deleting
    Background layer, 273
    backgrounds, 155
    captions, 59
    layers, 165
    normal layers, 273
    selections, 147
depth of field, simulating short, 281
deselecting selections, 137
details, viewing, 110
digital cameras, 26, 28–29
digital collages, creating, 5
disabling Auto Smart Tone effect, 229
displaying
    images from Organizer in Photo Bin, 97
    rulers, 22
    slide shows in Full Screen mode, 54–55

Distort command, 283
distorting, 151, 282–283
document size, 106–107
Dodge tool, 210, 236
drawing. *See* painting and drawing
drop shadows, adding to layers, 314–315
Dry Brush filter, 294
duplicating
    layers, 164
    photos, 40
    selections, 146
Dust & Scratches filter, 288

E

E (Eraser) tool, 13, 272–273
editing
    adding frames in Quick mode, 113
    adjusting
        image canvas size, 108–109
        image print size, 106–107
        image view, 102–103
        on-screen image size, 104–105
    applying effects in Quick mode, 112
    captions, 59
    with Clone Stamp tool, 188–189
    creating photo panoramas, 198–199
    cropping images, 114–115
    fixing keystone distortion, 200–201
    keyword tags, 73
    layer masks, 180–181
    magnifying with Zoom tool, 100–101
    managing open images, 96–99
    merging groups shots, 194–195
    photos from within Organizer, 47
    in Quick mode, 110–111, 184–185
    recomposing photos, 196–197
    removing
        red eye, 186–187
        spots, 190–191
    reverting images, 119
    rotating images, 116–117
    selections, 197
    sharpening images, 192–193
    undoing changes to images, 118
Editor
    opening, 8
    opening Organizer from, 47
    setting program preferences in, 20–21

Editor *(continued)*
switching
modes, 14–15
to Organizer from, 11
workspace, 9
Editor button (Organizer), 10
effects. *See* styles and effects
Effects panel, 289
Elements 12. *See* Photoshop Elements 12
Elliptical Marquee tool, 123
e-mailing images with Photo Mail, 336–339
Emboss dialog box, 292–293
Eraser (E) tool, 13, 272–273
erasing. *See* deleting
events
adding photos to, 83
creating albums using photos from, 61
defining, 82–83
filtering by date, 85
organizing photos by, 45
Smart Events, 84–85
working with tags for, 86–87
Expert mode, 14–15, 249
exporting photos, 356–359
exposure, fixing, 212–213
extending objects, 145, 250–251
Eyedropper (I) tool, 13

F

F (Smart Brush) tool, 12, 264–267
Facebook, 77, 350–353
favorites, 328–329
Feather option (marquee tools), 123
feathering selection borders, 154–155
file formats, 7, 35, 334–335
filename, searching by, 63
files
hiding in Media Browser, 51
size of, 7, 337
fill layers, creating, 172–173
filling selections with color, 263
film photos, 27
Filter Gallery dialog box, 284–285, 286–287
Filter Gallery interface, 294–295
filtering
events by date, 85
by keyword tags, 74
by ratings, 65

filters
adding noise with, 288–289
applying, 294–295
blurring, 243, 280–281
choices of, 283
distorting, 282–283
embossing with, 292–293
pixelating with, 290–291
turning images into paintings with, 284–285
turning images into sketches with, 286–287
Fit Screen option, magnifying images with, 103
flattening, 159
Flickr, 26, 351
Flow slider, 219
folders, importing photos by selecting, 32–33
foreground color, 13, 256–257
formatting, changing in text, 300–301
frames, 37, 113
friends, tagging in photos, 353
Full Screen mode, 52–55

G

G (Gradient) tool, 13
Gaussian Blur filter, 280–281
geo-tagging, 79
GIF (Graphic Interchange Format), 333
glass, covering with, 320–321
Glass filter, 282–283
glow, adding to portraits, 237
Gradient Editor, 274–275
Gradient (G) tool, 13
gradients, 274–275
Graphic Interchange Format (GIF), 333
Graphic Novel filter, 287
graphics, 7, 277, 328
Graphics panel, 276–277
Group Shot tool, 194–195
Guided mode
about, 14–15, 110
adding motion with Zoom Burst, 242–243
applying
Lomo camera effects, 240–241
Low Key effects, 252–253
reflections, 248–249
fixing colorcast in, 239
improving portraits, 234–237
miniaturizing objects with tilt shift, 244–245
panels in, 19
putting objects out of bounds, 250–251

Puzzle Effect, 246–247

restoring old photos, 232–233

shifting colors, 238–239

H

H (Hand) tool, 12, 99, 102, 103

Hand (H) tool, 12, 99, 102, 103

hard-edged lines, painting, 259

Height option (marquee tools), 123

Help menu, 15

hiding

files in Media Browser, 51

layers, 162

shapes, 311

Tool Options panel, 17

High Key effect, 253

highlighting objects using gradients, 275

histogram, 204

history, searching by, 63

Horizontal Type tool, 111, 299

I

I (Eyedropper) tool, 13

image tabs (Editor), 9

image window (Editor), 9

images. *See* photos

Import button (Organizer), 10

importing

about, 26–27

automatically stacking photos when, 91

from card readers, 28–29

from digital cameras, 28–29

from folders, 32–33

from scanners, 30–31

Impressionist Brush tool, 259

increasing

magnification, 100

saturation, 219

Inner Glows option, 319

Instant Fix, 88–89

Instant Fix panel, 47

intersection, 141

inverting

colors, 211

selections, 136

iStockphoto, 26

J

J (Spot Healing Brush) tool, 12, 190–191, 236

JPEG (Joint Photographic Experts Group), 35, 332–333

K

K (Paint Bucket) tool, 13, 221

keystone distortion, 200–201

keyword tags, 44, 72–75

keywords, searching for content by, 277

L

L (Lasso) tool, 12

labels, adding, 335

Lasso (L) tool, 12

layer masks, 178–181

layers

about, 158–159

adding

color shading to, 315

coverings to, 320–321

drop shadows to, 314–315

layer masks, 178–179

outer glows to, 318–319

adjustment, 159, 174–175, 177

applying commands to, 158

background, 161, 273

blending, 176–177

changing opacity of, 168

copying and pasting into, 161

creating, 160

deleting, 165

duplicating, 164

editing layer masks, 180–181

erasing, 273

fill layers, 172–173

hiding, 162

linking, 169

merging, 170

moving, 143, 163

moving selections in, 143

opacity of, 225

placing selections in new, 153

removing styles from, 321

renaming, 171

reordering, 166–167

Layers panel, 18, 166

layouts, managing open images using, 98–99

lettering, vertical, 311

levels, adjusting, 204–205

Levels dialog box, 204–205

lighting and color

adding

color to black-and-white photos, 224–225

color with Brush tool, 258–259

lighting and color *(continued)*
  adjusting
    brightness and contrast, 208–209
    color in text, 302–303
    color with Color Curves, 226–227
    color with Smart Brush, 264–267
    color with Sponge tool, 218–219
    levels, 204–205
    shadows and highlights, 206–207
    skin color, 216–217
  applying
    Auto Smart Tone tool, 228–229
    color to new selections, 266
  Blur tool, 214
  Burn tool, 211
  converting color into black and white, 222–223
  Dodge tool, 210
  filling selections with color, 263
  fixing exposure, 212–213
  inverting color, 211
  painting color onto layers, 179
  replacing color, 220–221
  setting color in backgrounds, 256–257
  Sharpen tool, 215
  shifting color, 238–239
  Smudge tool, 215
  using brushes to replace color, 262–263
lines, drawing, 270–271
linking layers, 169
loading selections, 135
Lomo camera effects, applying, 240–241
Low Key effect, applying, 252–253
Luminosity effect, 177

M

M (Marquee) tool, 12
Magic Eraser tool, 273
Magic Wand tool, 128–129
Magnetic Lasso tool, 126–127
magnifying, with Zoom tool, 100–101
Marquee (M) tool, 12
marquee tools, customizing, 123
masks, painting with Selection Brush, 133
matting, 108
measurement units, 22
Media Browser, 10, 50–51
media type, searching by, 63
memory, allocating, 22

merging, 170, 194–195
metadata, viewing, 56–57
metal, covering with, 321
miniaturizing objects with tilt-shift techniques, 244–245
mobile devices, viewing Revel photos on, 359
mode buttons (Editor), 9
Monochromatic setting (Add Noise dialog box), 289
Mosaic filter, 291
motion, adding with Zoom burst, 242–243
Motion Blur filter, 280–281
Move (V) tool, 12
moving
  guides, 23
  layers, 143, 163
  photos to different places, 81
  selection marquees, 141
  selections, 142–143
Multiply effect, 177
music, adding to slide shows, 343

N

N (Pencil) tool, 13, 259
noise, adding with filters, 288–289
notes, searching by, 63

O

O (Sponge) tool, 12, 218–219
Ocean Ripple filter, 282
100% magnification, reverting to, 101
on-screen size, changing, 104–105
opacity, layer, 168, 225
Open button (Editor), 9
opening
  Editor, 8
  frames from video clips, 37
  Organizer, 46–47
  photos, 34–35
Organizer
  about, 44–45
  adding
    captions, 58–59
    images to, 33
  albums, 60–61
  creating catalogs, 48–49
  displaying
    images in Photo Bin from, 97
    slide shows in Full Screen mode, 54–55
  editing photos from within, 47
  finding photos, 62–63
  opening, 46–47

rating photos, 64–65

removing photos from, 67

rotating photos in, 89

saving photos as albums in, 39

setting program preferences in, 21

switching to Editor from, 11

viewing

photo information, 56–57

photos in Full Screen mode, 52–53

photos in Media Browser, 50–51

versions of photos, 66

workspace, 10

Organizer button (Editor), 9

Orton effect, 245

outer glows, adding to layers, 318–319

outlines, adding along selections, 271

P

P (Straighten) tool, 13, 117

Paint Bucket (K) tool, 13, 221

painting and drawing

adding

color with Brush tool, 258–259

content from Graphics panel, 276–277

adjusting

brush styles, 260–261

color with Smart Brush, 264–267

applying

Eraser tool, 272–273

gradients, 274–275

colors onto layer content, 179

hard-edged lines, 259

lines, 270–271

masks with Selection Brush, 133

setting foreground and background colors, 256–257

shapes, 268–269

using brushes to replace color, 262–263

paintings, turning images into with filters, 284–285

panel bin (Editor), 9

panel bin (Organizer), 10

panels, 18–19

Paste command, 146

Pattern Stamp tool, 189

Pencil (N) tool, 13, 259

People Recognition dialog box, 77

Perfect Portrait tools, 234–235

Perspective command, 201

pet eyes, 187

Photo Bin, 9, 96–97

photo books, creating, 346–349

photo collage, 247

photo details (Organizer), 10

Photo Mail, e-mailing images with, 336–339

photo panoramas, creating, 198–199

Photomerge Exposure tool, 212–213

Photomerge styles, applying, 324–325

photos

acquiring, 6

adding

to events, 83

to Organizer, 33

saturation, 241

vignetting, 241

adjusting

canvas size, 108–109

date and time on, 57

on screen size, 104–105

print size, 106–107

view, 102–103

backing up, 360–361

bitmap, 6

black-and-white, 222–225

blurring with filters, 280–281

cataloging, 5

closing, 41

creating blank, 36–37

cropping, 114–115

defining people in, 76–77

digital, 6–7

displaying from Organizer in Photo Bin, 97

distorting with filters, 282–283

duplicating, 40

editing from within Organizer, 47

e-mailing with Photo Mail, 336–339

exporting, 356–359

finding, 45, 62, 63, 92–93

importing

from card readers, 28–29

from digital cameras, 28–29

from scanners, 30–31

by searching, 33

by selecting folders, 32–33

managing open, 96–99

manipulating, 4

moving to different places, 81

opening, 34–35

organizing, 5, 93

printing, 340–341

photos *(continued)*

    raster, 6

    rating, 64–65

    rearranging in slide shows, 343

    recomposing, 196–197

    removing, 61, 67, 75, 81

    repairing, 4

    restoring old, 232–233

    retouching, 4

    reverting, 119

    rotating, 89, 116–117

    saving, 38–39, 332–333

    sharing, 350–355

    sharpening, 192–193, 233

    stacking, 90–91

    tagging friends in, 77, 353

    turning into

        paintings with filters, 284–285

        sketches with filters, 286–287

    undoing changes to, 118

    unstacking, 91

    viewing

        in Full Screen mode, 52–53

        information for, 56–57

        in Media Browser, 50–51

        versions of, 15, 66

Photoshop Elements 12. *See also specific topics*

    about, 4–5

    digital images, 6–7

    Editor workspace, 9

    Organizer workspace, 10

    setting program preferences, 20–21

    starting, 8

    switching

        between Editor and Organizer, 11

        Editor modes, 14–15

    tools, 12–13

    viewing rulers and guides, 22–23

    working with

        panels, 18–19

        tools, 16–17

Picture Stack feature, 247

Pixelate dialog box, 290

pixelating, with filters, 290–291

pixels

    about, 6

    Levels dialog box, 205

    selecting, 125

places

    creating shortcuts for, 87

    defining, 78–79

    moving photos to different, 81

    placing on geographical map, 45

    removing photos from, 81

    working with tags for, 86–87

PNG (Portable Network Graphics), 35, 333

Pointillize filter, 290

Polygonal Lasso tool, 125

Pop Art feature, 251

Portable Network Graphics (PNG), 333

portraits, improving, 234–235

preferences, program, setting, 20–21

previewing image print size, 107

Print Preview dialog box, 107

print size, changing, 106–107

printing photos, 340–341

Process Multiple Files dialog box, 335

projects, creating and sharing, 45

PSD (Photoshop Document), 35

Puzzle effect, 246–247

Q

Q (Content-Aware Move) tool, 13, 144–145

Quick mode

    about, 14

    adding

        frames in, 113

        text in, 111

    applying effects in, 112

    editing in, 184–185

    panels in, 19

    sharpening images in, 193

    working in, 110–111

Quick Selection (A) tool, 12, 130–131

R

R (Blur) tool, 12, 214

raster images, 6

rating photos, 64–65

rearranging photos in slide shows, 343

Recompose (W) tool, 13, 196–197

Rectangular Marquee tool, 122

Red Eye Removal (Y) tool, 12, 186–187

Refine Edge dialog box, 152

reflections, applying, 248–249

Regular Lasso tool, 124

removing. *See also* deleting
        elements from scenes, 195
        items from Favorites panel, 329
        keyword tags from photos, 75
        merged styles, 325
        photos, 61, 67, 81
        red eye, 186–187
        spots, 190–191
        styles from layers, 321
renaming layers, 171
reordering layers, 166–167
repairing
        colorcast in Guided mode, 239
        exposure, 212–213
        keystone distortion, 200–201
        photos, 4
Replace Color command, 220–221
resampling, 104
resizing
        background patterns, 317
        panels, 19
        shapes, 269
        thumbnails, 329
resolution, choosing, 37
restoring, 20, 232–233, 361
retouching. *See* editing
reverting, 101, 119
Ripple filter, 282
rotating
        images, 89, 116–117
        selections, 148

S

S (Clone Stamp) tool, 12, 188–189
saturation, 218, 219, 241
Save For Web dialog box, 105, 332–333
Save Photo Bin dialog box, 39
saving. *See also* sharing
        advanced searches, 71
        backing up photos, 360–361
        converting file types, 334–335
        layered files, 159
        photos, 38–39, 332–333
        selections, 134, 135
scaling selections, 149
Scanner Preferences dialog box, 31
scanners, 26, 30–31
Screen effect, 177
scroll bars, adjusting image view with, 103

searching
        advanced, 70–71
        catalogs, 45
        for content by keyword, 277
        importing photos by, 33
        photos, 45, 62, 63, 92–93
        for photos in folders, 32–33
security settings, changing for catalogs, 49
selecting
        areas with
                Elliptical Marquee tool, 123
                Magic Wand tool, 128–129
                Magnetic Lasso tool, 126–127
                Polygonal Lasso tool, 125
                Quick Selection tool, 130–131
                Rectangular Marquee tool, 122
                Regular Lasso tool, 124
                Selection Brush tool, 132–133
        brushes from predefined sets, 260
        objects, 110–111
        pixels, 125
        resolution, 37
        tools, 16
Selection Brush tool, 132–133
selections
        adding
                outlines along, 271
                to selections, 140
                text along, 308–309
        adjusting
                about, 131
                precision of Magnetic Lasso tool, 127
        applying
                color to new, 266
                Content-Aware Move tool, 144–145
        deleting, 147
        deselecting, 137
        distorting, 151
        duplicating, 146
        editing, 197
        feathering borders of, 154–155
        filling with color, 263
        inverting, 136
        loading, 135
        moving, 142–143
        refining edges of, 152–153
        rotating, 148

Office
InDesign®
Facebook®

THE WAY YOU WANT TO LEARN.

HTML
Photoshop®

DigitalClassroom.com

Flexible, fast, and fun, DigitalClassroom.com lets you choose when, where, and how to learn new skills. This subscription-based online learning environment is accessible anytime from your desktop, laptop, tablet, or smartphone. It's easy, efficient learning — on *your* schedule.

- Learn web design and development, Office applications, and new technologies from more than 2,500 video tutorials, e-books, and lesson files
- Master software from Adobe, Apple, and Microsoft
- Interact with other students in forums and groups led by industry pros

Learn more! Sample DigitalClassroom.com for free, now!

We're social. Connect with us!

facebook.com/digitalclassroom
@digitalclassrm